HISTORY OF WORLD ARCHITECTURE

Pier Luigi Nervi, General Editor

PRE-COLUMBIAN ARCHITECTURE OF MESOAMERICA

Doris Heyden and Paul Gendrop

Translated by Judith Stanton

Harry N. Abrams, Inc., Publishers, New York

Series Coordinator: Giuseppe Positano de Vincentiis

Produced under the supervision of Carlo Pirovano,
editorial director of Electa Editrice

Design: Diego Birelli, art director of Electa Editrice
Photographs: Paul Gendrop and Doris Heyden
Drawings: Studio of Enzo Di Grazia

Library of Congress Cataloging in Publication Data

Heyden, Doris.
  Pre-Columbian architecture of Mesoamerica

  (History of world architecture)
  Translation of Architettura mesoamericana.
  Bibliography: p.
  Includes index.
  1. Indians of Mexico—Architecture. 2. Indians
of Central America—Architecture. 3. Mexico—Antiq-
uities. 4. Central America—Antiquities. I. Gen-
drop, Paul, joint author. II. Title.
F1219.3.A6.H4913   720'.972   75-8993
ISBN 0-8109-1018-7

Library of Congress Catalogue Card Number: 75-8993
Copyright © 1973 in Italy by Electa Editrice, Milan
Published by Harry N. Abrams, Incorporated, New York, 1975
All rights reserved. No part of the contents of this book may be
reproduced without the written permission of the publishers
Printed and bound in Japan

PREFACE

Architectural criticism has nearly always been concerned with the visible aspect of individual buildings, taking this to be the decisive factor in the formulation of value judgments and in the classification of those "styles" which appear in textbooks, and which have thus become common knowledge. But once it is recognized that every building is, by definition, a work subject to the limitations imposed by the materials and building techniques at hand, and that every building must prove its stability, as well as its capacity to endure and serve the needs it was built for, it becomes clear that the aesthetic aspect alone is inadequate when we come to appraise a creative activity, difficult enough to judge in the past, rapidly becoming more complex in our own day, and destined to become more so in the foreseeable future.

Nevertheless, what has struck me most, on studying the architecture of the past and present, is the fact that the works which are generally regarded by the critics and the general public as examples of pure beauty are also the fruit of exemplary building techniques, once one has taken into account the quality of the materials and the technical knowledge available. And it is natural to suspect that such a coincidence is not entirely casual.

Building in the past was wholly a matter of following static intuitions, which were, in turn, the result of meditation, experience, and above all of an understanding of the capacity of certain structures and materials to resist external forces. Meditation upon structural patterns and the characteristics of various materials, together with the appraisal of one's own experiences and those of others, is an act of love toward the process of construction for its own sake, both on the part of the architect and his collaborators and assistants. Indeed, we may wonder whether this is not the hidden bond which unites the appearance and substance of the finest buildings of the past, distant though that past may be, into a single "thing of beauty."

One might even think that the quality of the materials available not only determined architectural patterns but also the decorative detail with which the first simple construction was gradually enriched.

One might find a justification for the difference in refinement and elegance between Greek architecture, with its basic use of marble—a highly resistant material, upon which the most delicate carvings can be carried out—and the majestic concrete structures of Roman architecture, built out of a mixture of lime and pozzolana, and supported by massive walls, to compensate for their intrinsic weaknesses.

Would it be too rash to connect these objective architectural characteristics with the different artistic sensibilities of the two peoples?

One must recognize, therefore, the importance of completing the description of the examples illustrated with an interpretation of their constructional and aesthetic characteristics, so that the connection between the twin aspects of building emerges as a natural, logical consequence.

This consequence, if understood and accepted in good faith by certain avant-garde circles, could put an end to the disastrous haste with which our architecture is rushing toward an empty, costly, and at times impractical formalism. It might also recall architects and men of culture to a more serene appraisal of the objective elements of building and to the respect that is due to a morality of architecture. For this is just as important for the future of our cities as is morality, understood as a rule of life, for an orderly civil existence.

PIER LUIGI NERVI

5

TABLE OF CONTENTS

Chapter One THE BACKGROUND

The Peopling of Mesoamerica

Citlalicue, the sky goddess, gave birth to a flint knife, which so shocked her other children, the stars, that they threw it out of the heavens. The knife fell to the earth and broke into thousands of fragments, each one turning into a god. But the gods had no one to serve them, and so they asked their mother for permission to create men. Citlalicue instructed them to get bones from the underworld and to give them life by letting blood upon them. But in stealing the bones, one of the gods fled in such haste that he fell and broke all the bones into pieces of many sizes. This is why some men were created tall, some short. Thus a sixteenth-century chronicle explains the appearance of man on this earth.[1]

Quite different from this myth, however, is the true story of the peopling of America. Men from the Old World crossed the Bering Strait 40,000 or more years ago, moving from what is now Siberia to Alaska over a natural bridge then formed of ice and land, ignorant of the fact that they were crossing from one continent to another. Undoubtedly they were small bands of hunters following the fauna of the Pleistocene age. That man originated in the Old World we know because no remains of his predecessors, the apelike primates, have been found in America; nor are there apes here today. As men moved on down the American continent, they eventually came to the area we call Mesoamerica. Here many groups settled, while others continued further south.

Mesoamerica

At the time of the European Conquest of Mexico, in A.D. 1521, the geographical limits of Mesoamerica were—in the north—from the Panuco River in the east to the western Sinaloa and—in the south—from the outlet of the Motagua River in what is now Honduras to the Gulf of Nicoya. These borders lie somewhat south of the present-day frontier between Mexico and the United States, and include not only Mexico itself but Guatemala, El Salvador, and parts of Honduras, Nicaragua, and Costa Rica. Mesoamerica is bounded on the east by the Atlantic Ocean and on the west by the Pacific.

In his definition of Mesoamerica, the area encompassed in this book, Paul Kirchhoff lists both the presence and the absence of cultural traits within a given area which serve to define its limits.[2] One of the features characteristic of Mesoamerica during pre-Hispanic times was the use of truncated stepped pyramids, to which we shall often refer in this book. Among other traits considered typically Mesoamerican, Kirchhoff includes stucco floors; ball courts; steam baths; *chinampas,* or artificial raft-islands filled with lake mud and used for agriculture; specialized markets; hieroglyphic writing; positional numeration; books folded screen-style or codices; the establishment of a solar year of 18 months consisting of 20 days each, plus 5 days at the year's end; the combination of 20 day signs with 13 numbers, forming another calendrical period of 260 days (the ritual calendar); and the combination of these two time cycles to form a greater cycle—or "century"—consisting of 52 years.

In studying the traits mentioned, one fact becomes obvious: they define an advanced culture, for only a true civilization produces writing, complex mathematics, calendrics, and monumental architecture. Mesoamerica and the other high-culture region in the New World—the Andean area—are together called Nuclear America.

Mexico, the largest region of Mesoamerica, has often been called a mosaic. Much of the land is mountainous, yet there are great deserts in the north and tropical rain forests in the south. Each region is different, each valley constituting a separate ecological system. These geographical facts explain why Mesoamerica in ancient times was made up of so many separate city-states, each an independent entity within its own geographical environment. It also explains why trade was so active in the pre-European American world: cotton and cacao from the lowlands were coveted in the cool highlands, which in turn exported its own special products.

Because of its striking ecological contrasts, Mexico experienced either too much or too little rain. E.R. Wolf mentions that water played such a vital role there that the country is dotted with hundreds of place names referring to it: Apan ("On the Water"), Atocpan ("Watery Field"), and so forth.[3] This same author calls the people of Mesoamerica "Sons of the Shaking Earth," since they live constantly menaced by earthquakes. Changes in natural phenomena—such as the sudden birth of a volcano in a corn field, dry river beds that change overnight into raging torrents, or sudden temperature changes—have given men in Mesoamerica a unique view of creation and life. History is seen in closed cycles, in contrast to the Western point of view of history as a continuum.[4] The myth of the Five Suns, each one a cosmic world, each world or era ending in a cataclysm (discussed in the Teotihuacán section), is an example of this.

Geographic conditions in Mesoamerica determined its art. In the coastal area, where life was easier due to favorable agricultural conditions, the people were extroverted, as is evidenced in Veracruz's "laughing figurines." In the harsh highland areas, not even the Aztec god of song, dance, and flowers—Xochipilli—is shown laughing. The Aztec smile is rather a grimace.

1. *Principal cultural centers of Mesoamerica.   A. western Mexico*
B. central plateau of Mexico   C. Gulf Coast   D. Oaxaca area
E. Maya area

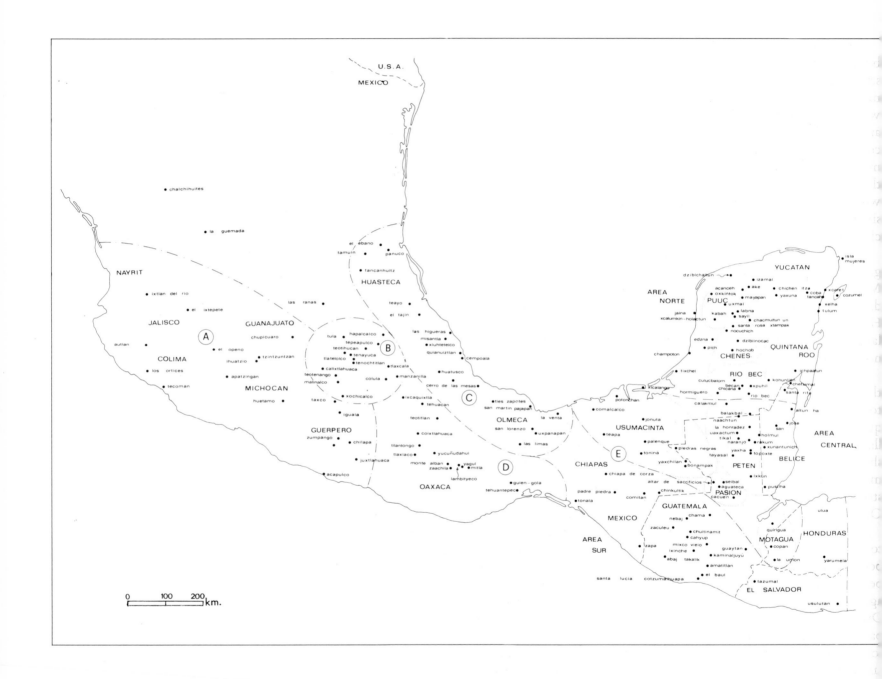

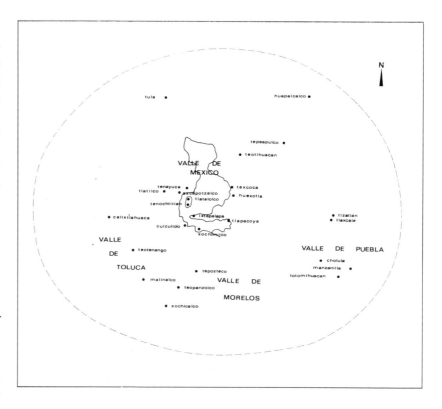

Mexico's central plateau, a corridor which runs north and south, by its very nature invited change. Sedentary groups were constantly finding new and often hostile neighbors—nomadic peoples moving down from the north, who in turn adopted sedentary ways while new groups flowed in and repeated the process. The Maya area, on the contrary, being the isolated "toe" of a geographical cornucopia, developed in a fairly uninterrupted fashion over the millennia. The Maya, who experienced few cultural innovations through new groups, were at the end of their long-lived splendor when the Spaniards reached American shores at the beginning of the sixteenth century, but the Aztecs were still a young and vigorous civilization.

Among the numerous languages spoken in Mesoamerica, two great strains stand out: Uto-Aztecan, whose roots were in western Mexico and the southwestern United States, and whose best-known division is Náhuatl; and Macro-Mayan, from which both Mayan and Huaxtec derive. Wolf claims that prior to 4000 B.C. all Mesoamerican languages may have been related, but different tongues branched off not much later.[5]

When early settlers were not searching for food or defending themselves against animals or hostile bands, they turned their hand to art. Probably the earliest work of Mesoamerican art is the Tequixquiac sacrum (c. 10,000 B.C.), intentionally worked to resemble a llama's head. During this early period people lived in caves, rock shelters, or temporary outdoor camps. The latter consisted of huts made of perishable materials. Some may have been shelters constructed of long tough agave leaves, such as we see in the Mexican Otomi region today.

Big game was becoming scarce in some regions and men began to rely more and more upon seed gathering, storing some for lean periods. It was perhaps in storage that some seeds sprouted, or perhaps some dropped upon the ground and took root. At any rate, agriculture came into existence: in Tehuacan and Tamaulipas, Mexico, Dr. Richard S. McNeish found an agricultural complex that dates back 9,000 years. Yet the cultivation of plants was not a prerequisite for sedentary life, inasmuch as collecting wild food, hunting game, and relying on fish and water products naturally led to sedentarism.[6] Nevertheless, plants that accompanied sedentary life were pumpkins, squash, beans, avocado, chili pepper, corn, amaranth, sapote, maguey, and cacti. Corn or maize, the basic cereal of Mesoamerica, made a fairly late appearance in this agricultural complex, between 5000 and 3000 B.C. Twelve types of domesticated maize were found in Tehuacan as well as the wild variety. Manioc and millet also appeared in this satisfying diet, which has changed little over the millennia. Grinding stones—*metates* and *manos*—for making meal or flour were used in Tehuacan as early as 4800 B.C. Michael D. Coe, in regard to Harvard botanist Paul C. Mangelsdorf who worked with McNeish, says that "we hear about the glories of Maya astronomy, the marvels of the Inca highway system, and the massiveness of the Teotihuacán pyramids, but these are nothing compared to the achievement of the Coxcatlan phase (5000–3500 B.C.) people, who made the most important discovery ever attained by the American Indians. For this plant (maize) created and fed native New World civilization."[7]

Many plants native to Mesoamerican soil later found their way to Europe and other parts of the world, among them maize, squash, lima beans, pumpkins, avocados, cacao, tomatoes, pineapple, and tobacco. Domesticated animals were the turkey, the dog, and the bee. The fat hairless dog, like the turkey, was used for food and the bee provided honey. Completing the diet were fish and shellfish, deer, hare, rabbit, turtle, pheasant, boar, and duck. (Ducks are still hunted on Mexico's Lake Pátzcuaro with a type of *atlatl*, the spear thrower that has been used throughout Mesoamerican history.) Special delicacies were mosquito eggs *(ahuauhtli)* scraped off Lake Texcoco's surface, dried and then prepared with chili and vegetables; or toasted maguey cactus worms. These two are still popular dishes.

The people of Mesoamerica, irrigating their fields, deforming their crania and filing their teeth as signs of beauty, weaving their cloth of agave fibers or cotton, each individual fitting into his niche in a highly stratified society, looked to the gods as guides in every phase of life. For religion was the great driving factor, the uniting force of this civilization, tightly interwoven into every act, public or private. Heads of state were also ecclesiastical leaders; the supreme ruler was considered a living deity. The pantheon was crowded with gods for every function, from the rising of the sun to the appearance of the planet Venus, from birth to death, from planting to sowing. There were gods of trade, of the ball game, of drink, of "the hills, the water, the springs, the cliffs, the trees, the clouds, the rainstorms—in sum, all created things . . ."[8]

Led by this profound religious feeling, the people created their art not only for themselves but for their gods. Their outstanding artistic manifestation was the building of majestic cities, whose centers were places of worship for the *centzon teteo,* or innumerable deities. Assured of their food supply, men settled in permanent villages, living in pit houses first, then in huts of wooden poles interwoven with branches and straw, finally plastered with mud (wattle-and-daub). Roofs were thatched. This type of construction has survived until the present day in many regions.

The Pre-Classic or Formative phase is usually divided into three periods: Early (2000–1300 B.C.), Middle (1300–800 B.C.), and Late (800–200 B.C.). During these two millennia the main patterns of Mesoamerican civilization were formulated, patterns that were maintained in the period of efflorescence which followed, the Classic. Cultural traits appearing at this time include architecture, ceremonialism, social differentiation, characteristic technology (pottery, weaving, stone- and woodwork), hieroglyphic writing and calendrics, and the establishment of trade and commercial relationships.[1]

In central Mexico, five lakes joined together to form a basin, now almost entirely occupied by Mexico City. In the Early Pre-Classic, people built their houses on the higher lands and planted their crops along the low river banks and lake shores, where flooding provided natural irrigation. Román Piña Chán calls the Early Pre-Classic the village or rural period.[2] Sedentary farming groups cultivated the basic corn-beans-squash-chili crops. Their villages were small, and their houses of perishable materials like those of previous periods. Clay figurines from this phase show people nude but adorned with body paint, wearing turbanlike headdresses and jewelry. Most Early Pre-Classic figurines from central Mexico are feminine, indicating a fertility cult or a possible matriarchy.

The Middle and Late Pre-Classic periods are termed urban and transitional by the same author. As agriculture guaranteed a steady diet, population increased and rural villages gradually turned into towns. Toward the end of the Middle Pre-Classic new villages (among them Cuicuilco) appeared on the southwestern shore and at the northwestern end of the multiple lake (Zacatenco and El Arbolillo). Ayotla, near Tlapacoya—on the lake's eastern edge—and Tlatilco, on the west, were earlier settlements.[3] Tlatilco was a large burial ground where beautiful figurines and pottery have been found at different levels. The dead were interred underneath house floors and were accompanied by utensils, vessels, and figurines, all to be used in the other world (religion, still in a formative phase, consisted primarily of magic practices). The clay figurines reflected the people themselves, and among them we find shamans wearing masks or strange headdresses, dancers, acrobats, musicians, and ball players. Figurines in the Middle Pre-Classic were mainly masculine, some of them with "baby-face" features, although many female figurines were now so lovely that Covarrubias calls them "pretty girls."[4] Pottery was shaped in many forms: ducks, bedgers, peccaries, fish, armadillos, rabbits, turtles—all good indications of the Pre-Classic diet. The presence of jade, shell, cotton, turquoise, kaolin, and other raw materials foreign to central Mexico indicates increased trade between the lowlands and the highlands.

A cult to a jaguar deity (related to rain and earth), the use of masks, the practice of cranial deformation, and feline motifs in pottery provide evidence of Olmec influence from the Gulf Coast (the Olmec, said to be the "Mother Culture"[5] of all others in Mesoamerica, or "America's first civilization,"[6] will be discussed further on). Such influence was far-reaching and is seen in many Pre-Classic cultures in the central basin, Puebla, Morelos, and of course in the heartland in the southern lowlands.

Outside the central basin, in other parts of Mesoamerica, the Pre-Classic period has yielded rich remains in figurines and vessels, especially in the western region. Western lake shores, plains, and valleys were occupied from early Pre-Classic times. The Capacha phase at Colima has yielded composite vessels and pottery forms earlier than similar wares in central Mexico and Morelos, and can be dated at 1450 B.C.[7] At El Opeño in Michoacán, Oliveros found ball-player figurines in a shaft tomb, dated at 1350 B.C.[8] From Chupícuaro in Guanajuato (500–200 B.C.) have come thousands of delightful clay figures and handsome polychrome vessels. The Chupícuaro style exerted considerable influence on central Mexico.[9] In the Gulf Coast region, Remojadas in central Veracruz was outstanding for its beautiful Early Pre-Classic clay figurines (some decorated with tar), which were to continue through the Classic period and constitute some of Mesoamerica's most handsome clay sculpture. Farther north, in the Panuco River zone, what was to be the Huaxtec culture was emerging, its architecture characterized by circular earth mounds.

In Oaxaca, a key area located between the highland and lowland cultures, a long history of occupation began just northwest of the present-day city of Oaxaca, in the valley of Etla. By about 1500 B.C. people living in settled villages farmed the rich area by means of wells sunk into the fields.[10] Early Oaxaca ceramics (1500–900 B.C.) show a strong Olmec influence, and in turn the remains of workshops suggest that San José Mogote in the state of Oaxaca supplied the Olmecs with ilmenite mirrors, hematite, magnetite, mica, and green quartz—all important elements for art and ritual use.[11]

In the Middle Pre-Classic period Oaxaca's ties were closer with Puebla and the Gulf Coast, but the so-called *Danzantes* engraved on rock slabs at Monte Albán from a slightly later period (900–400 B.C.) have definite Olmec features. Calendric inscriptions, hieroglyphs, and numerals at Monte Albán indicate another Olmec heritage, as do carvings (some of them humanized jaguars) at Dainzú. Glyphs, numerals, and the calendar also point to Maya influences. Montenegro, in the Mixteca region of Oaxaca, was founded around 600 B.C. but seems to have been abandoned about three hundred years later.

Zapotec culture came into being in Oaxaca in the Middle Pre-Classic period. Although both the Maya and Olmec form part of its family tree, Zapotec culture soon acquired unique vigorous characteristics, reflected in its splendid pottery urns and in that amazing city built on an artificially flattened mountain top, Monte Albán.

In the Maya region, a more or less uniform proto-Maya cultural substratum ran through the three zones of the area during Pre-Classic times (1500–200 B.C.), but the Classic period (200–900 A.D.) —the golden age of the Maya—flourished first in the central zone (tropical lowlands), then in the southern zone (Chiapas and the Guatemala highlands), and finally in the north (Yucatán peninsula). The earliest groups in the Maya region had the same linguistic and cultural roots as those of the people who inhabited Mexico's Gulf Coast from the Early Pre-Classic period. Hieroglyphic writing, dot-and-dash numeration, the calendar count, and colossal heads from El Baúl and other sites reveal the Olmec heritage.

Proto-Mayan groups separated from the Olmec as early as 1500 B.C., crossing Mexico from the Gulf Coast to the Pacific by way of Tehuantepec, continuing south into Guatemala, then turning north and moving into the highlands. From here they went into the lowlands of El Petén and finally into Yucatán.[12] By 800 B.C. the Proto-Maya were building ceremonial centers in Chiapa de Corzo, Izapa, Kaminaljuyú, and Dzibilchaltún. The earliest Maya period (1200–800 B.C.) is called *Mamon* ("grandmother"), a fitting term for a beginning.

It is probable that Mesoamerica and South America were connected by sea trade during Pre-Classic times. There is a striking similarity between Ocos pottery from coastal Guatemala and Chorerra ceramics from Ecuador (1500–900 B.C.).[13] Even earlier, some Guatemalan vessels from the Pacific coast find a counterpart in Valdivia, Ecuador. The greatest evidence for contact among the various centers of Nuclear America is to be found before 300 A.D.[14]

The Olmecs

The name Olmec is derived from *olli,* the Náhuatl word for rubber, and from *mecatl,* meaning lineage. The Olmecs undoubtedly did not call themselves "the Rubber People" but the name serves to designate the Olmec heartland: northern Tabasco and southern Veracruz, Mexico's rubber country. Olmec civilization spanned the years from 1500 to 200 B.C.—the main part of the Pre-Classic period—although Olmec influence continued to be seen in Mesoamerica for many centuries after this.

Among the greatest contributions of the Olmecs were the calendar, a numbering system, hieroglyphic writing, and astronomical observations. The dot-and-dash system of numbering, later developed by the Maya, is seen on Stele C from Tres Zapotes in Veracruz, dated at 291 B.C. according to Correlation A—"our first positive evidence of the use of the zero" in America.[15] The date on the Tuxtla statuette now in Washington, D.C., is set at 162 B.C. according to the so-called Long Count.[16]

Although the Olmecs lived in a stoneless area, their favorite material was stone, which they imported from other regions. They were the first great Mesoamerican lapidaries. The most dramatic Olmec sculptures undoubtedly are the colossal basalt heads. Their features are rounded, the lips are full, and they wear helmets *(plate 4)*. They have been said to represent decapitated ball players. At the other end of the scale are delicate small sculptures—some representing humans, others canoes or celts—made of fine bluish-green jade or of serpentine, hematite, aventurine quartz, rock crystal, amethyst, or steatite. These sculptures give us a good idea of the Olmec physical type, or rather, of two types: one a plump figure with Negroid features, the other a slender one with Mongoloid features, slanted eyes, and artificially deformed head.

Olmec art is so permeated with jaguar motifs that these people have been called "the Jaguar's Children."[17] Not only does sculpture exist in which a jaguar is seen copulating with a human,[18] but many humans are depicted with feline features, the snarling jaguar mouth, a cleft head, and wavy "eyebrows."

Inasmuch as the Mesoamerican Classic cultures were theocratic, it has been claimed that the Olmec was so also. Coe disputes this and draws a parallel with the Maya of the Classic era, whose inscriptions speak of a secular leadership, with power in the hands of a hereditary lineage.[19] Coe believes that the Olmecs were ruled by great civil lords, and offers as proof the altars showing an adult male seated within a niche, either holding a jaguar baby or else grasping a rope with which two captives are bound *(plate 7)*. These are themes of lineage and personal conquest, intended to glorify rulers. We have written proof that the later Aztecs, the cultural heirs of many groups that preceded them, created sculptured portraits of their leaders; the colossal Olmec heads may represent "busts" of Olmec sovereigns.[20] Nevertheless, religion was such an intrinsic part of life that it is difficult to tell where it stopped and civil activity began, if indeed there was such a separation. According to Coe, the major gods in Mesoamerica took definitive form in Olmec times.[21] He has identified in Olmec iconography Xipe, lord of spring and regeneration; Quet-

...alcóatl, god of wisdom, life, and the wind; and the gods of fire, death, and rain.

There are still many questions to be answered about Olmec culture. Can it be called an empire, as Caso, Coe, and Bernal believe?[22] Certainly trade was widespread, and Olmec expansion in one form or another reached out to almost every corner of Mesoamerica. Bernal believes that leagues of city-states, one of the political characteristics of Mesoamerica, may have appeared in Olmec times. He feels that the Olmec social organization was a military theocracy, and thus the first Mesoamerican empire.

Other scholars regard the Olmec as an art style.[23] But it cannot be merely regarded as such: the Gothic style in Europe spread from France to Germany, England, and Spain—yet we cannot properly speak of a Gothic empire. Nor, probably, can we call the Olmec world an empire. The spread of its influence into many parts of Mesoamerica (Puebla, Morelos, Guerrero, the central basin, Oaxaca, Chiapas, Guatemala) has been attributed to a messianic movement,[24] the carrying of Olmec ideas from their heartland to other regions, accompanied by trade (the usual concomitant of religious pilgrimages) and by the inevitable art style created by the figurines or other objects transported to those regions. Many aspects may be said to have formed this great culture whose achievements and ideas were basic to the development of all other Mesoamerican civilizations.

The First Ceremonial Centers

With the Olmecs, and dating from the Middle Pre-Classic period, appear the oldest known planned ceremonial centers in Mesoamerica. Usually located on islands, or on land elevations that became islands during the rainy season, the ceremonial centers of this epoch consisted basically of terraces and platforms of packed earth or, in some cases, of adobes—bricks of sun-baked clay. But of the temples or palaces that may have stood on these mounds—probably simple huts of perishable materials—no trace remains.

San Lorenzo, one of the first Olmec ceremonial centers (1200–900 B.C.), rises on a plateau totally reconstructed through a gigantic earth-transport project. Its man-made mounds were topped with many *lagunas,* or depressions, of various sizes, which provided water during the dry season. The water level could be regulated through an ingenious network of drainage canals built of large basalt blocks—the first sign of advanced hydraulic engineering on the American continent. A careful study of the map of San Lorenzo, even after three millennia of abandonment and the erosion wrought by rain, reveals that the placement of these *lagunas* was quite regular, and reflects a calculated symmetry in the positioning of many of the mounds. Such is the case in the groups designated C and D, and similarly in the elongated ridges of earth lying to the southwest and southeast of the complex *(plate 3)*. Even more evident are several groups of regular platforms, along a north-south axis, forming plazas in the middle of which there rises a higher base—probably a "pyramid"—or what seems to be a ball court, of the type known as Palangana, almost completely enclosed by platforms.

Now, for the first time, we perceive some elements basic to the planning of many Mesoamerican ceremonial centers: a distinct orientation, with principal structures distributed along a particular axis (suggesting an incipient astronomy); the existence of ball courts; terraces and elevated platforms arranged to form plazas; and all enhanced by monumental sculptures placed along the main axis. The population comprising the dominant class has been calculated at about 1,000 inhabitants, who lived in housing groups atop the elongated terraces noted above.

For reasons unknown, the site of San Lorenzo was abandoned about 900 B.C.—but not before its great monolithic sculptures had been mutilated and buried with solemn ceremony. Among these was the largest, and one of the most beautiful, of the fifteen known colossal Olmec heads *(plate 4)*.

At this same time, we can follow the development of the ceremonial center of La Venta (1100–400 B.C.), beginning with the erection of its great clay "pyramid," over 98 1/2 feet (30 m.) high and 426 1/2 feet (130 m.) in diameter—a construction exhibiting a strange series of depressions and protrusions, unique in Mesoamerica but so regular in pattern as to seem intentional. Lying more or less in the center of a swampy island about 1 4/5 miles square (5 sq. km.), the pyramid was gradually surrounded by lower structures, along a perceptible north-south axis as in San Lorenzo, with principal elements concentrated in the northern part of the complex. Around the Great Pyramid are hemispherical mounds ("house" mounds), while the sides of the elongated terraces form a ceremonial plaza similar to that found in San Lorenzo. To the north, the complex is closed off by a stepped pyramid (perhaps the first of its kind in Mesoamerica), before which there rises a broad, man-made esplanade of adobes, partially enclosed between what might be called palisades—large monolithic columns of basalt, in natural formations.

At the end of these two palisades, on both sides of the access platform, we find two pits, completely closed on four sides. These sacred receptacles concealed, under many successive layers of adobe and stone, huge stylized masks carefully executed in mosaics of green

3. *San Lorenzo, Veracruz: general plan*

4. *San Lorenzo: colossal monolithic head. Jalapa, Anthropological Museum of the University of Veracruz*
5. *La Venta, Tabasco, Mexico: aerial view of Complexes C and A, occupying the main part of the ceremonial center*

serpentine. Their hidden presence must have served the Olmecs as a magic contact with the forces of water, earth, and sky *(plate 6)*.

Within the stepped base that bounds the complex to the north, three tombs have been discovered, one of them formed of basalt columns that probably came from the palisade described above. Another tomb contains one of the only two monolithic sarcophagi known in Mesoamerica (the other being that found in the famous crypt at Palenque). Finally, the principal sculpted monoliths—colossal heads, stelae, and altars *(plate 7)*—were located along the main axis of the mounds and plazas. We will see this practice (the carving of stelae and altars) evolve in some of the later Indian cultures such as the Zapotec and the Maya, in actual building construction, in the commemoration of historic events, and most especially—among the Maya—for the recording of astronomical observations, sidereal computations, or regular intervals of time.

In the ceremonial centers of San Lorenzo, La Venta, and Tres Zapotes we see set forth for the first time fundamentals that would prevail in Mesoamerican architecture for twenty-five centuries—namely, the use of a truncated pyramid as a temple base and the conscious placement of terraces, platforms, and temples to form plazas. This skill in the handling of large open spaces, utilizing fixed axes or some kind of symbolic orientation combined with structural masses, would prove an important cultural constant in the evolution of this architecture. But if it was the Olmecs who created the first clay architecture in Mesoamerica, other peoples, strongly influenced by Olmec culture, would lay the foundation for what was to become great architecture in stone.

The Beginnings of Stone Architecture

Of all the regions infiltrated by Olmec culture during the Late Pre-Classic period (800–200 B.C.), three apparently were to establish the basis of a more lasting architecture: the region of Oaxaca, certain centers in the Maya area, and the central plateau of Mexico. During this period, the most important from a cultural standpoint may have been Oaxaca, since it evolved the first system—albeit a primitive one—of "glyphic" writing, and the earliest known representations of deities among Mesoamerican peoples aside from those that were clearly Olmec. They were deities with well-differentiated characteristics, and we will watch them evolve in this area in the course of twenty centuries. As for architecture, there appeared in Monte Albán, starting with this period, structures faced with large stones carved in relief, such as the ancient building of the *Danzantes (plate 11)* and the curiously arrowhead-shaped Mound J *(plates 12, 13)*, thought to be

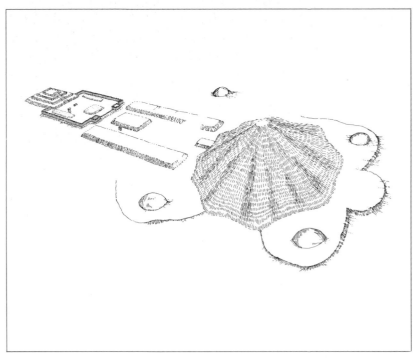

6. *La Venta: colossal mask in green serpentine mosaic. Villahermosa, Park-Museum*
7. *La Venta: monolithic altar. Villahermosa, Park-Museum*

8, 9. *Dainzú, Oaxaca, Mexico: bas-reliefs*
10. *Dainzú: bas-relief on the base of a large truncated pyramid* ▷

the oldest astronomical observatory in Mesoamerica. Another site of this period, Dainzú, shows us the first reliefs associated with the ritual ball game *(plates 8–10)*. We might also mention an incipient urban layout in Montenegro, complete with streets and plazas, including temples in the shape of great houses whose mode of construction—again for the first time—involved steps and bases solidified with stone and mud, and most important, with thick columns of the same material.

During this period, the southern Maya region enjoyed one of its most productive phases. Although the area would ultimately prove marginal to the great Classic development of the Maya, elements evolved here that seem to fall midway between the Olmecoid and those we can later define as totally Mayan. In Izapa—perhaps the key site of this area, as was Monte Albán for the region of Oaxaca—we find ball courts and large stepped bases decorated with boulders, as well as important carved monoliths. Furthest from the Maya region, in the north of the Yucatán peninsula, Dzibilchaltún erected its first stucco-covered platforms and stairways. But we must wait until the Proto-Classic period (roughly between the second and third centuries B.C. and the third century A.D.) to see, in sites such as Uaxactún and Tikal, the emergence of the more decisive elements of Maya architecture.

Among the initiators of stone architecture, the peoples of the Mexican plateau rank high. During the Late Pre-Classic period we already find ceremonial centers built on great earthen bases, as with the Olmecs—Totomihuacán, for instance, in the Puebla Valley, its stepped pyramids rising nearly 500 feet (over 150 m.) from the base and concealing a series of tunnels that lead to subterranean chambers.[25] But in the basin of Mexico, from the earliest days of this same period, we find sites such as Cerro del Tepalcate, and masonry bases that, aside from their modest dimensions, anticipate the silhouette of the later pyramids *(plate 16)*. The great circular stepped base built at Cuicuilco toward the end of the Pre-Classic era was, at 492 feet (150 m.) in diameter, perhaps the largest of its time *(plate 18)*.

Cuicuilco's importance at this point seems to have been considerable, and might have remained so had it not been for a volcanic eruption in the third or second century B.C. that was large enough to have buried the whole southwestern zone of the Valley of Mexico under lava. Other foundations recently found at this site point to the role it played as a large ceremonial center, in which appeared the truncated pyramidal stepped bases *(plate 17)* that were to become the rule soon thereafter in Teotihuacán, along with the stairways flanked by the typical *alfardas,* or railing-like lateral safeguards. Another

12. *Monte Albán: partial view of the Great Plaza from the southwest. Mound J is in the foreground*
13. *Monte Albán: Mound J*

antecedent of Teotihuacán may well have been the stepped base at Tlapacoya, set into an enormous hill that lends it a certain monumentality. Here we see a complicated series of platforms, reflecting three stages of superpositional construction and amplification. The different levels are joined by flights of stairs ingeniously combined with huge masonry walls, and the effect stands out sharply *(plates 14, 15)*.

In the course of one millennium—from approximately 1200 to 200 B.C.—we thus see born the first elements of Mesoamerican architecture, from the Olmec ceremonial centers, set on their clay-mound bases, to such advanced techniques and forms as the manufacture of sun-baked adobes; the removal and hauling of stone; the use of mortar as an agglomerative; the covering of structures with stone and stucco as protection; the beginnings of stairways, protective *alfardas,* columns, etc.; and the evolution of funerary architecture. Primitive forms of worship, content with simple edifices, would begin in time to call for the construction of more durable propitiatory temples. And so, Mesoamerican religious architecture was to crystallize around the stepped pyramidal form, conceived as a monumental base for a temple erected on a higher platform, with one or more stairways providing access.

Like any great cultural complex, Mesoamerica could and did create its own architectural language. At first glance, the Mesoamerican pyramid might be likened to the ziggurat of Mesopotamia or the graded pyramid of Saqqara. But it was in fact a distinctly different entity, for while the Egyptian structure was designed to perpetuate the memory of a pharaoh and invariably concealed his tomb, there are few examples in Mesoamerica of burial chambers or tombs within the nucleus of a pyramidal base. (One famous exception is the crypt at Palenque, of which we shall speak later.) Finally, the Mesoamerican "pyramid" is not, strictly speaking, a true pyramid. It comprises a stepped superposition of bodies in the form of truncated pyramids, truncated cones, or more complex shapes.

What inspired a design that could endure for twenty-five centuries? Its main function, evidently, was to lend substance to some symbol or effigy of the deity, be it inside the temple—where only priests might enter—or on the platform without, easily visible to the multitude of faithful gathered at the foot of the pyramid. Let us not forget that the Mesoamerican sanctuary was not generally accessible to mortals—as we will perceive in examining the narrow dimensions of some of these temples.

Certain pyramids must have been dedicated to the worship of the stars, and the majority of these to the sun. During the Aztec

Feast of the Sun, a captive of war, adorned with symbolic insignia, would be made to ascend the pyramid steps one by one, reflecting the sun's course from dawn to midday (midday being represented by the temple summit). Here, his face raised toward the sun, the captive delivered a message that had been entrusted to him. The priest then sacrificed him over a stone carved with solar symbols, and allowed the corpse to roll back down the steps to signify the path of the sun from noon to sunset.[26]

In some parts of Mesoamerica, the pyramid, with its superimposed bodies, symbolized the heavens, which people visualized as a series of layers—almost always thirteen—each occupied by some deity. On the highest layer dwelled the primordial couple, the Supreme Duality, from whom the other gods and man himself had descended.[27]

The Classic period (200–900 A.D.) left a spectacular mark on Meso-america, with the peaks of civilization being reached at Teoti-huacán in the Mexican highlands, Monte Albán in Oaxaca, and the Maya region. These will be treated separately.

Prior to this apogee, a transition between formative rural cultures and more urbanized ones followed the Pre-Classic period. In the basin of Mexico, as we have mentioned, Tlapacoya was a typically civic-religious center of Late Pre-Classic proportions, yet it possessed many features that were to be characteristic of the Classic world, such as fresco painting on pottery and a pyramid with sloping walls that probably served as inspiration for Teotihuacán's great structures. The eruption of Xitle volcano near Cuicuilco, which spewed lava over most of the southern part of the basin, forced the inhabitants to migrate, undoubtedly to Tlapacoya and Teotihuacán.

The Classic was a period of planned urban centers with astronomical orientation for streets and buildings, monumental architecture, intellectual achievements such as the perfection of the calendar, mathematics, writing, and astronomy (the latter especially among the Maya). A golden age of arts and architecture flowered, reflected in the magnificent pyramid-temples at Teotihuacán and Tikal, in mural painting, ceramics, and mosaics. Professional people and artisans were organized in guilds. Traders (pochteca) were also well organized, and in large and efficient markets goods from many regions changed hands. Society was both stratified and theocratic.

Teotihuacán was the most highly urbanized center of its time in the New World.[1] The life-span of this center was roughly 500 B.C. to 750 A.D. The beginnings of Teotihuacán were in the Late Pre-Classic and, although its chronological end was earlier than that of the Maya region, the later Aztecs continued to use the ceremonial center as a sacred place, burying their deceased rulers there.

In their study of Mesoamerica, Sanders and Price tell us that the Teotihuacán Valley was occupied for approximately one thousand years by a sedentary agricultural society prior to the rise of the city.[2] The settlement pattern was one of a tribal society that occupied primarily the elevated portions of the valley. By 300 B.C., a series of small chiefdoms existed, and in the next three centuries the population doubled every generation. By 100 A.D. the settlements had shifted to the alluvial plain, with half the population concentrated in the huge center which was to be the Classic city. Sanders feels that this great number of people in the valley made possible the construction of the Pyramid of the Sun, and about a century later the Pyramid of the Moon and Avenue of the Dead. In fact, there may have been forced

19. *Teotihuacán, Mexico: aerial view of the Pyramid of the Sun*
20. *Teotihuacán: Pyramid of Quetzalcóatl. Elevation*
21. *Teotihuacán: Pyramid of Quetzalcóatl. Lateral detail of one of the alfardas*
22. *Teotihuacán: Pyramid of Quetzalcóatl. Detail of the facade* ▷

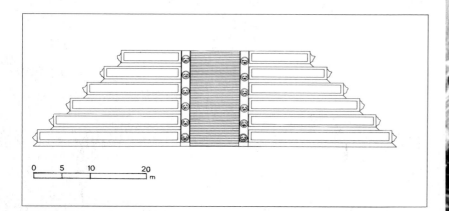

23. *Teotihuacán: Pyramid of Quetzalcóatl. Detail of the facade*

24. *Teotihuacán: Temple of the Feathered Shells. Detail of a corner of the facade*

labor in this gigantic construction project. In the early days of Teoti-huacán, dispersed settlements around the valley were without cere-monial architecture, indicating that the population worshiped in the one ritual center. Later, sites on the periphery began to have their own temple-pyramid complexes.

The city covered more than 13 square miles (20 sq. km.) and at-tained a maximum population of 200,000.[3] Although this sounds small compared to our modern metropoli, the city was larger than imperial Rome. Frequent pilgrimages to this sacred center swelled the popula-tion. Teotihuacán was, furthermore, the civic, religious, political, and economic center for all the surrounding valleys; thus hundreds of thousands more were brought under its influence. As René Millon states, other contemporary Mesoamerican centers such as Tikal or Dzibilchaltún may have covered larger areas, but "none seems to have been so highly urbanized; that is, none seems to have combined great size, high population density, large populations, foreign enclaves, and thousands of craft specialists in a market-place and ritual center of immense, monumental proportions" as did Teoti-huacán.[4]

The city's name means "birthplace of the gods." Myth tells us that after the sun had died the gods gathered here to create a new one (in ancient Mesoamerica a "sun" was equivalent to an era):

It is told that when yet [all] was in darkness, when yet no sun had shone and no dawn had broken—it is said—that the gods gathered themselves together and took counsel among themselves there at Teotihuacán. They spoke, they said among themselves: "Come hither, O gods! Who will carry the burden? Who will take it upon himself to be the sun, to bring the dawn?"[5]

Tecuciztécatl, a rich god dressed in costly clothing, came forward, as did Nanahuatzin, a poor god arrayed in garments of paper and covered with sores from disease. But the rich god hesitated before the roaring flames, and it was Nanahuatzin who threw himself into the fire and became the sun. Tecuciztécatl took heart from his rival's example and jumped into the fire, thus becoming the moon.

Very early in its history a strong religious attraction in Teoti-huacán, together with its favored location in a fertile valley, next to a lake (now non-existent), with a nearby source for the obsidian industry (the valley itself being a natural corridor between the high-lands and the eastern and southern lowlands), all combined in a self-generating process to make Teotihuacán a unique urban center as well as a religious, economic, and political leader in Mesoamerica.[6]

◁ 25. *Teotihuacán: aerial view of the Citadel. In the center, the remains of the Pyramid of Quetzalcóatl, partially covered by a later construction*

26. *Teotihuacán: Citadel. Detail of the platforms with stairs and of the stepped bases leading to the interior plaza*

27. *Teotihuacán: Citadel. Detail of a stepped base displaying the Teotihuacán principle of the* talud-tablero

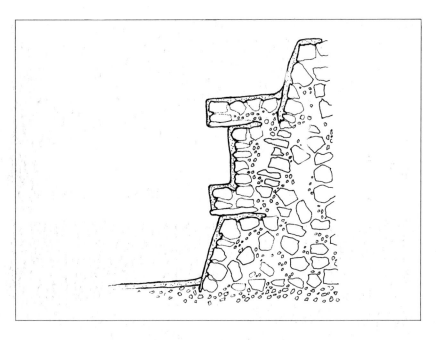

The recent discovery of a sacred cave underneath the center of th Pyramid of the Sun, reached by a natural tunnel from west to ea and bearing remains of man-made adaptations, not only fits th Florentine Codex's description of the burial place for Aztec sover eigns ("And when the rulers died, they buried them there [in Teoti huacán]. Then they built a pyramid over them . . ."),[7] but also lead us to believe that this cave, undoubtedly a center of worship as cave in Mexico have been over the centuries, actually determined the sit of the Pyramid of the Sun. A small structure has been discovere inside the pyramid,[8] which in all likelihood was a primitive altar temple, later covered by the larger pyramid around the beginning c the Christian era.

Any holy place attracts multitudes of pilgrims and permaner settlers as well, the latter to feed and attend the transients. This alon will not cause a great city to spring up around a shrine; optimur ecological and economic conditions must also combine with th sacred attraction. Teotihuacán was indeed a sacred place. The politic sovereigns were also priests, considered of divine origin. The nobilit —leaders and government officials—also had priestly functions an were the intermediaries between men and the gods. They acquire divine characteristics when they dressed in the gods' clothing; thus i Teotihuacán's mural paintings and pottery decoration we see pries dressed as Tláloc, the rain deity, as the mother goddess, or as jagua coyote, and bird divinities. Aside from some images which may hav been emblems indicating members of a lineage,[9] most of the symbo in Teotihuacán's art seem to have had religious meaning: the butterfl to some historians represents fire, to others the soul, or "inner fire," the jaguar an earth cult, and the "mantle" plaques on braziers th cardinal points because of their colors.

In all Mesoamerican art, religious symbolism is prevalent. I Teotihuacán, however, the genealogical representations in May stelae and Mixtec codices, or the court-life scenes of Bonampak ar lacking—unless, of course, they have not yet been discovered. Th predominance of religious representation at Teotihuacán, plus th presence of an altar in the central courtyard of each house testific to the importance of religion in Classic society. This world wher religious, civic, and secular duties overlapped was sharply stratified We can imagine a series of invisible circles to illustrate this strat fication as symbolized by the city planning. The innermost circl which covers the very heart of the ceremonial center would hav been occupied by the sovereign—the living representative of the mo revered god—and by the highest priest-chieftains. The next circl would correspond to noblemen with slightly lesser civic and religiou

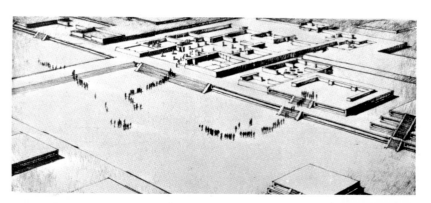

29. *Teotihuacán: Citadel. Perspective reconstruction of the so-called Viking Group and of a section of the Avenue of the Dead*

30. *Teotihuacán: perspective reconstruction of several triple complexes in the northwest section of the Avenue of the Dead. In the foreground, the complex of the Four Little Temples; in the center, the Plaza of the Columns*

functions, this circle encompassing smaller religious edifices and the "palaces," as well as government buildings. The third would correspond to the merchants, men of wealth who also lived in palatial homes, and perhaps to the poets, musicians, and actors (the latter were highly respected and took part in both religious and secular ceremonies). The next circle would encompass specialized artists and artisans, who lived in multiroomed "apartment houses" with home altars. This would be followed by laborers, servants, and slaves; on the periphery would live and work the farmers.[11]

The people carried out their crafts within their one-story apartment dwellings, which Millon compares to the Roman atrium house that offered a maximum of privacy in a crowded city.[12] Dwellers of these compounds, which might properly be called mazes, were linked by ties of kinship or by a common occupation, or both.[13] There were more than 2,000 of these apartment complexes in the city, housing numerous families, each with its own set of rooms, kitchen, and small patio, various families sharing the courtyards and probably sharing sanitation facilities also. Archaeological remains of more than 500 craft workshops have been found within the city.[14]

The enormous numbers of pilgrims who poured into Teotihuacán for religious ceremonies both brought and took away with them craft objects and foodstuffs. The civic center and the vast marketplace were located across the road from the Citadel, but other small markets existed in different sections of the city, much the way today's cities have various shopping centers. Merchants carried Teotihuacán's goods and ideology to the far corners of Mesoamerica and returned with feathers from tropical birds, cotton, cacao, jade, turquoise, and other desirable items. They had their own god who protected them on their journeys.

Although there are considerable indications of a militaristic aspect in Teotihuacán's society (especially in its later history)—weapons and proof of cannibalism having been excavated[15]—it is illogical to suppose that Teotihuacán was a predominantly warring culture. Theocracy and militarism are not mutually exclusive, but it is difficult to imagine constant pilgrimages to Teotihuacán by people from far away unless these pilgrims were assured of a peaceful reception. Nevertheless, in view of isolated mandibles found in kitchen refuse and human bones discovered in cooking pots, Sanders feels that "warfare with its attendant ritual practices seem to parallel very closely those reported by the Spaniards of the Aztec."[16] Sharp social stratification is usually accompanied by oppression and there is evidence both in Teotihuacán and beyond its borders that the military were increasingly important from the fifth century A.D. on.[17]

31. *Teotihuacán: Pyramid of the Moon seen from the Avenue of the Dead*
32. *Teotihuacán: Plaza of the Moon and Pyramid of the Moon*

33. *Teotihuacán: Pyramid of the Moon. Detail of a corner of the additional base* ▷

We do not yet know who the Teotihuacanos were. They left no written documents as such. Their story will one day be revealed in the symbolic writing on their murals and pottery.[18] It may be that Teotihuacán manuscripts, if they existed, were destroyed by later groups, as the Aztecs destroyed the Toltec codices. We can, however, make certain assumptions: the Teotihuacanos probably were mainly of the Utonahua linguistic family, like the later Toltecs and Aztecs. This language originated in northwestern Mexico and overlapped with Otopame in the central valleys. But Teotihuacán was a multilingual city. People from Oaxaca, Guerrero, the Gulf Coast, and the Maya region lived and worked in special sectors of the city. Add to this the influx of pilgrims and it is easy to see that Teotihuacán was a veritable Tower of Babel.

Clay figurines, stone masks, and fresco paintings show us what the Teotihuacanos looked like. Except for some plump figures with coastal features and broad heads represented in the masks, people were slender, of medium height, practiced cranial deformation by applying boards to the heads of newborns, and filed their teeth for cosmetic purposes. In early Teotihuacán people followed the Pre-Classic norms of decorating their bodies with painted designs. During the Classic age dress was rich and varied. Fine weaving, embroidery, a lavish use of feathers, ritual use of paper, and intricate zoomorphic headdresses were common, at least among the privileged classes. Heads were partially shaved and, as among the Post-Classic Aztecs, each hairdo was symbolic of its wearer's position in society.

The decline of Teotihuacán (650–800 A.D.) was due partly to internal forces. Weakened by dissent that may have been caused by a decadence in religion, or possibly even because of climatic changes— an increasing need for wood for construction entailed the cutting down of forests and consequent erosion, food shortages, and lack of arable land—as well as by a rebellion against growing militarism, Teotihuacán suffered a decline in population. Part of the city was burned by the inhabitants themselves around 700 A.D. As Muriel Weaver says: "The Teotihuacanos had managed to establish a prestige and influence unsurpassed in the history of Mesoamerica. Why, just when their art and architecture were being copied, their pottery popular and much prized, and even their religion was spreading—why at the seeming peak of their power did the great city suddenly and completely collapse?"[19] In reality, that collapse was probably not so sudden. Only in rare instances is a culture dissolved with a single blow. Rather, there is a shifting of economic, political, and military power to other centers—and in the case of Teotihuacán these new centers undoubtedly were Cholula, Xochicalco, and El Tajín.

34. *Teotihuacán: Building of the Altars at the foot of the Pyramid of the Moon*

35. *The "five regions of the world" from the Fejérvary-Mayer Codex*

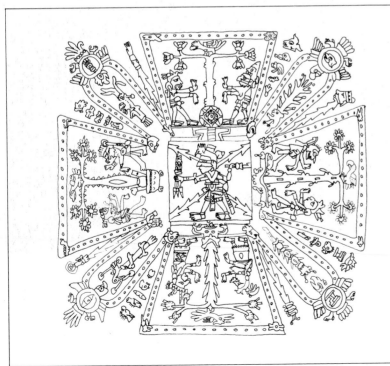

Teotihuacán's two local black obsidian deposits and the fact that the city was en route to the even more highly prized green obsidian deposits in Hidalgo gave it virtual control of the entire obsidian trade. Obsidian—volcanic glass—was, in the economy of ancient Mesoamerica (where metal did not come into use until around 900 A.D.), as important as steel is to modern industrial nations, since most tools and weapons were made of obsidian.[20] It was imported to the southern Olmec region from Teotihuacán as early as 1200 B.C., "several centuries earlier than any known occupation" of the Teotihuacán Valley.[21] Control of the obsidian route must have been equivalent to control of a major portion of Mesoamerica's trading economy and another factor in the rise of Teotihuacán. Loss of this control—and there is evidence of this at the time of the city's internal collapse, when obsidian traders probably went directly to the Puebla deposits near Cholula and/or combined this route with the cotton route through Xochicalco, down into Guerrero and then eastward[22]—would have been the *coup de grâce* for an already weakened state.

Other theories exist for the disappearance of Teotihuacán as a great power. Piña Chán believes that the myth of the gods throwing themselves into the fire symbolizes the change in Teotihuacán's social structure.[23] The peaceful agricultural gods abandoned the city, which was then occupied by cults dedicated to fire, sun, and war. The high priest was not only the civil leader but also the military chieftain, according to this scholar. Nevertheless, although there was a decline in population at the end of the Classic period, neighboring groups coexisted with surviving Teotihuacanos and blended the local arts and philosophy with their own. These people became the Toltecs (*toltecatl* means artisan).

It may seem surprising that although the urban center of Teotihuacán was practically moribund during the Toltec period (800–1300 A.D.), the Teotihuacán Valley was densely occupied at that time, and even more so in the Aztec period (1300–1521 A.D.). Sanders feels that possibly the Pyramids of the Sun and the Moon never stopped functioning, although in Post-Classic times the use of the ceremonial center would have been limited to a very small area.[24] Although minor Aztec structures displaying a poor construction technique are attached to earlier and finer buildings, Aztec towns in the Teotihuacán Valley had their own civic and religious centers. At the end of the Classic era, colonies or satellites of Teotihuacán—Azcapotzalco, for example—became independent, just as modern suburbs at times eventually break off from their mother city.

36. *Teotihuacán: view of the Plaza of the Moon and the Avenue of the Dead from the summit of the Pyramid of the Moon; in the background, left, the Pyramid of the Sun*

37. *Teotihuacán: aerial view from the south*

Architecture and Urbanism in Teotihuacán

The monumental architecture of Teotihuacán first appears in the Proto-Classic period, early in the Christian era, with one of the most ambitious undertakings in all of Mesoamerica: the Pyramid of the Sun. Built over a cave held sacred since more ancient times, the pyramid generally retains the simple outlines of the Pre-Classic stepped bases, with steeply sloping outer walls *(plate 19)*. These principles, realized a millennium earlier in the earthen pyramids of La Venta, are set forth here on a gigantic scale. The pyramid's massive bulk looms over the other remnants of the great city; its unique dimensions can be fully appreciated only from a distance. The ground plan reveals a square base some 738 feet (225 m.) across; its total height, including that of the temple that once stood on the upper platform, is estimated to have been about 246 feet (75 m.)—loftier than any other pre-Hispanic structure discovered to date.

Dating from somewhat later in the same period is the Pyramid of the Moon, in which structural bodies protrude forward, resulting in a somewhat more complex interplay of volumes *(plate 32)*. The structure itself is of more modest dimensions than the Pyramid of the Sun, although its placement in the northern part of the valley, on gradually rising terrain, brings the upper platform to roughly the same altitude.

These two edifices, their severe contours playing against the mountainous landscape on the horizon, were to dictate the features of the city's future growth. Though the Avenue of the Dead[25]—one day to be the city's mainline—did not yet exist, some kind of urban plan must already have evolved, since there are too many intriguing relationships to warrant our supposing them to be mere accident. For example, the Pyramid of the Sun is oriented toward the precise point on the horizon where the sun sets over Teotihuacán the day it reaches its zenith; this orientation would prevail throughout the subsequent centuries of the city's growth. Furthermore, the Avenue of the Dead, which runs strictly parallel to the main facade of the Pyramid of the Sun, is perfectly aligned with the axis of the Plaza of the Moon and that of the Pyramid of the Moon *(plate 36)*. This axis ultimately terminates in a slight depression atop Cerro Gordo—where, incidentally, we find the remains of a temple *(plate 37)*. And from the top of the Pyramid of the Moon, a line of sight runs to the summit of the Pyramid of the Sun and from there straight on to the peak of a mountain in the far distance *(plate 38)*.

All this suggests that in Teotihuacán, with the great pyramids

completed, a gigantic urban plan began to emerge, reflecting current ideas about astronomy and a desire to truly identify with the semiarid but serene landscape of the Mexican plateau. And so we are able to witness the gradual evolution of an enormous city in every sense of the word, based on a strict plan grander and more complex than anything ever known on the American continent.

A second stage in Teotihuacán's architecture begins between the second and third centuries A.D.—around the start of the Mesoamerican Classic period—and signals an abrupt spurt in urban growth. Now the Avenue of the Dead appeared, and around this *via sacra* arose a number of ceremonial complexes, including the typically symmetrical "triple complexes" so frequent in Teotihuacán—structural arrangements, apparently, of a very special kind *(plates 30, 39)*. It was during this epoch that the Pyramid of the Sun received the last segment of its stepped base, and saw new platforms built at its foot. And the residential sector, which had once centered mainly to the northwest of the two great pyramids, in a place where the land lent itself less to farming, now suddenly began to grow in all directions, outward from the Avenue of the Dead and from the broad East and West Avenues perpendicular to it *(plate 38)*.

From the standpoint of urban planning in Mesoamerica, this expansion, which assumed a fairly regular checkerboard pattern, seems to have signified a real revolution. Extraordinary for its time in this part of the world, the phenomenon might reflect a happy combination: on the one hand, the special importance of religious temples around a great ceremonial area where elaborate ritual performances must have been held, attracting multitudes of pilgrims from distant regions; on the other, the manufacture of many specialized craft products—what René Millon calls a "pilgrim-temple-market complex."[26] An important architectural refinement during this same phase—one that would come to influence many aspects of Meso-american architecture—was the definitive crystallization of the *tablero*. By the second century, this element (which may have been created at Tlalancaleca some centuries earlier) had become an inseparable feature of all Teotihuacán's religious structures—whether a simple altar, ceremonial platform, small temple, or majestic stepped pyramid. The Teotihuacán *tablero* was a heavy rectangular molding, outlined by a thick frame that accentuated its marked horizontal trend, and it projected from the inclined plane (the *talud*) from which it was detached *(plate 28)*. In this particular combination of *talud-tablero,* the *tablero* usually predominated—at least in Teotihuacán, where its height was generally double or triple that of the *talud*. This combination could be adapted to the structure of the typical stepped

Legend:

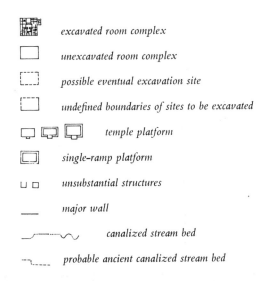

    excavated room complex

    unexcavated room complex

    possible eventual excavation site

    undefined boundaries of sites to be excavated

    temple platform

    single-ramp platform

    unsubstantial structures

    major wall

    canalized stream bed

    probable ancient canalized stream bed

1. *Pyramid of the Moon*   2. *Pyramid of the Sun*
3. *Citadel*   4. *Temple of Quetzalcóatl*
5. *Avenue of the Dead*   6. *Great Compound*
7. *West Avenue*   8. *East Avenue*
9. *Market*   10. *Tlamimilolpa*   11. *Xolalpan*
12. *Palace of Tepantitla*   13. *Fresco of the Priest*
14. *Plaza I*   15. *House of the Eagles*
16. *"Ancient City"*   17. *Oaxaca Quarter*
18. *Palace of Atetelco*   19. *La Ventilla A*
20. *La Ventilla B*   21. *Teopancaxco*
22. *San Lorenzo River*   23. *San Juan River*
24, 25, 26, 27. *Cisterns*   28. *Plaza of the Moon*
29. *Palace of the Quetzalbutterfly*   30. *Group 5'*
31. *Group 5*   32. *Complex of the Four Little Temples*
33. *Building of the Altars*   34. *Temple of Agriculture*
35. *Fresco of the Mythological Animals*
36. *Fresco of the Puma*   37. *Plaza of the Columns*
38. *Excavation of 1895*   39. *Palace of the Sun*
40. *Patio of the Four Little Temples*   41. *House of the Priest*
42. *Viking Group*   43. *Avenue of the Dead*
44. *Excavation of 1917*   45. *Superimposed Buildings*
46. *Excavation of 1908*   47. *Palace of Tetitla*
48. *Patio of the Palace of Zacuala*   49. *Palace of Zacuala*
50. *Yayahuala*

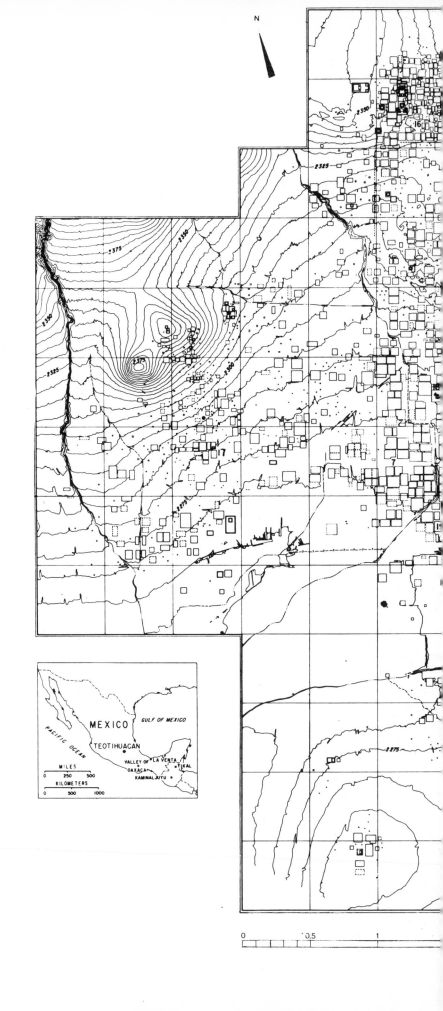

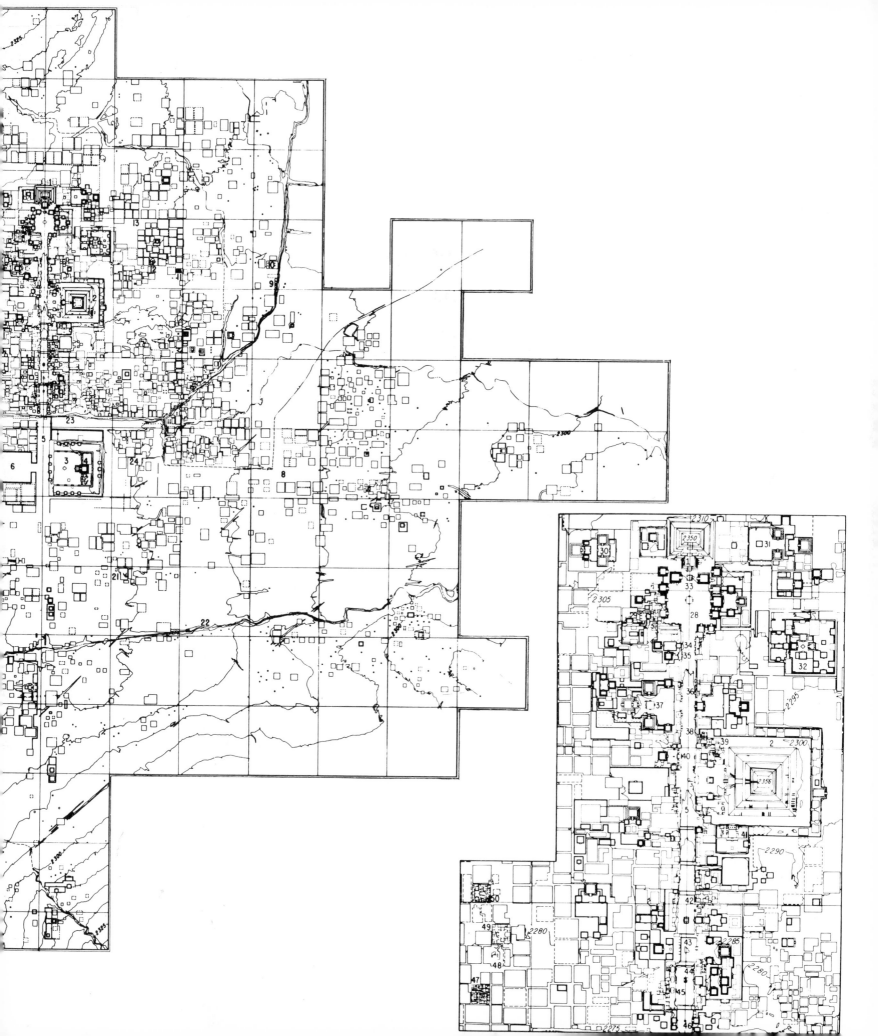

40. *Teotihuacán: Palace of the Quetzalbutterfly. Porticoed patio*
41. *Teotihuacán: Palace of the Quetzalbutterfly. Detail of the pillars around the patio*

42. *Teotihuacán: Palace of the Quetzalbutterfly. Detail of one of the pillars around the central patio* ▷

bases that made up the ceremonial center, and it lends Teotihuacán's religious architecture an unmistakable stamp—providing unity and emphasizing the visibly horizontal orientation that characterized the urban phase. We find early examples of *tableros* in the so-called Underground Buildings; in the first "triple complex" *(plate 27)*; and in the Temple of the Feathered Shells, which forms the substructure of the Palace of the Quetzalpapálotl (Quetzalbutterfly).

Perhaps the most splendid example of the *tablero* lies in the Pyramid of Quetzalcóatl, one of the most fascinating buildings of ancient Mexico *(plates 22, 23)*. Built, it would seem, during this same transitional period between the Proto-Classic and the Classic phase, the pyramid was luckily preserved, thanks to its partial burial under a more recent structure. Its principal facade, which faces west like the Pyramid of the Sun, shows an ornamental richness unparalleled in Teotihuacán's architecture.

Jutting out from the *alfardas* that border the stairway, we see the enormous heads of Quetzalcóatl, the Plumed Serpent *(plate 21)*, centered in the thick *tableros* that form the stepped segments of the base; we find the same serpent—its feathered halo, its undulating body covered in stylized feathers, its tail ending in the characteristic ring of a rattlesnake—alternating with heads of Tláloc, a deity associated with water and rain (whose cult, as we shall see, apparently flourished in Teotihuacán). On the *taludes,* too, we see reliefs with the profile of plumed serpents, their bodies undulating—like those on the *tableros*—amid various kinds of seashells, many of which still reveal the original stucco and the colors that had once covered the entire facade (mainly pink and green).

This marks the arrival on the Mexican plateau's cultural horizon of one of its most fascinating mythological entities—the plumed serpent, whose historical development was to prove as rich as it was complex. Here, it appears directly associated with marine symbols and with the god of water and rain, as certain painted murals and ceramic motifs suggest. In other cases, Quetzalcóatl seems to relate to a certain bearded figure, as we shall see in various myths from the time of the Spanish Conquest.

Aside from the vast symbolic and aesthetic appeal of the Pyramid of Quetzalcóatl, a study of its structure reveals the technological advances of the period. The entire nucleus of the pyramid, for example, is reinforced with a skeleton of limestone. The colossal heads are deeply anchored in the core of the *tableros*—a veritable *tour de force*—and all the exterior joints show a precision almost incredible in the light of the primitive tools then available in Mesoamerica, where the use of hard metals was not known. We should also observe the side

43. *Teotihuacán: plan of the Palace of the Quetzalbutterfly and adjoining buildings*
44. *Teotihuacán: plan of the Palace of Zacuala*

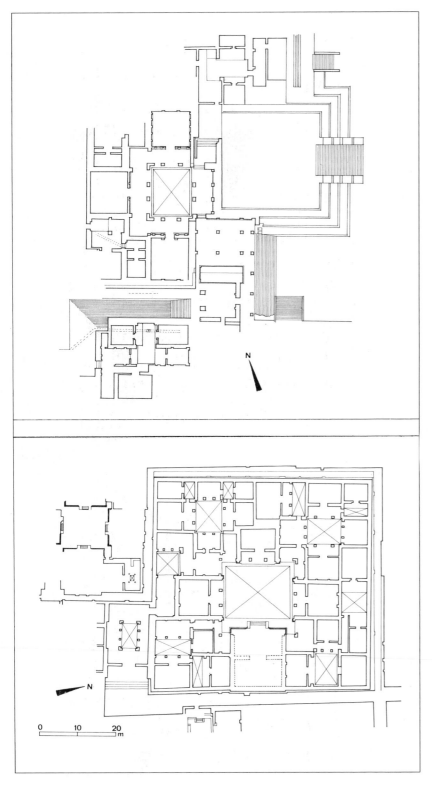

of the stairways *(plate 21)*, where, to avoid slippage and to transfer the weight directly to the ground, the builders devised an ingenious way of fitting the stones that would seem to have been inspired by the true arch—except that this form was unknown in the pre-Columbian world.

With the construction of this pyramid, perhaps more accurately named the Pyramid of Quetzalcóatl and Tláloc, Teotihuacán made its triumphant entry into what we now call the Mesoamerican Classic period. But the enormous effort that must have gone into the pyramid's construction was to prove unique in the city's overall visual severity; we might almost refer to it as its baroque phase. Indeed, except for an occasional ruin of a contemporaneous building also decorated with carvings, such as one of the bases near the Pyramid of the Sun or the Temple of the Feathered Shells *(plate 24)*, most structures in the ceremonial center show only the remains of painted murals. Perhaps the immensity of their urban plan forced the builders of Teotihuacán to renounce the idea of polychrome sculpture in favor of designs that, while well-contrasted, were applied to smooth surfaces only. We still find enough traces of polychrome stucco *in situ* to suggest that the city was once entirely painted, including the surfaces of streets, thoroughfares, and plazas. We even know that in the ceremonial sector the predominating colors were red and white.

Once its two great pyramids and the splendid temple honoring Quetzalcóatl were built, Teotihuacán's early zeal for monumentality yielded to a more horizontal type of growth. During the entire period of the city's Classic glory, which runs more or less from the end of the second to the middle of the eighth century, the ceremonial center was remodeled and completed, the residential zones experienced a controlled expansion, and great engineering projects were initiated—including the channeling of the rivers and streams that traversed the city, and the building of large open-air reservoirs.

To this gigantic urban layout, for reasons that remain unknown, there eventually was added a new stepped base, almost completely covering the main facade of the Pyramid of Quetzalcóatl; and around it appeared the high platforms crowned with secondary temples that—when taken with the central platform, its four stairways, and subsidiary structures—would form one of Teotihuacán's most imposing ceremonial entities, known (inaccurately) as the Citadel *(plates 25, 26)*.[27] With its broad access stairway, and the severely symmetrical sequence of platforms and stepped bases delineated in the subtle lines of the now-classic *tableros*, the complex must indeed have created a majestic effect. Everything suggests that as the Mesoamerican "Mecca"—a role that Teotihuacán fulfilled for several centuries—

this mega-complex forming the ceremonial center was the heart of the city. Its axis coincided not only with those of the East and West Avenues, but with what is known as the Great Compound, which faced it across the Avenue of the Dead, and which seems to have been both the administrative center of the city and the site of an important outdoor market. The Great Compound and the Citadel, with their broad surrounding thoroughfares, formed what according to René Millon "seems to have been one of the most outstanding architectural works in the history of pre-Columbian peoples."[28]

North of the Citadel, along a stretch of the Avenue of the Dead between the San Juan River and the Pyramid of the Sun, Teotihuacán's urban architects arrived at a clever device to compensate for the difference in height resulting from the slope of the land from north to south, which was slightly more pronounced in this section. Here, a series of wide, bridge-like partitions crossed the Avenue from side to side, so that the high platforms bordering the *via sacra* could meet at the same level. This resulted in new ceremonial complexes, as suggested by structures found in the center of some of the small plazas thus formed. Yet while they afforded a series of flat transverses across the Avenue of the Dead, these platforms constituted a kind of obstacle course for the many processional groups that must have paraded along it. And in the opinion of Matthew Wallrath, such impediments were designed precisely for the purpose of controlling and regulating the flow of these pilgrims, so that as they approached the Pyramid of the Sun they would maintain the good order and dignified composure that circumstances required.[29]

Hardoy suggests, in poetic terms, the psychological impact of such transitional elements on pilgrims who, making their way toward the Citadel from the Pyramid of the Moon, found themselves suddenly facing "a series of sequences, simple, yet rich in sensation, resulting from the changing view of the Pyramid of the Sun, and from its continual appearance and disappearance along the axis, intermittently shutting off the vista beyond."[30] Having reached the vicinity of the Pyramid of the Sun, the various processions could then turn right and at last, by mounting an access platform perpendicular to the previous ones, reach the sunken plaza at the foot of the pyramid. Or, they might continue along the Avenue of the Dead, bordered here by high platforms and secondary temples hiding some of the most grandiose "triple complexes"—such as the Plaza of the Columns *(plate 30)*—and slowly approach the Pyramid of the Moon, gazing in wonder as it grew larger in a veritable towering crescendo—while behind it, on the same axis, Cerro Gordo would seem to shrink until it had all but disappeared *(plate 31)*.

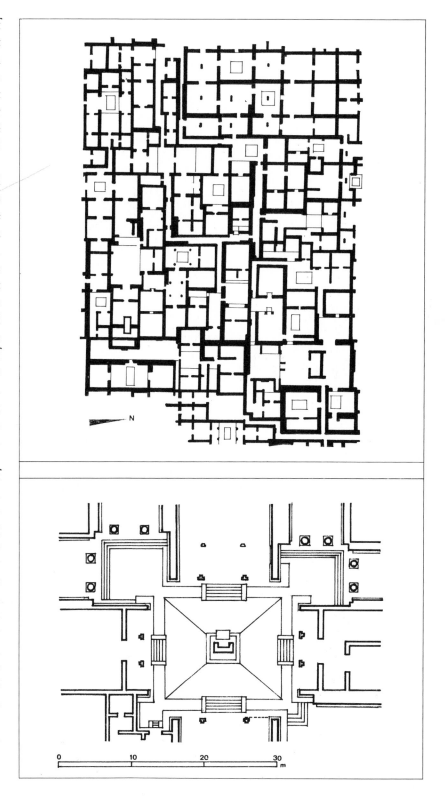

N

0   10   20   30
m

It must have been an overwhelming experience, after suffering the hardships of travel—often from remote regions—to find oneself abruptly in the middle of this broad, paved avenue, flanked by temples shrouded in clouds of *copal* (the Indian incense), witnessing spectacular rituals and celebrations. The grand design of this vast and well-orchestrated ceremonial area was on a scale that sought to approach the grandeur and power of the gods, reducing the human condition almost to insignificance. Even today, as it stands in ruins, we can sense Teotihuacán's almost inhuman majesty.

And what might be said of the Pyramid of the Moon, which possibly for religious reasons, we suspect played a role of primordial importance, and may well have served as the final chord in this great architectural cantata? Planned with astonishing strictness and symmetry, the Plaza of the Moon must have provided a worthy setting for this final drama. The additional base of the Pyramid of the Sun was too small; that of Quetzalcóatl was excessively large. But the base added to the foot of the Pyramid of the Moon is in complete harmony with its bulk, and creates a smooth transition between it and the other pyramids that make up the plaza *(plate 32)*. Between the ceremonial platform, which occupies the center of the plaza, and the foot of the stairway leading to the Pyramid of the Moon, a small and rather strange structural element underscores the role of this site as a *sanctum sanctorum*. It consists of an enclosure with only one entrance, facing west, with a series of altars *(plate 34)*, in *talud-tablero* form, whose broken angles suggest, as Otto Schöndube observes, "the five regions of the world in the Fejérvary-Mayer Codex, wherein appear the deities that occupy each segment of the universe *[plate 35]*; as this far transcends a mere formal resemblance, it is evident that this place was one of the most sacred in Teotihuacán—just as the dimensions of the Plaza and Pyramid of the Moon would make one suppose."[31]

Looking down from the summit of the Pyramid of the Moon at the farms and cultivated fields that cover most of what is left of the city, we can still appreciate the grandeur and clarity of Teotihuacán's urban plan, with the immense plaza down below, the Avenue of the Dead stretching to the hillsides some 3 miles (5 km.) to the south and the Pyramid of the Sun, its profile majestic against the form of the mountain Patlachique, which sits afar like a distant echo *(plate 36)*. It is easy to see why the Aztecs, who knew this city only as a ruin some five centuries after its abandonment, gave it a place in their mythology and called it Teotihuacán—City of the Gods; it must have been hard for them to believe that such a place could have been created by mere mortals. And so arose the beautiful Aztec legend of the Fifth Sun, in which we learn how the gods gathered in Teotihuacán to give

birth to the sun—that same sun, so the legend goes, that lights our planet today.

In our time, aerial photography makes it far easier to grasp the overall design of architectural complexes *(plates 25, 38)*; but in the case of Teotihuacán, a careful study of its urban plan as it appears in maps painstakingly drawn up under the direction of René Millon can be even more eloquent. With its quadrants, formed by the Avenue of the Dead and the East and West Avenues; its span of 13 square miles (20 sq. km.); and a population of between 75,000 and 200,000,[32] the city emerges as a living entity by 600 A.D., in a state of constant renovation and, judging by the many still uninhabited sectors, likely to keep on growing. Even peripheral housing zones were aligned with the city streets *(plate 39)*. The regularity of the city blocks and the density of some of the residential sectors are astonishing. Add to this the channeling of the rivers; large reservoirs; steam baths; specialized workshops; *tianguis,* or open-air markets; administrative buildings; theaters; areas set aside for ball games and other public functions—and we come to realize the kind of advance that Teotihuacán represented in pre-Columbian city planning.

The immense ceremonial center in the core of the city is, of course, the outstanding element. The incredible quantity and concentration of religious elements here have earned a special niche in history. Noteworthy, among other things, are the thick walls on the Citadel's upper platform and around the Pyramid of the Moon and other areas that enclosed large architectural groupings, shutting them off and thus transforming them into so many independent complexes within the ceremonial mega-complex.

Hardoy, analyzing the city's plan, concludes that "the three basic aspects of urban Teotihuacán: arrangement along axes; the symmetry of elements within groups; and the use of simple masses, in isolation or connected by platforms of lesser height . . . are most decisively planned."[33] As for the vigorousness of the layout, we need only mention that it is based on an urban module of 187 feet (57 m.), as are the proportions of many "standard" blocks in the residential zones. This same measure, probably a multiple of a much smaller pattern, emerges as the distance from axis to axis between each of the stepped bases that border the Citadel. Bruce Drewitt points out the modules' pattern of repetition in the overall composition: from the center of the platform in the Plaza of the Moon to the axis of the Pyramid of the Sun, ten times; from the latter to the axis of the Citadel and the Great Compound, twenty-one times; in the channeled stretch of the San Juan River to the north of these, twenty-four times; and so forth.[34]

This planning eventually reached a point at which the checker-board pattern serving as a general model was used not only for th[e] valley proper but for the sides of the surrounding hills as well; eve[n] the river that crosses the valley had its course changed artificially t[o] conform to the grid pattern of 187 × 187 feet (57 × 57 m.). A sma[ll] array of circles divided by a cross seems to have served the topogra[-] phers as a guide, since one circle lines up with another as though the[y] had been placed there to act as a theodolite. Two of the patterns ar[e] to be found two miles apart, creating a line exactly perpendicular t[o] the north-south axis of the city.[35]

The use of such modules, in addition to the city's controlle[d] growth and the other factors we have cited, imply the existence of [a] particularly energetic ruling group, both spiritual and temporal. I[t] all seems to indicate that for several centuries Teotihuacán represente[d] not only a commercial capital, but the religious and cultural heart o[f] what may have been a very large segment of Mesoamerica. Som[e] authors speak of a possible Teotihuacán "empire"—although w[e] should perhaps limit this idea to spiritual, cultural, and economic aspects[.]

Before considering the matter of Teotihuacán's influence o[n] other regions of Mesoamerica, let us pause to discuss some of th[e] buildings found in its residential zones, beginning with the Palace o[f] the Quetzalpapálotl, or Quetzalbutterfly, which, in view of its loca[-] tion at the southwest angle of the Plaza of the Moon *(plate 38)*, ma[y] have been the residence of a high priest. The wide, porticoed ante[-] chamber adjacent to that angle of the plaza, flanked by two of th[e] pyramids that border it, shows a subtle technique employed b[y] Teotihuacán's city planners to establish a link between ceremonia[l] spaces and the streets that led to residential areas. In this case *(plat[e] 43)*, the antechamber is divided into two parts: the main section— the actual vestibule of the Palace of the Quetzalpapálotl—and [a] subsection serving as a transitional element between the vestibule an[d] the adjacent buildings; and, most important, between the stairwa[y] of the Plaza of the Moon and that which runs into a city street. Bu[t] the main attraction of the palace is its porticoed central patio, bounde[d] on three sides by spacious rooms covered by the usual flat roof, an[d] with an east gallery leading to other buildings. Almost completel[y] reconstructed by Jorge Acosta, this patio exhibits an unusual opulence[:] its massive pillars entirely covered in stone bas-reliefs *(plates 40, 41)*.[36]

The motifs carved into the pillars of the west gallery appear t[o] be owls, portrayed in frontal position; those in the other gallerie[s] denote the mythological *quetzalpapálotl,* the Quetzalbutterfly *(plat[e] 42)*. We should note too the ceiling frieze, in *tablero* form; the typica[l] stepped merlons carved in stone; and, on the inner faces of the pillars[,] a series of rings driven into the stone plaques or embedded in th[e] masonry at a height we usually associate with hinges. These served t[o]

tie the cords supporting the curtains that were Teotihuacán's equiva-lent of modern windows and doors.

To the southwest, in the center of a dense residential district in a rather regular grid pattern of 187 × 187-foot (57 × 57 m.) blocks we find the Palace of Zacuala—an excellent example of what may have been the luxurious residence of a rich Teotihuacán merchant or of a high functionary *(plate 44)*. Minutely explored and studied by Laurette Séjourné, this palace is outstanding for its clarity of composi-tion, its ample spaces (both open and closed), the privacy it afforded, and the high level of urban life it suggests in comparison to the rest of Mesoamerica.[37] The narrow streets form a typical urban crisscross pattern, and the *cul de sac* in front of the palace entrance widens to take in part of a neighboring block.

Entering through the wide doorway, we come to a spacious porticoed vestibule, a kind of *impluvium,* leading off to the right into a second, elongated vestibule offering indirect access to one of the apartments and direct access to an enormous central patio that is the building's key element. Opening onto this patio are three important porticoed chambers—probably reception areas—and a medium-sized temple (the palace's private "chapel") that, like so many of Teoti-huacán's sanctuaries, faces west. The three other corners of the patio, reflecting a custom characteristic of this city, lead to other apartments in which covered and uncovered spaces alternate. Such "patio-gal-leries," which served as a link between various rooms, were a source of light and air in this Mesoamerican architecture wherein windows were almost unknown. In some of Teotihuacán's buildings—the Palace of Tetitla, for example—the "light patio" had shrunk to the size of a skylight.

In violent contrast to the opulence and spaciousness of the Palace of Zacuala, the more densely populated artisans' quarter of Tlami-milolpa, east of the ceremonial center, reveals a veritable labyrinth of passageways, patio-galleries, and chambers. Here, in 176 rooms, twenty-one small patios and five large ones, plus alleys, large family groups probably lived and worked, crowded into perhaps 11,700 square feet (3,500 sq. m.) of space.

Moving on, we find an instance of the interesting and typical Teotihuacán solution to the problem of connecting the open angles of the principal patio, using secondary patios, passageways, and stair-ways. It occurs in the Palace of Atetelco, another structural complex in the western sector, which—from the number of "chapels" it housed (there is another example at Tetitla)—must have served some monastic function, perhaps as seminary, spiritual retreat house, or lodging for pilgrims *(plate 46)*. This judgment seems confirmed by a large altar in the center of the main patio, resembling a temple in miniature.

by the Classic *tableros* of its base—a constant feature of Teotihuacán's religious architecture; and by the moldings crowning the flat roof of its sanctuary, as depicted in a painting on a vase found at Tikal *(plate 47)*. This instructive documentation, plus some smaller models in stone *(plate 48)* and various ceramic representations, graffiti, and mural paintings, give us an idea, however superficial, of the probable appearance of Teotihuacán's temples.

Though only rubble is left of Teotihuacán's buildings, patient exploration is slowly revealing the wonderful purity of the wall fragments—the lower parts generally showing the sloping *talud*— and of floors that were, according to a description by the chronicler Fray Juan de Torquemada, ". . . of plaster; and after whitewashing them . . . they polished them with pebbles and very smooth stones; and they looked as well finished and shone as beautifully as a silver plate . . . so smooth and clean that one could eat any morsel off them without a tablecloth, and feel no disgust."[38]

Fragments of frescoes on certain walls reveal the soul of Teotihuacán. Indeed, were it not for the rich tapestry suggested by what remains of this culture's minor arts and paintings, its entire vast urban plan would be nothing more than an immense skeleton, devoid of spiritual content. In a highly esoteric symbolic language worthy of their majestic surroundings, the paintings display a thousand facets of Teotihuacán's religious thought. We meet the Teotihuacán pantheon in sculpture; in paintings on ceramics; in figurines; and, above all, in mural form. We make the acquaintance of the water deities: Chalchiuhtlicue, Tláloc's consort; the old fire god, Huehuetéotl, carrying a brazier on his head; Quetzalcóatl, associated with water in the Classic epoch; and the deities of commerce, of twins, of the morning star, of spring, flowers, music—and death.

There are curious mythological animals, such as the plumed jaguar with a forked serpent's tongue *(plate 49)*; richly dressed priests with their inevitable pouches of *copal;* seashells and other water symbols; and, finally, numerous representations of Tláloc, god of rain and water, who appears in his multiple roles—holding lightning in his hand, sowing or reaping maize, sprinkling large raindrops, or liberally dispensing abundance and wealth in the guise of a shower of jade jewels *(plate 50)*. Jade—associated with water and new vegetation— was the symbol of rebirth and of all that was "precious"; except for quetzal feathers, it was the material pre-Hispanic peoples prized most.

As an example of the "sacrifice of entreaty" that in Kubler's opinion[39] characterizes Teotihuacán's art, the paintings in the Palace of Tepantitla deserve special mention. We can admire here, in a truly enchanting freshness of style, scenes of Tlalocan (or Tamoanchan)— the paradise of Tláloc (or of the mother goddess)—where fortunate souls protected by the gods of earth and water abandon themselves to innocent games in a heaven replete with water, flowers, and butterflies. An ingenuous tropical paradise—and a worthy dream for men who dwelled on the semiarid Mexican plateau.

One fragment of these scenes portrays a lively ball game— a sport that in Teotihuacán, as in some of the western regions of Mexico (but unlike almost all other areas of Mesoamerica), was played with a stick. It is interesting that the painstaking exploration of Teotihuacán has failed so far to unearth any sign of the I-shaped ball courts that abound in almost all other Mesoamerican cities, where they were built especially for the practice of this important ritual game, as we shall see. Perhaps the intensive farming of this region erased all traces of them; or perhaps such courts never existed here, and the game was played on simple fields marked off by stelae, or *marcadores,* similar to the beautiful one found in the southern part of La Ventilla *(plate 51)*.

We should point out that in the nearby Puebla Valley, the ceremonial center of Manzanilla *(plate 52)*—which displays strong Teotihuacán influences in its ceramics and stone sculpture—had two important I-shaped courts (one even boasting a Teotihuacán *tablero*), and may have been the first center to introduce this feature on the Mexican plateau.

This brings us to the subject of outside influences. It would be wrong to suggest that the cultures of other Mesoamerican regions had had no impact on Teotihuacán. In its ceramics, we find forms and motifs of Maya inspiration and elements characteristic of the central Veracruz area—such as the unmistakable interlaced volutes clearly visible on the stele from La Ventilla—to say nothing of Oaxaca's contribution. But during the early centuries of the Christian era, Teotihuacán influences generally predominated. An active commerce conveyed products of Teotihuacán manufacture—ceramics in particular—to remote regions of Mesoamerica, where they were imitated, along with Teotihuacán ideas and architectural forms. Deeper and more subtle still is the impact of Teotihuacán's iconography, whose motifs appear in the most unexpected places, sometimes in the midst of a totally foreign artistic idiom. We shall see examples of this in certain buildings of the purest Maya style.

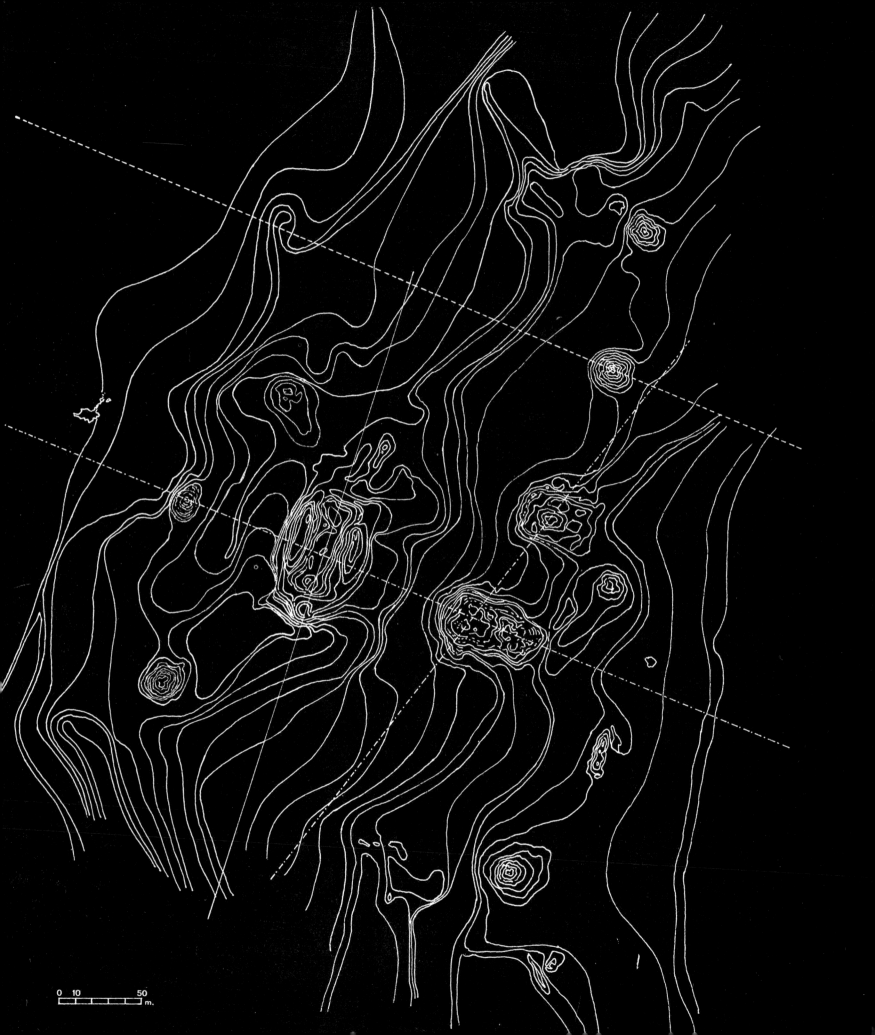

0 10   50
                m.

Cholula

Cholula, in the present-day state of Puebla, some 80 miles (129 km.) east of Mexico City, has been continuously occupied for thousands of years and was in part coeval with Teotihuacán. It had a Pre-Classic settlement, and in Classic times was a large and bustling city. Its art and architecture were largely influenced by Teotihuacán, although during the Classic efflorescence Teotihuacán's relations with Puebla seem to have bypassed Cholula to some extent and made themselves felt farther to the east, in Manzanilla and Tecamachalco, for example, where much Teotihuacán thin orange ware has been found.[1] That these sites are en route to the Mixtec area in Oaxaca and the permanent settlement of Oaxaca potters in Teotihuacán indicates a close relationship between these two regions.

According to Florencia Müller,[2] archaeologist and head of the ceramics department of Mexico's Institute of Anthropology, a summary of Cholula's history is as follows:

Although Pleistocene hunters must have roamed this once swampy valley—mammoth bones have been unearthed here—the earliest settlement dates from 800–500 B.C. and is located on the site where the University of the Americas now stands. The ceramic tradition of Cholula is related to the Olmec style of Morelos. Other early sites, near where the Great Pyramid of Tepanapa was to be constructed, show closer ties with the Olmec culture of Tlatilco in the basin of Mexico, and a little later (200–100 B.C.) the settlement pattern shows a village culture with a ceremonial center as yet unplanned, similar to Tlapacoya. Architectural planning appeared after this period, between 100 and 200 A.D.

In Early Classic times, between 200 and 450 A.D., the planned urban site, with the ceremonial center containing the pyramid-temple, plazas, and civic buildings, was erected. In a plan similar to Teotihuacán, two main avenues crossed at the heart of the city, where the pyramid stood. But unlike Teotihuacán, which expanded from the center outward, Cholula developed from east to west as new structures were built. The reason for this was the marshy land of an ex-lake bed on which the pyramid and related edifices were built: as slow sinking of the heavy stone and earth structures became evident, repairs and partial superpositions were undertaken, but by the Middle Classic period (450–500 A.D.), the new ceremonial center was moved west to the area occupied by the modern city of Cholula.

By 700–800 A.D. the pyramid (which Dr. Müller refers to as an acropolis due to its distribution of buildings, plazas, and monumental stairway, closer in plan to a Greek acropolis than to a true pyramid) was abandoned for ceremonial purposes and little by little became

53. *Cholula, Puebla: Great Pyramid (or "Acropolis") of Tepanapa seen from the east*

54. *Cholula: Great Pyramid of Tepanapa. Detail of the base*

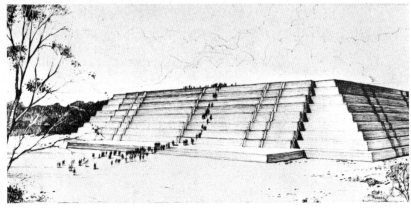

used as living quarters, as people took advantage of the solid walls, against which they built their houses. When the Spanish arrived at the beginning of the sixteenth century, they found the great temple to Quetzalcóatl on the site now occupied by the Franciscan monastery.³ The 164-foot-long (50 m.) mural of a drinking scene in one of the acropolis-pyramid structures dates from Early Classic times.

Divided into *barrios* or neighborhoods like Teotihuacán (originally four), Cholula's agricultural population made use of irrigation canals, aqueducts, and probably *chinampas*—man-made raft-islands covered with lake mud. The strong Teotihuacán traditions felt early by Cholula in both its ceramics and architecture gradually were replaced—or at least infiltrated—by influences from El Tajín in the Gulf Coast region, Monte Albán in Oaxaca, and the Maya region. These influences became felt around 500–700 A.D. Maya influence may be seen in the arrangement of plazas: as the center grew, ceremonial, civic, and residential structures encroached upon these plazas and reduced them in size, often necessitating stairways to lend access from one level to another. In the plazas, vertical stelae are associated with horizontal altars, as in Tikal. Yet a step-and-fret design, typical of the Oaxaca region, is on the walls of the plaza's buildings. Maya influence is also revealed in Cholula's people: teeth have been unearthed in nearby Xochitécatl, Tlaxcala, that are filed and inlaid in a manner similar to that used in Uaxactún and Piedras Negras before the Classic era, about 600 B.C.

Toward the end of the Classic period drastic changes took place in the Cholula region. The acropolis-pyramid was almost completely abandoned and there are signs that a fire had occurred. Teotihuacán tradition in ceramics had become minor by 800 A.D., but influence was still felt from the Maya area, the Gulf Coast, and most important, from the Mixteca region of Oaxaca.

Although Müller begins her Post-Classic ceramic sequence in 800–900, we shall include this new phase here, since the time period is considered still Classic in most of Mesoamerica. In this century two new traditions appeared in Cholula: one, found at Xicoténcatl in Tlaxcala, bearing ceramic characteristics similar to Casas Grandes in northern Mexico and Hohokam in the southwestern United States; the other seemingly originating in Tabasco and bringing with it Upper Mixtec traits. Furthermore, there was a change in the physical type, as can be seen from skeletal remains. These facts all point to a probable conquest of the region by the people we know as the Xicalanca-Olmecs (or Historical Olmecs, to distinguish them from the Pre-Classic Olmecs). Much can be learned about people from their funeral customs. From the Classic period in Cholula some skele-

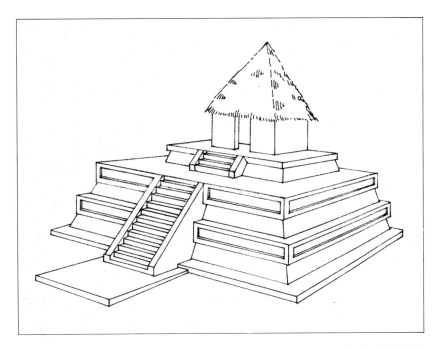

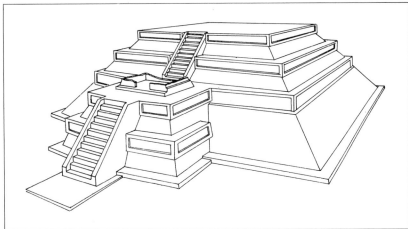

tal remains of children were found within an altar. This indicates sacrifice to a rain god, probably to the powerful Teotihuacán Tláloc, since children were the preferred sacrificial petitions for water. In the Xicalanca-Olmec period burials of remains within urns occurred for the first time; the deceased were also interred under the floors of their homes. The latter custom still exists in some regions of Mexico such as the Lacandon, where a chieftain's grave is dug beneath his own floor, after which the house is abandoned for a time. Aside from its impact on such peripheral cities as Tepeapulco and on remote "colonies" such as Kaminaljuyú in the Guatemala highlands *(plate 58)*, whose buildings are purely in the style of Teotihuacán, the City of the Gods seems to have influenced architecture in very diverse ways. In the Puebla Valley, in addition to Manzanilla (mentioned above), the great city of Cholula arose, and ultimately began to rival Teotihuacán. Its importance as a religious center must have grown steadily up to the time of the Spanish Conquest.

The fruit of innumerable stages of amplification and superposi-tioning carried out between the second and eighth centuries (and paralleling Teotihuacán's dominant period), Cholula's Great Pyramid of Tepanapa *(plates 53, 54)*, which today is no more than a heap of rubble, extended over 1,300 feet (400 m.) on one side. In the midst of its multiple phases of reconstruction—from which we find mural fragments, including the section called "*Los Bebedores*," or "The Drinkers"—there are combinations of *talud-tableros* inspired directly by the classic Teotihuacán forms. Local variants predominate however—versions in which the Teotihuacán *tablero* is enclosed in two heavy moldings and rises from generally higher *taludes*, many of these concave in shape and rare in Mesoamerica *(plate 55)*.

Among various facets of Cholula's architecture, we should take note of the way local architects turned to advantage the elementary problem of draining off the water that poured down the stepped base during a rainfall. In Teotihuacán, the Pyramid of the Moon was drained by two enormous conduits located between the pyramid and the new base next to it *(plate 33)*. In Cholula, except for the occasional instance of ceramic pipes (rather like amphorae without bottoms joined together and hidden in the sloped base), we find a series of clearly visible, open conduits on the exterior panels. Running down the facade in parallel lines, they divide it into regular sections and form an element of its structure. We see such conduits on a base to the west of the Great Pyramid of Tepanapa *(plate 57)*, where the *tableros* display a restrained interlaced motif, and where the execution—based on huge stone blocks—is comparable to the quality we admired in the Pyramid of Quetzalcóatl at Teotihuacán. One of the last superposi-

ional layers that form the central body of the Great Pyramid shows a imilar use of open-air conduits, which stand out in sober contrast to he sloping bodies of the totally stepped base *(plate 56)*.

The Teotihuacán Talud-Tablero and Its Propagation

Teotihuacán's impact on surrounding areas can be seen in other rchitectural elements, such as the lower parts of the reinforced sloping valls and either the serpents' heads or the "dadoes" that project from he *alfardas* on the stairways. We see this in an unexpected clay model rom Nayarit, with its pumpkin-shaped temple *(plate 60)*. But the oncept that seems to have penetrated deepest into the architecture of ther Mesoamerican regions is that of the *tablero*. Not only do examples of *tableros* obviously inspired by Teotihuacán crop up in such ar-away contemporary sites as El Ixtépete in the western area, and in n important Maya city such as Tikal; but this characteristic projecting element, whose mass breaks the continuity of the sloping bodies nd outlines each of the stepped layers of the base in strong shadow, may have inspired the development of the important regional variants ve find at Xochicalco, El Tajín, and Monte Albán *(plate 61)*. The opularity of the *tablero* seems to have been so widespread that it ould almost be called the Mesoamerican equivalent of the Classical rders.

The Gulf Coast

ast of Teotihuacán and Cholula, in the lowlands bordering the Gulf Coast, the exuberance of nature was reflected in the arts of the people. Here we find the intricate scrollwork of El Tajín, rivaling in sensual orm and design that of the Maya; textiles in the Huaxtec zone so olorful and ornate that to this day they are outstanding among ndian costumes. The land in this region was so rich and productive nat in time of famine in the highlands people were forced to exchange neir children with residents of Veracruz for a handful of corn.[4] reedom from economic worry probably gave the Gulf Coast people n optimistic disposition: most of their sculptured figures are shown ughing.

As in all parts of Mesoamerica, trade flowed to and from the Gulf Coast, accompanied by influences from other regions. During the arly Pre-Classic there evidently was a proto-Maya settlement along ne coast which eventually was divided by a cultural wedge that eveloped into the Totonac culture. The Huaxtecs still speak a Mayoid tongue and, farther south, Nopiloa Late Classic figurines from eracruz (600–750 A.D.) are so similar to Maya examples that they n be mistaken for Jaina or Jonuta clay sculptures.

61. *Sketch of various profiles of* tableros *found in Mesoamerica.*

1. *Teotihuacán*   2. *Cholula*   3. *Xochicalco*
4. *El Ixtépete*   5. *Kaminaljuyú*   6. *Monte Albán*
7. *Yaxhá*   8. *El Tajín*   9. *Tikal*   10. *Tula*
11. *Lambityeco*   12. *Calixtlahuaca*   13. *Chichén Itzá*
14. *Mitla*   15. *Misantla*

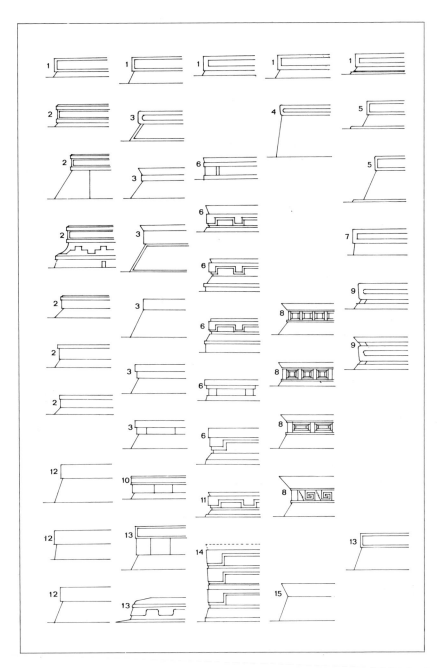

During the Classic period Olmec influence disappeared from the Gulf Coast but other groups left striking reminders of their culture, mainly the yoke, axe, and *palma*. These three forms were intricately carved of hard stone, usually with scrolls, volutes, and fantastic heads. The yoke was probably an imitation of the padded waist-protector worn by ball players, and was placed over them when they were buried. Durán, however, refers to a wooden yoke "carved in the form of a snake" that was placed on the throat of a sacrificial victim to hold his head down while his chest was being cut open.[5] The *palma*, a long tongue-shaped carved stone, is seen set into a waist-protector in a relief at El Tajín. Undoubtedly *palmas* were ceremonial objects, possibly used to identify the rank of chieftains. The axes have stems to hold them in a wall, and may have been ball-court markers, although Proskouriakoff[6] suggests that they could represent heraldic attributes of families or ball teams, and Covarrubias[7] reports that they have been found in funerary mounds inside yokes.

The ball game, with which these three forms are closely linked, possibly originated in the Gulf Coast region, where rubber for making balls was plentiful.[8] Sixteenth-century Spanish writers, unfamiliar in Europe with rubber, describe it as a material with a life of its own:

> . . . this ball was as large as a small bowling ball. The material that the ball [was made of] was called *ollin*, which . . . is resin of a certain tree. When cooked it becomes stringy. It is very much esteemed and prized by these people . . . Jumping and bouncing are its qualities, upward and downward, to and fro. It can exhaust the pursuer running after it before he can catch up with it.[9]

While Teotihuacán introduced the *talud-tablero* architectural complex to El Tajín, the Gulf Coast introduced the style of interlaced scrolls and the ball game to Teotihuacán. That the game took a strong hold in central Mexico is indicated by a sixteenth-century account of this sport—which, incidentally, was also considered a religious ceremony:

> It was a highly entertaining game and amusement for the people, especially for those who held it to be a pastime or entertainment. Among them there were those who played it with such skill and cunning that in one hour the ball did not stop bouncing from one end to the other, without a miss, [the players] using only their buttocks [and knees], never touching it with the hand, foot, calf

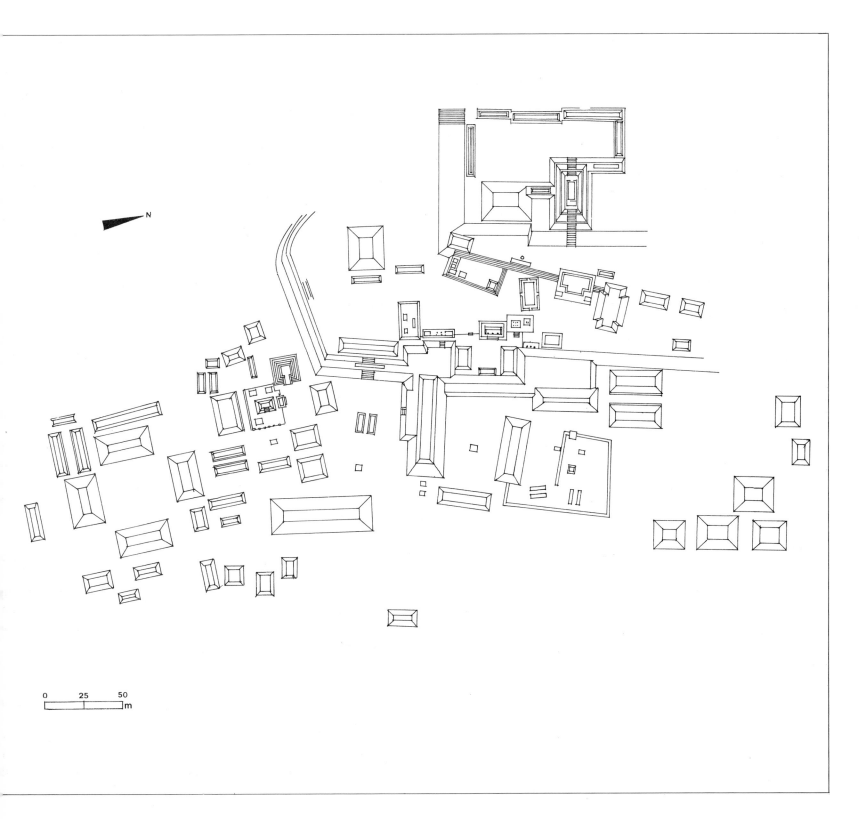

0 25 50
m

or arm. . . . If watching a handball game among Spaniards gives us such pleasure and amazement on seeing the skill and lightness with which some play it, how much more are to be praised those who with such cunning, trickery, and nimbleness play it with their backsides or knees! It was considered a foul to touch [the ball] with the hand or any other part of the body except the parts I have mentioned . . . Through this demanding sport excellent players were formed, and, aside from being esteemed by the sovereigns, they were given notable dignities, were made intimates of the royal house and court, and were honored with special insignia. . . . Ball courts exist in all the illustrious, civilized, and powerful cities and towns, in those ruled by either the community or the lords, the latter stressing [the game] inordinately. . . . [The ball courts] were enclosed with ornate and handsomely carved walls. The interior floor was of stucco, finely polished and decorated with figures of the god and demons to whom the game was dedicated and whom the players held to be their patrons in that sport. These ball courts were larger in some places than in others. They were built . . . narrow in the middle and wide at the ends. The corners were built on purpose so that if the player's ball fell into one it was lost and was considered a foul. The height of the wall was anywhere between eight and eleven feet high, running all around [the court]. . . .

The ball courts were anywhere between 100, 150, and 200 feet long. In the square corners [which served as ends or goals] a great number of players stood on guard to see that the ball did not penetrate. The main players stood in the center facing the ball, and so did the opponents, since the game was carried out similarly to the way they fought in battle or in special contests. In the middle of the walls of this enclosure were fixed two stones facing one another, and each had a hole in the center. Each hole was surrounded by a carved image of the deity of the game . . .

[The players] bet jewels, slaves, precious stone, fine mantles, the trappings of war, and women's finery. Others staked their mistresses. . . . This took place . . . among the nobility, the lords, captains, braves, and important men. Countless lords and knights attended this game and played it with such pleasure and enjoyment, changing places with one another occasionally, taking their turns so that everyone could take part in that pleasant sport, to the point that sometimes the sun set upon them while they enjoyed themselves.

[If a player and bettor] who lost . . . did not possess [valu-able articles] or find a way to make payment, he was sent to jail, and if his wife or children did not ransom him, he became a slave of the creditor. The laws of the republic permitted that he could be sold for the sum he owed and not for more.[10]

But these ball courts are not the only elements in the art of the Gulf Coast. Striking Veracruz sculpture is found at Remojadas, where clay figurines predominate over architecture as an art form. These figurines are full of vitality and movement, representing all types of daily life from girls on swings to persons laughing and displaying ornamentally filed teeth, to victims ready for sacrifice. They are frequently painted with tar, whose black adornment probably carried with it some magic significance.

In the southern part of this region sites such as Cerro de las Mesas (where an early stele is dated 468 A.D. in the dot-and-dash Long Count) and Tres Zapotes inherited Olmec tradition but displayed more Maya and Teotihuacán influences. In northern Veracruz and eastern San Luis Potosí, the Huaxteca came into its own during the Classic period but reached its apogee in the Post-Classic. This region produced many centers notable more for fresco painting than for architecture. But more spectacular is Huaxtec stone sculpture especially figures of Quetzalcóatl, the creator god, whose cult is said to have originated in the region. The eternal Mesoamerican concept of duality between life and death is seen in some of these sculptures. (Huaxtec architecture will be discussed in the Post-Classic chapter.)

The Architecture of El Tajín

El Tajín—a city consecrated to and named after the god of lightning and rain, equivalent to the Mexican Tláloc—represents the architectural culmination of a cultural evolution that began, as we have seen, in the central Veracruz area in the Early Pre-Classic period about 1500 B.C. We know little about the beginnings of this architecture. Its origins may lie somewhere in the last centuries before the Christian era; but what is left of it today belongs mainly to the last phase of the Classic period (sixth to tenth century A.D.) and to the beginning of the Post-Classic (eleventh to thirteenth century).

The numerous buildings that comprise the city's ceremonial center *(plate 62)* are set out, in no apparent order, on a graduated series of platforms and artificial esplanades surrounded by hills. The locale is a fertile valley that lent itself to the cultivation of vanilla, and the whiteness of the city's partially restored structures stands out against their background of luxuriant vegetation. From some reasonably well-preserved remains we learn that here, as in other

Mesoamerican centers, the structures were decorated, at the height of their splendor, in rich polychrome stucco *(plate 63)*. The fertility of this land, the centuries of abandonment, and the deficiencies of some of the local building techniques have produced a deterioration more advanced than that found at Teotihuacán and Monte Albán.

The first thing one notices, in the diverse architectural tapestry of El Tajín, is an entirely new type of *tablero*. It is a form that seems to have developed toward the middle of the Classic period, due perhaps to the still potent Teotihuacán influence seen in Monte Albán and elsewhere. Let us also remember that the City of the Gods shows frequent cultural ties with the Veracruz region, as in the structural use of interlaced volutes, the typical ornamental motif of this area. But at El Tajín, as in Monte Albán, the architects created an interesting variation on the Teotihuacán model, adapting the *tablero* to their own architectural style.

Unlike its Teotihuacán counterpart, the Totonac *tablero* is usually a heavy projecting molding adorned with a horizontal series of fret designs in sharp relief *(plates 65, 66)*, or, more commonly, with a set of concentric rectangular frames forming a niche of greater or lesser depth. A large beveled cornice—probably influenced by the Maya architecture of the Yucatán—crowns the elongated body of the *tablero*, inverting the angle of the *talud*—the inclined segment of the base, whose proportions may vary considerably with respect to the *tablero*.

Finally, we should note with what flexibility the same element was used on stairways, either as a finial for the *alfardas* (in place of the classic Teotihuacán "dado") or to divide the stairs into various ramps *(plates 66, 67)*. In the case of Building 5 *(plate 64)*, this interesting partitioning of the stairway that leads to the first level serves to emphasize the statue of the god Tajín; the stairs then continue throughout the rest of the *tablero* that girds this first body, as in other buildings. In Building 3, on the other hand, these ramps with niches contrast sharply with the pyramid's stepped bodies, the latter severely outlined by a series of moldings in either horizontal or vertical relief *(plate 69)*. In the famous Pyramid of the Niches, these same elements, smaller than the *tableros* that encircle the base, contribute to a much more complex and dynamic composition *(plates 66, 67)*.

In the rich array of architectural solutions found in the Totonac metropolis, probably the most outstanding is Building 1—the above-mentioned Pyramid of the Niches, which borders the west side of one of the plazas leading to the lower part of the ceremonial center. Combined in this building are many of the features we have observed elsewhere, making it not only representative of the culmination

65. *Tajín Chico : rear corner of Building C*
66. *El Tajín : Pyramid of the Niches ▷*

67. *El Tajín: Building 3. The Pyramid of the Niches is in the background*

of Totonac architecture, but a prototype of the Classic style in this region. In no other building at El Tajín can we see so clearly how the local *tablero* form differed from the Teotihuacán version. With strong effects of light and shadow enlivening its facades, constantly shifting throughout the day, the Pyramid of the Niches seems to be in a state of perpetual tension; it emits, as the poet Octavio Paz says, "a vital breath, as we see in the lines and undulations that give [this] pyramid an animation that remains unchecked by its solemnity. These stones are alive and dancing. . . . Unlike Teotihuacán, El Tajín is neither petrified motion nor time suspended. It is geometry dancing; undulation; rhythm. The Totonacs are not always sublime; but they seldom overwhelm us as do the peoples of the plateau."[11]

Despite its modest dimensions—115 feet (35 m.) across and a maximum of 82 feet (25 m.) high—and the advanced deterioration of its facades, the Pyramid of the Niches stands out indeed, thanks to the lively play of chiaroscuro and to the way it varies the balance between the horizontal and vertical thrusts underlying the different compositional elements. The cornices and steps emphasize the horizontal; but their effect is offset by the deep niches sunk into each *tablero*, which, with its meandering fret design, interrupts the vertical line of the stairway framed by the moldings of the *alfardas*. We should note the proportions of the stepped base, which appear to be a compromise between both directional tendencies *(plate 68)*. We should also observe the solar symbolism of a building with 365 niches, including some hidden under the stairs along with the entrance to the sanctuary.

The Pyramid of the Niches provides the most beautiful and typical example of architecture during the Classic period in El Tajín. But some of the structures built in the first centuries of the Post-Classic period show innovations in technique and form that are no less interesting. Building 3 *(plate 67)*, across a plaza from the Pyramid of the Niches, may belong to a transitional phase between the two periods, although the greatest concentration of this later epoch's buildings appears to be on higher ground, atop an enormous artificial platform of irregular shape. This group of structures is known as Tajín Chico *(plate 72)*. Here, in many of the ruins, José García Payón has found significant traces of heavy plaster roofs whose interior faces, slightly concave and carefully polished, suggest a support of corresponding shape and finish—most likely a fill, similar to what we find in a modern concrete archway.

The largest edifice at Tajín Chico, Building A *(plates 70, 74)*, is the product of several phases of superpositioning, and presents a large number of new, even unusual features. Separated into horizontal

68. *El Tajín : Pyramid of the Niches. Elevation and plan*

69. *El Tajín : Building 3. Detail of a corner*
70. *Tajín Chico : Building A*
71. *Tajín Chico : Building A. Detail of the access stairway*

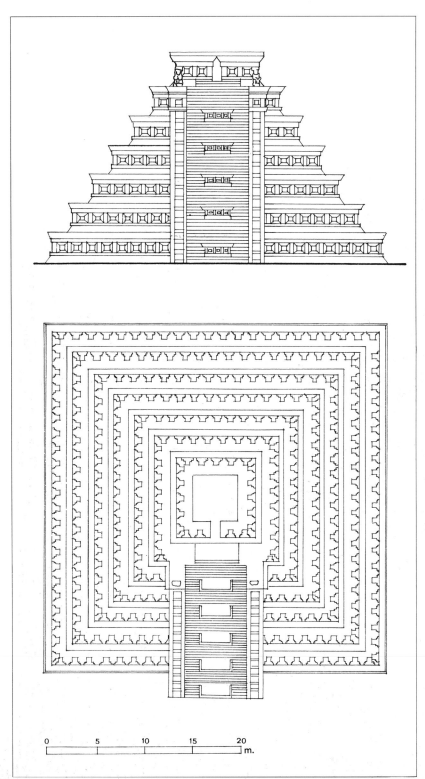

0   5   10   15   20
m.

73. *Tajín Chico: Building A. Detail of the stucco decoration along the corridor*

74. *Tajín Chico: plan of Building A*

75. *Tajín Chico: plan of Building Q. First phase of construction*

76. *Tajín Chico: plan of the Building of the Columns and Tajín Chico*

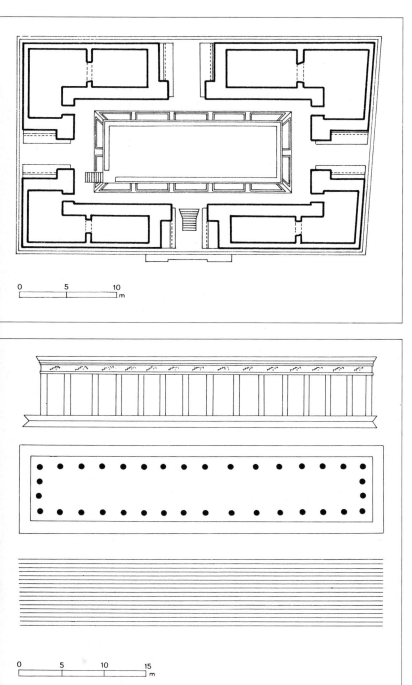

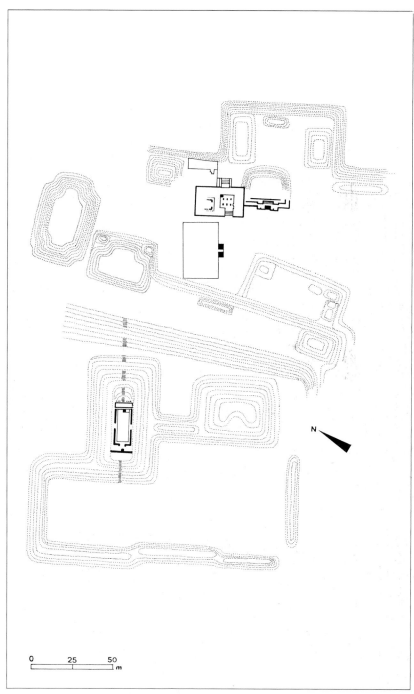

bands by a variety of moldings—the most prominent being a heavy double-beveled strip about halfway up the base—the vertical panels of the lower facades boast great rectangular frames similar to those of Building 3 *(plate 69)*; the upper part offers variants of the *Xonecuilli* (double S or "Blue Worm") and *Xicalcoliuhqui*, or stepped fret design —the latter a motif repeated in the building's interior passages, where large areas of the original stucco and paint still remain *(plate 73)*. In the center of the principal facade, we see a surprising solution to the problem of providing access: a stairway that, after repeated remodelings, appears more decorative than real. Flanked by flattened *alfardas* decorated with a fret pattern and topped with niches, this simulated stairway has a narrow flight of real steps cut through its center *(plate 71)*. The corbel arch that covers the upper part of the stairway, plus the profusion of beveled cornices and geometric motifs on many of the buildings, seem inspired by the Maya—an influence Hardoy notes in the distribution of some of the structural groups: "The platforms, *taludes,* and stairways enfold and unite the middle- and upper-level structures. . . . Even the south group, where the orthogonal layout of structures is maintained, has similarities to Maya centers such as Yaxhá."[12]

Among the buildings at Tajín Chico, we should note the Quadrangle of the Niches, whose sloping surfaces (also decorated with stepped frets) end in large, deep niches crowned with the classic beveled cornices, and which leave, between these niches, roofed openings at the intersections of the adjacent cornices, connected to the exterior by flights of stairs. Another novel solution is found in Building Q, located west of Building A, on the edge of a higher platform *(plate 75)*. Here there is an elongated rectangular base that rises up from a socle in the form of beveled moldings, and whose supports, consisting only of thin columns, must have borne the weight of a light roof. This structure may have served as a transition between Tajín Chico's plaza and the adjacent levels.

The city's most imposing structure—in both the dimensions of its pyramidal base (650 × 295 feet, or 196 × 90 m.) and its elevated placement, which allows it to dominate the whole city from the northwest—is unquestionably the Building of the Columns *(plate 76)*. Its access portico (measuring 59 × 20 feet, or 18 × 6 m.) was covered by a heavy vault of the type made of lime concrete slabs. The remains of the main stairway are well preserved, with *alfardas* covered in stylized designs of rattlesnakes. A simple geometric motif runs along the broken planes around the base of the building. Toward the front of the portico are the ruins of six columns that were built of stone drums over 3 1/2 feet (1 m.) in diameter. These are entirely covered in

fine relief carvings—a unique discovery in Mesoamerica *(plate 77)*. The columns are being partially reconstructed, thanks to the patient work of García Payón, and will soon dominate the city once again. Their delicate relief work, in which we see warriors and other personages, glyphic dates, classic interlaced volutes, and mythological animals (including a plumed serpent of probable Teotihuacán origin), counts among the most exquisite examples of carving at El Tajín—a city with a prodigious wealth of bas-reliefs of unmistakable style.

To conclude this discussion of the art of the Totonac metropolis—an art that Octavio Paz describes as "midway between Teotihuacán severity and Maya opulence"[13]—we might mention other reliefs, such as a tablet that seems to represent the cocoa tree—a plant of Mexican origin used traditionally to prepare a "drink of princes." Nor should we overlook the scenes carved in bas-relief on the center and ends of the walls of the city's numerous ball courts (seven at least). The most outstanding of these is found on the court located south of Building 5; one of its walls forms part of the platform supporting this building. Delicately carved in four large blocks of white stone, some over 20 feet (7 m.) long, and perfectly fitted without mortar, these scenes form rectangles bordered on their tops and bottoms with fantastic serpents embodying, respectively, heaven and earth—their conventional features (eyes with brows; fangs and feathers) lost in a complex, somewhat rigid labyrinth of interlaced volutes, the *leitmotif* of central Veracruz art. Several scenes seem related to the ritual ball game, and in one we can see the ceremonial sacrifice of one of the players at the hands of others wearing the characteristic equipment of the region (heavy belt, chest protector, etc.). The sacrifice is being witnessed by an enthroned personage and, from the opposite side, by the god of death, while another deity is seen descending upon the victim from heaven *(plate 78)*.

El Tajín has yielded us only a few fragments of a rich and delicate polychromatic art. But many mural paintings have recently been discovered in Las Higueras, another small Totonac ceremonial center not far from the Gulf of Mexico, and they demonstrate aspects of Totonac painting of the last centuries of the first millennium. These freely drawn works reveal various facets of Totonac ritual: processions of priests, parasol-bearers, and others; scenes depicting the ball game, fishing, solar deities, or the relinquishing of command.

Oaxaca

The Classic period made its appearance earlier in Oaxaca than in many other regions of Mesoamerica. In Monte Albán I (600–300 B.C.) we find a culture that is usually described as pre-urban, but which Bernal

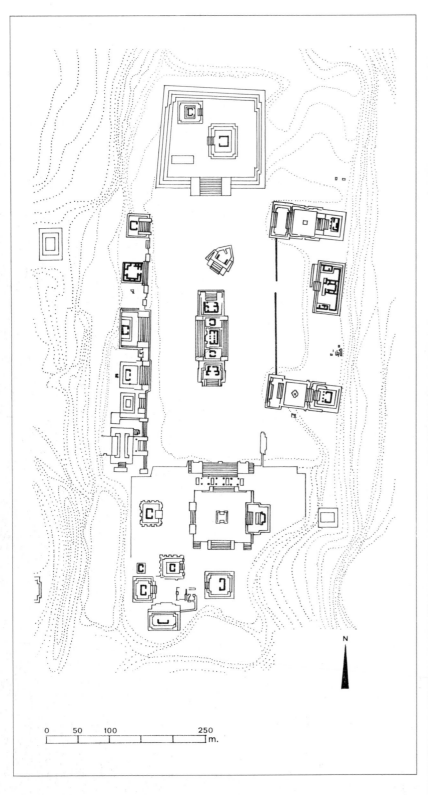

81. *Monte Albán: plan of the Great Plaza*
82. *Monte Albán: aerial view of the Great Plaza from the north* ▷

0   50   100   250
|__|__|__|__|_____|
                         m.

83. *Monte Albán: base of one of the buildings situated on the north platform*

84. *Monte Albán: west side of the Great Plaza seen from the north platform. In the foreground, Complex IV; in the background, Complex M; toward the center, Building of the* Danzantes

85. *Monte Albán: east side of the Great Plaza seen from the ground* ▷

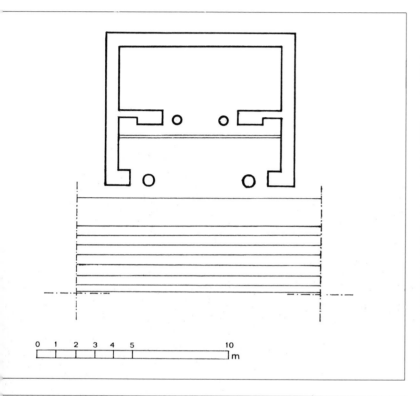

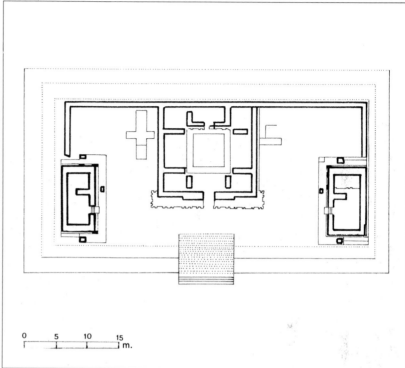

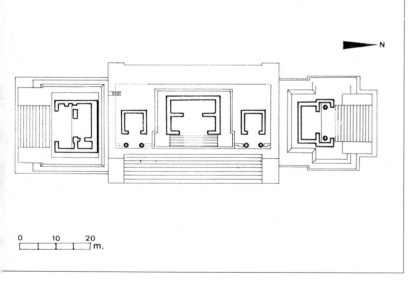

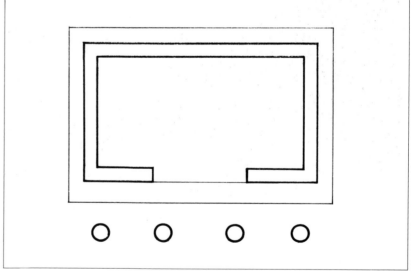

claims has the elements of a true civilization, one of them being stone architecture.[14] Paddock declares that these Oaxacans were possibly the first city dwellers in America.[15]

The Zapotecs had developed hieroglyphic writing, calendrics, dot-and-dash numeration, and astronomical observation from their Olmec heritage; later these were to be developed to their full splendor by the Maya. One of Mesoamerica's most outstanding intellectual contributions, the calendar round, formed of two simultaneous calendrical wheels—one a 365-day solar calendar and the other a 260-day religious and probably agricultural calendar, coinciding to create a 52-year "century" (see Chapter Five)—was brought to a working development at Monte Albán before the Christian era.

Although the present-day state of Oaxaca is dotted with numerous ancient sites, many still occupied by Zapotec-speaking inhabitants, Monte Albán, with its advanced degree of planning and urbanism, has provided archaeologists with a ceramic and architectural sequence that has enabled them to establish a chronology for the Oaxaca area. Recent excavations by Richard Blanton have shown that a huge urban center existed on this site at the time of Monte Albán II (300–100 B.C.).[16] Residential quarters were grouped on small terraces around the hillside, water for daily use channeled here from dams above which held rain water, and from the terraces to the agricultural fields below. By the time of Monte Albán IIIb (600–800 A.D.) the population was at least 50,000.

As in Teotihuacán, priest-rulers controlled the intellectual and religious life of Monte Albán. A period II carved glyph on Mound J representing a conquest—a mountain, pyramid, and upside-down head of a warrior with eyes closed as in death are shown—indicate that, as in other Classic cultures, religion was not the only driving force. Defensive walls in the city have also been identified by Blanton.

Around 200 A.D., the Zapotec culture began to incorporate strong influences from Teotihuacán. (This influence was felt mainly in architecture and will be described separately.) This culture left many monuments to their gods and to the dead. Baroque funerary urns in the shape of deities and their "companion urns" were placed in tombs. The tombs themselves were built in the form of a cross with vaulted roof, adorned with mural paintings, niches and antechambers, and filled with rich offerings; such tombs are found on the slopes of the hills that form the periphery of Monte Albán. Other tombs are underneath mounds, floors, and platforms.

Unlike Teotihuacán, where mural painting was an art for the living, in Monte Albán it seems to have been an art for the dead, confined mainly to tombs. The fresco technique was the same as in

93. *Monte Albán: partial view of the buildings along the southwest side of the Great Plaza. In the foreground, Complex M with its access platform; in the background to the right, the Building of the Danzantes*

other regions: mineral colors were used, combined with an agglutinating organic substance, perhaps cactus juice. This was applied to a white base on the wet wall. The same type of painting on pottery is usually referred to as "dry fresco" because the vessel was not dampened each time color was applied, and therefore chips off more easily. Depicted in Oaxaca tomb murals were gods, priests, cosmic and earth symbols, and at a later period, rulers—for example, at Zaachila.

The Zapotecs believed they were descended from trees and great rocks, whereas their successors, the Mixtecs, were cloud people. The Zapotecs inhabited the valleys, the Mixtecs both the mountains and the "hot land." The most important gods of the Zapotecs were Xipe Tótec, who is said to have originated on Oaxaca's Pacific coast and who was a god of the earth's fertility and patron of jewelers; the rain god Cocijo, called Tláloc in the central region, Tajín in Veracruz, and Chac in the Maya area; "Thirteen-Serpent," the mother goddess; Pitao Cozobi, lord of corn, called Yum Kax among the Maya and Céntéotl in the central plateau; Quetzalcóatl, the wind god, shown with a duck's beak in the central area and with a serpent's mask in Oaxaca, named Kulkulkán by the Maya; Xochipilli, god of flowers, song, and dance; a bat god; and a nameless fire god, equivalent to Teotihuacán's Huehuetéotl and the Aztec Xiuhtecuhtli.

Parallel to the Zapotec, Mixtec culture developed in Oaxaca, although its period of efflorescence was in the Post-Classic and therefore will be discussed later. Due to relatively meager explorations of Mixtec sites, our knowledge of this culture is scant until late times, when the pictorial codices tell us of their feats and genealogies. Nevertheless, linguistic reconstruction has shown Mixtec words for weaving, market, and *pulque* (the liquor from the maguey agave plant) as early as 1000 B.C.[17] A Carbon 14 date for Montenegro has been given as 649 B.C. In Diquiyú Olmecoid stone sculpture has been found.[18] Dr. Paddock follows Jiménez Moreno's designation in distinguishing early Mixtec from Post-Classic Mixtec by referring to the region where the former is found and the style here as Ñuiñe ("hot land"):

"Ñuiñe is the Mixtec name for the Mixteca Baja; the other two main provinces of the Mixtec region, which occupies the western part of the state of Oaxaca and small portions of adjoining southern Puebla and eastern Guerrero, are the Mixteca Alta and the Costa, or Pacific coast. . . . The Ñuiñe . . . has recently been shown to have been . . . the home of a distinctive regional art style previously unknown. In addition it seems to have been a meeting ground for the major early traditions whose capitals were at Teotihuacán, in the Valley of Mexico, and Monte Albán, in the Valley of Oaxaca."[19]

The beginnings of early urbanism in the Mixteca, continues Paddock, may be inferred from their reflection in the Tehuacan Valley (described in Chapter One), which corresponds to early urbanism in the Mixteca, and begins around 200 B.C. In Tequistepec, relief carvings show glyphs almost identical to the Monte Albán glyphic system, associated with dot-and-dash numerals. These carvings date from the Classic period. As for ceramics, Paddock sees a forerunner of the famous late Mixtec polychrome in both Teotihuacán Classic fresco-painted ware and Maya polychrome. Thin orange ware, one of the hallmarks of the Classic, has been shown by Carmen Cook to have been produced in southern Puebla, in the Ñuiñe region. There was large-scale exporting of thin orange ware to almost all Classic sites between 200 and 500 A.D., which tells us that this region was important long before the massive invasion of Monte Albán in the Post-Classic by the people who are truly called the Mixtecs.

The Architecture of Monte Albán

Architecturally, what first engages one's interest about Monte Albán is the placement of its ceremonial center, on a mountain crest commanding three valleys from an average altitude of 1,300 feet (400 m.), with the rest of the city spread out on the slopes below. In contrast to Teotihuacán—where civic will transformed a broad and sprawling valley to accommodate its ceremonial center and residential quarters—Monte Albán's founders chose, at the cost of considerable human effort, a much more dramatic site as the only setting worthy of their gods. After some fifteen centuries of constant remodeling, the immense complex of Monte Albán displayed an incredible array of man-made terraces and esplanades—some 2,200 in all—and of platforms and mounds, leaving the physiognomy of the original mountains completely altered. Despite its many phases, the finished product, whose form crystallized toward the end of the first millennium, exhibits an astonishing balance *(plates 80, 82)*.

The American continent may contain sites with even more dramatic locations, such as Machu Picchu in the Andes; but we find here, as Hardoy puts it, "one of the loveliest civic areas ever created by man, and certainly the most beautiful in America."[20] In addition to its extraordinary setting, Monte Albán's main appeal lies in a feeling of completeness that reaches into the very heart of its ceremonial center—namely, the Great Plaza, which lies bounded on the north and south by two immense platforms *(plates 81, 84)*.

This "unity in diversity" is so evident that at first glance, from any angle of the plaza, it is precisely the whole that impresses us. Only then can we begin to appreciate the features of each segment.

nd the avoidance of the relative monotony of Teotihuacán. The center, observes Hardoy, appears as "an enclosed space with no view of the valleys that surround the hill on three sides. The impression is of omething finished, something that cannot be continued either in xtension—due to topographical limitations—or in intention, in view f the stupendous scale and the magnificent oneness achieved . . ." To conclude, he emphasizes that "the individuality of each new uilding was sacrificed for the unity of the whole."[21]

We find, nevertheless, great diversity in the conception of this mposing complex. Forming the east side of the Great Plaza, for xample, is a row of bases of various sizes, connecting with the plaza n an impressive series of stairways *(plate 85)*. One of these leads to the all court, sunken and half hidden between other buildings *(plate 86)*. Built in the classic I-shape, it lacks rings but has niches for the figures f deities. The opposite side of the plaza, on the other hand, is occupied nainly by three isolated groups: the Building of the *Danzantes* in the niddle, and two almost-matching complexes flanking it on either ide *(plate 89)*. The south platform is limited in its span and supports nly two temple bases, while the considerably broader north platform subdivided into other ceremonial complexes that include a num- er of buildings and some small plazas, among these the so-called unken Court, bounded to the south by the remains of an immense ortico that once dominated the Great Plaza, and that survives today nly in the stumps of its once thick masonry columns, some 6 1/2 eet (2 m.) in diameter *(plate 84)*. Here, symmetry becomes secondary o the relationship between open spaces and structural masses.

In this "parade of asymmetrical harmony," as Flores Guerrero escribes it, we note the absence of fixed axes.[22] The placement of he buildings is not only informal—with neither a uniform alignment or orientation—but at times departs from any visible order. This is he case with Mound J, one of the oldest in the city and the fruit of everal remodelings *(plate 12)*. Following the dictates of ritual, or erhaps the requirements of the astronomer, it is located in the middle f the Great Plaza, where it stands out both for its strange arrowhead hape and for its orientation—so different from that of the other uildings. A particularly fortuitous solution was the more recent ddition of three other structures to form a single block in the center f the plaza, for while these do not touch Mound J, they do create the mpression of incorporating it within a single complex *(plate 82)*.

Despite its irregularities, the ceremonial center appears as one armonious unit, laid out around a plaza 1,000 feet (320 m.) from north o south and 460 feet (140 m.) from east to west, taking as the western mit the wall that enclosed the Building of the *Danzantes* and that

was aligned with the access platforms of Buildings IV and M, and with other minor structures. This side of the Great Plaza thus acquires a more private ceremonial character, like that of many of Teotihuacán's enclosed complexes.

In Monte Albán's flexible yet balanced composition, there breathes an intuitive feeling for space. Paul Westheim speaks of "a system of living spaces that complement each other to form an organic unit . . . a symphony of space . . ."[23] This ability of Mesoamerican peoples to combine architectural volume with great open space undoubtedly reached one of its most sublime expressions in Monte Albán.

Turning now to some of the buildings in the ceremonial center, we find the concept of interior space less complex than that in Teotihuacán, although both are based on similar principles and modes of construction—flat roofs supported by walls and columns, and so forth. Monte Albán's architecture puts greater emphasis on the use of columns, and combines this with more flexibility. We see an example in the heavy columns that stood at the front of the north platform (*plate 82*), and in the feeling of lightness afforded the building through the frequent use of more slender columns (both monolithic and masonry) along the walls. Examples are found in Mound X-sub (*plate 87*) and Buildings G, H, and I (*plate 88*), and again in front of the main facade as in Temple-system IV. In the latter (*plate 90*), and in its near-twin, Complex M, we see the interesting combination of individually styled ceremonial complexes using a wide access platform and two lateral walls that bordered a small interior plaza containing a central altar, and adorned with a stele and altar-niche placed at the foot of the pyramid (*plate 91*). Of the stairs that lead directly to the temple, the last flight is the narrowest, giving the facade more animation and causing the building to appear lighter.

There is nevertheless a quality of massiveness inherent in Monte Albán's architecture. It reflects, in part, the strong seismic activity that periodically shook the region of Oaxaca. The visual impact of these sober, elongated masses, wide stairways set into their bodies as in the Building of the *Danzantes* or more often projecting out and flanked by heavy *alfardas*, might have been rather cumbersome had it not been for the ingenious arrangement of shapes, which produced a striking chiaroscuro even while it emphasized and confirmed their massive character. The interplay of light and shadow resulted from a skillful blending of *taludes* and moldings (and at times horizontal rows of stone discs), plus interesting regional *tableros*—the Zapotec version of a theme we watched develop in Teotihuacán from the end of the second century.

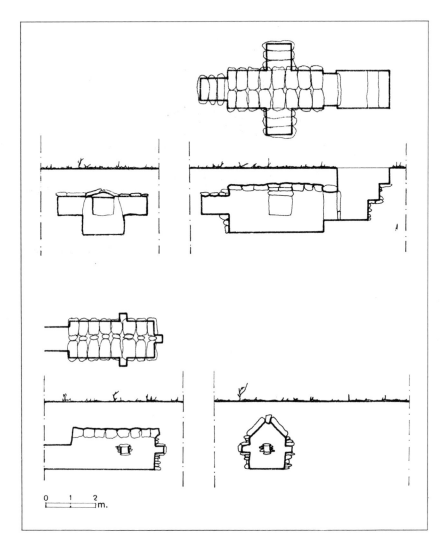

The use of the *talud-tablero* as an architectural element may have been inspired by the City of the Gods, with which Monte Albán maintained close ties. Indeed, a western sector of Teotihuacán was called the "Oaxaca Quarter" because of a Oaxaca-style stele found there, along with a large quantity of Zapotec ceramics manufactured by Oaxacan residents living in Teotihuacán. However, it does not appear that this *tablero* was ever slavishly copied by Zapotec builders. They knew how to imbue this Teotihuacán suggestion with a spirit that better met their own architectural needs. In Teotihuacán, the uncompromisingly horizontal frames of the *tableros* always rise from a short *talud* and usually run completely around the base, stopping at the stairways, where narrow *alfardas*—generally with projecting dadoes—serve as an element of transition *(plate 27)*. In Monte Albán, on the other hand, there emerged a rich variety of *tableros*—among them the famous "scapulary" type, almost invariably formed by a broken panel with a second one sitting on top of it, thus creating an overhanging double molding on the upper part *(plates 92, 93)*.

Starting with the second or third century A.D., the *tableros* became the most important element in nearly all Zapotec buildings, accompanied as they were by two, three, or more "scapularies," by heavy moldings, straight or beveled cornices, socles for either vertical or sloping panels, platform bases, and, most particularly, by the *alfardas* of the stairways. Thanks to some lovely stone models, we know that *tableros* were used to crown roofs *(plates 94, 95)*, and we see them employed often on the entrances to tombs *(plate 98)*. With "that subtle break in the *tablero* created by two lines, defined in shade as the sole decoration," of which Flores Guerrero speaks, this architectural element served to outline the basic shapes of the buildings and conferred a unity on the diversity of the whole.[24] Perfectly adapted to formal, massive structures, the *tablero* emerges as a common denominator of style. Closely linked to the stairway *alfardas*—as is the dado to the Teotihuacán *alfarda*—it maintains a balance in the relative proportions of the bases. Such is the case in the imposing front of the north platform, some 656 feet (200 m.) in length, whose central stairway—almost 130 feet (40 m.) wide—is flanked by exceptionally broad *alfardas* and *tableros*, of a width of 40 feet (12 m.) *(plate 83)*.

After studying Monte Albán's monumental architecture, which Flores Guerrero calls "a play of *alfardas, tableros,* and sun,"[25] we turn

o its funerary architecture, which played a vital role, and made this acred city of the Zapotecs the first Mesoamerican necropolis. Paralleling the copious production of funerary urns that constitute the most typical item of Zapotec pottery, a great number of tombs were uilt, generally hidden under the floors of temples, palaces, platforms, nd patios. Dating for the most part from the Classic period, Zapotec ombs vary in form from a simple rectangular grave to a cruciform lan with niches, an antechamber with stairs, and so forth. The walls re of masonry, and the funerary chamber is usually covered with a at or triangular roof made of large stone slabs, sometimes supported y a central stone functioning as a keystone *(plate 97)*. Some of these hambers show traces of mural painting in a style that incorporates ertain Teotihuacán and Maya influences. Ornamentation was most ften concentrated around the tomb's entrance, sometimes on a nonolithic lintel, with jambs covered with reliefs—a frequent practice fter the end of the first millennium A.D., as we shall see at Mitla— nd sometimes in the form of sculptures in terracotta or stucco. We nd the latter at the entrance to Monte Albán's Tomb 104, where, in kind of central niche within one of the characteristic recesses of the *ablero,* there is a great clay urn representing one of the many gods in ne Zapotec pantheon *(plate 98)*.

The tombs recently discovered at Lambityeco, a small site in ne nearby valley of Tlacolula, dating from about 700 A.D., display ome interesting versions of *tableros* covered with rich sculptural ecorations in terracotta and stucco. Outstanding among these are arvings in the form of great masks that project from the planes of ne *tablero,* and heads modeled with particular delicacy. Lambityeco's eautiful tombs, whose *tableros* retain intact not only their carvings ut their original contrasting colors as well, provide documentation f exceptional interest and permit us to imagine how Monte Albán nust have looked at its apogee, all its buildings adorned in splendid elief, the different elements enhanced by a rich polychrome palette. xcept for its stelae, lintels, and tablets carved in stone *(plate 96),* lus some mutilated fragments of terracotta and stucco reliefs (inluding a large serpent modeled in clay, found at the northeast corner f the north platform and belonging to the first phase of construction), Monte Albán today is nothing more than a majestic skeleton—a set f sober ruins that seem to be holding a solemn dialogue with eternity.

This is the account of how all was in suspense, all calm, in silence; all motionless, still, and the expanse of the sky was empty.

This is the first account, the first narrative. There was neither man, nor animal, birds, fishes, crabs, trees, stones, caves, ravines, grasses, nor forests; there was only the sky . . .

There was only immobility and silence in the darkness, in the night. Only the Creator, the Maker, Tepeu, Gucumatz, the Forefathers, were in the water surrounded with light . . .

. . . Then they planned the creation, and the growth of trees and the thickets and the birth of life and the creation of man . . .

. . . they began to talk about the creation and the making of our first mother and father; of yellow corn and of white corn they made their flesh; of corn meal dough they made the arms and the legs of man. Only dough of corn meal went into the flesh of our first fathers . . . who were created.[1]

Thus was man created of maize, the Mesoamerican staff of life, according to the *Popol Vuh*, the sacred book of the ancient Quiché Maya. The Maya, whose myths and history are recorded in the *Popol Vuh* and other documents, have been called "the intellectuals of the New World."[2] Their writing system, their calendar, their arts and architecture were almost unparalleled in America. This civilization, which began with roots in the Olmec culture about a millennium before the Christian era, reached a stunning climax during the Classic period, and even after this experienced a renaissance under central Mexican influence. The Maya built more cities in a greater extension of territory than any other Mesoamerican civilization.

We no longer speak of the Old and New Maya empires—an outdated system based on Old World chronologies—but of the Pre-Classic or Formative phase (1500 B.C.–300 A.D.), Classic (300–900 A.D.), and Post-Classic (900–1500 A.D.), as we do in discussing other Mesoamerican cultures. Maya civilization developed in the region which reaches from the Grijalva River in Tabasco to the Ulúa Valley, Honduras, and the Lempa River in El Salvador. Three sub-regions are found here, occupying territories of great geographical contrast. This environmental variety influenced the way of life, costume, art, and architecture of its inhabitants.

The northern zone, of semi-arid plains, embraces the states of Yucatán, northern Campeche, and northern Quintana Roo in Mexico. Except for the low hills of the Puuc region, the land is flat and dry. Only a few lakes and timid streams show themselves on the surface, while the majority of the rivers run underground. Access to them is by way of *chenes* or *cenotes*, natural caves or wells. Among the sites in the northern zone are Uxmal, Kabáh, Labná (in the Puuc zone), Cobá, Dzibilchaltún, Chichén Itzá, Mayapán, and Tulum.

The central zone, the core region of Maya civilization, is one of great rivers such as the Usumacinta, Grijalva, La Pasión, and Lacanjá and of exuberant tropical jungle alternating with savannah. This is the interior drainage basin of the department of El Petén, Guatemala. Large lakes are here also, including the Petén Itzá, last stronghold of the Itzá family and not subdued by the Spaniards until 1697. In this central lowland are found southern Campeche and Quintana Roo, Belice, the Usumacinta and Grijalva basins in Chiapas and Tabasco, the Petén of Guatemala, and part of Honduras, with sites such as Palenque, Bonampak, Yaxchilán, Altún Há, Uaxactún, Tikal, Quiriguá, and Copán.

Towering mountains and high plateaus of cool climate, covered with pine forests, form the southern zone. Here are the highlands of Chiapas and Guatemala, dotted with rich intermontane valleys, rivers that flow both to the Caribbean and the Gulf of Mexico, and lakes such as Guatemala's Atitlán. Southern sites include Kaminaljuyú, Nebaj, Zaculeu, and Mixco Viejo.

The Classic efflorescence of the Maya terminated a century or so later here than in the central plateau of Mexico, ending in the Maya region around 900 A.D. The splendor of these six centuries has left breath-taking examples of the greatness of this civilization, in the lofty pyramids of Tikal and Uxmal, the exquisite carving of Copán, the rich murals at Bonampak, the stucco art of Palenque, the genealogy-recording stelae at Yaxchilán. Covarrubias aptly claims that Maya art "combines the precise hieraticism of the Egyptians, the decorative flamboyancy of China, and the sensuous exuberance of the art of India."[3]

But perhaps Maya scientific achievements are more spectacular. The *Haab* of 365 days—the solar calendar of 18 months consisting of 20 days each plus 5 "useless" days—was more accurate than the Julian calendar used contemporaneously in Europe. The *Tzolkín*, the religious calendar of 260 days, was used in conjunction with the *Haab*. The Maya calendric system functioned as two great wheels with meshed gears: as the wheels turned the gears meshed, the 365-cog wheel with the 260-cog circle. Each cog represented a day, and before ny given day in one wheel could coincide again with the same day in the other wheel 18,900 days had to pass. These constituted the calendar round or 52-year cycle equivalent to our century.[4] This combination of the 365-day *Haab* and the 260-day *Tzolkín* is referred to as the Short Count. The Long Count is a calculation of the number of days elapsed since the beginning of the Maya era, a mythical or actual event designated *4 ahau 8 cumhu*. This unidentified event was for the Maya what the birth of Christ is for Westerners or the initiation of the Olympic games for the Greeks. Thus the priest-astronomers fixed the tropical year at 365 days, the lunar month at periods of 29 or 30 days, and the "year" of the planet Venus at 584 days. Today, the figures of these same calculations are 365.24 days, 29.53 days, and 583.92 days, which shows the amazing accuracy achieved by the Maya.[5] Of the three surviving pre-Conquest Maya pictorial manuscripts, the Dresden Codex contains tables for the calculation of eclipses and of the average length of the sinodical revolution of Venus.[6]

The mathematical system of positional numeration and the use of zero (the latter invented only twice in the history of the world) were in use in America about the time that Alexander the Great was building his empire. In Maya mathematics, a glyph in the form of a shell symbolized zero, and numbers were represented by dots (. = 1) and dashes (— = 5) up to 20. The system was vigesimal and the Maya counted from bottom to top, each position having a value of 20 more than that below it. For example, if a dot is on the bottom line, it equals 1. Above this, on the second line, a dash (5) would have the value of $5 \times 20 = 100$. On the third line, two dashes (10) equal $10 \times 20 \times 20 = 4,000$. The addition of these lines totals 4,101. This may be represented as follows:

$$
\begin{aligned}
= \ = \ 10 \times 20 \times 20 &= 4,000 \\
— \ = \ 5 \times 20 \quad\ \ &= \quad 100 \\
. \ = \qquad\qquad\ \ &= \quad\ \ \underline{1} \\
&\quad\ \ 4,101
\end{aligned}
$$

By giving a value to the relative position of each digit, the Maya could make calculations in the millions by using only a few dots and dashes.

Like Teotihuacán, Maya society was stratified. We might compare it to a human pyramid with the "common man," usually farmers, slaves, and servants, at the bottom; artisans and civic workers in the middle; and noble chieftains, priest-rulers, merchants, and warriors at the summit. The *halach uinic* was the supreme leader, whose civic, religious, and military duties were hereditary. When we see in stelae reliefs a figure carrying a small scepter and wearing a ceremonial bar across his chest (at times the mask of a god), we are looking at the portrait of a supreme ruler of a chiefdom or city-state. The *halach uinic* was aided by a state council. Lesser chieftains handled military affairs, collected taxes, and attended to a multitude of everyday problems.

Unlike many Mesoamerican regions, but similar to the Oaxacan Mixtec area, women in the Maya zone seem to have enjoyed a certain amount of power and freedom. The Bonampak murals show us the chieftain's wife in a commanding attitude, and clay figurines from the island of Jaina off the Campeche coast portray women whose position and dress reveal a high status. These figurines constitute a treasure of ethnographic documentation and, together with richly carved stelae from Yaxchilán and other Classic sites, show us the luxury and splendor of Maya dress. Magnificently woven and embroidered textiles vie with a wealth of jade jewelry and abundant feathers from the highly valued quetzal bird to make the ancient Maya costume one of the most elegant and sumptuous of all time.

In art—and especially in architecture—considerable central Mexican influence is found in the Maya area. The Pipils, central Mexicans of Náhuatl speech and culture, probably were migrants (or merchants or missionaries) from Teotihuacán to the Guatemalan highlands, where they left such building concepts as the *talud* and *tablero* and certain Mexican deities, among them Tláloc. But the main characteristic of Maya architecture is its emphasis upon skillful and elaborate decoration rather than upon size, with aesthetic architectural refinements—such as lacelike roof-combs and intricately carved mosaic facades—rather than sheer imposing mass.[7]

As for war, the murals of Bonampak and Mulchic show us the capture, mutilation, and killing of enemies, but—as Betty Bell points out[8]—in the Classic Maya period there seems to have been internecine strife rather than organized warfare, with sporadic raiding between centers to obtain captives for slavery and sacrifice.

Following the general Mesoamerican pattern, the Maya pantheon was complex, inhabited by numerous gods, each one protecting a special aspect of Maya life. The supreme invisible god, Hunab Ku, called Tloque Nahuaque among the Aztecs, was the creator god who begot the creator pair, Itzamná and Ixchel. Itzamná was also a divinity of the firmament, associated with the sun, Venus, and the Pleiades. He was also connected with agriculture, maize, and rain, and was supposed to have invented writing and medicine. Kulkulkán, the plumed serpent, has many of the same qualities of his northern counterpart, Quetzalcóatl. He was originally a culture hero, and as a god represented the planet Venus. He was also a giver of life and a symbol of the wind. Chac was to the Maya what Tláloc was to the people of Mexico's central plateau and Cocijo to the Zapotecs. He created rain, lightning, and thunder. In this he was aided by four little Chaques, each one a different color and each at a different point of the compass. In Chac's house there were four rooms, each with a large tub of water: one with "good" water provided rain to make the plants grow; one with "bad" water gave too much rain, causing food to rot; a third with cold water brought hail and ice; and a fourth with hardly any water caused the maize to dry up. When the rain god ordered his assistants to provide rain, they took clay jars filled with water from these tubs, and with a jar in one hand and a stick in the other, each Tlaloque beat his jug. With the noise of thunder the jugs broke and water burst free. A survival of this myth can be seen today in the *piñata* celebration: a candy-filled clay jar is broken during Christmas festivals by children, who swing a stout stick in order to release the gifts.

Why did this rich, highly developed pre-Columbian civilization collapse? Why, indeed, did the Classic Mesoamerican world as a whole decline and in some places perish? One explanation may be that the Classic centers, which grew idle and rich through trade and production of many articles, including luxury items, attracted people from outlying areas to the exciting, bustling centers (a phenomenon that still takes place today) until these centers failed to contain the demographic explosion. It is logical to suppose that small groups eventually would break away and build their own temples, markets, and so on, the way suburbanites today group themselves around shopping centers with churches and schools nearby, independent of the mother city.

Other explanations have been offered:[9] 1) Intensified agriculture in the Late Classic allowed for a population increase and, through careful planning, a maximum diversion of man power to non-agricultural activities, but "short-term farming failures could have triggered long-term troubles." 2) Extensive clearing of land for agriculture would have shifted insect vectors from animal to human hosts and heavily increased disease and mortality. 3) Mounting competition in the magnificence of ceremonial centers and the capturing of victims for sacrificial rites would have diverted a great deal of labor from productive farming to the improvement of these sites. 4) A growing non-productive upper class would have increased the economic strains on society. 5) Long-distance trade, both a benefit and a hazard to the stability of society, brought conservative peoples

(the Maya) in contact with professional merchant groups, backed by military force (central Mexicans), who exercised external pressure and created strong competition.

When we observe the luxurious dress, we are well aware that an extremely wealthy upper class existed among the Maya. Thompson believes that a proletarian revolt against the elite brought the Maya centers to an end.[10]

MAYA ARCHITECTURE OF THE CLASSIC PERIOD

The Petén Area

We have already mentioned sites in the Maya region where a durable architecture had begun to evolve, along with a series of cultural elements that we can place between the Olmec heritage and that which later would become the true Maya culture. Such is the case with Chiapa de Corzo, Izapa, and Kaminaljuyú in the southern area, and Dzibilchaltún in the north of the Yucatán peninsula. But in many respects, it seems to have been the Petén area in northern Guatemala that early in the Christian era served as the birthplace of certain elements destined to be decisive in the subsequent Classic development of Maya culture. In the midst of this dense, steaming tropical forest, today the home of just a handful of men, we can watch the flowering of one of the most brilliant cultures produced on the American continent—a saga that occupied more than a thousand years.

Two of the key sites in this cultural development were Uaxactún and Tikal, located north of Lake Flores, in the heart of the Petén jungle. These two cities, separated by a scant 9 1/2 miles (15 km.) of forest, bear traces of intense human activity from some 600 years before the Christian era. But the oldest structural elements seem limited to the Proto-Classic period, roughly between the third century B.C. and the third century A.D. We can follow the uninterrupted evolution of this architecture through the entire Classic period to the end of the ninth century—spanning about twelve centuries in all.

Uaxactún

A beautiful reconstruction of part of Uaxactún, done by Tatiana Proskouriakoff, shows us how this medium-sized city may have looked toward the final years of its evolution when, by dint of incredible human effort, these forest dwellers managed not only to survive—clearing the land of huge trees and sowing their *milpas*, or maize fields—but to hack out the space they needed for a life that was both familial and collective. Patiently wresting large clearings from the more level parts of the forest, between the depressions of generally uneven terrain, the Maya grouped their buildings on platforms, creating in time a veritable man-made acropolis.

Under the rubble of a building designated E-VII, Sylvanus Morley discovered, almost intact, the famous pyramid known as E-VII-sub, the oldest ever found in this region *(plate 99)*. The structure's three phases of construction probably go back two centuries before the Christian era. Though it displays some almost primitive aspects—its four stairways set into the structural body, the small stairs at the base, and traces of four large wooden posts that may have supported a palm-frond roof over the temple—this building exhibits a number of characteristics that were to prevail for several centuries in the religious architecture of the region. Flanked by the stairways, we see great masks of stone and stucco, some of which still bear strong Olmecoid traits. We notice, too, a tendency to soften certain angles and raw edges, and to emphasize the well-differentiated levels on the upper platform where the sanctuary stood. Finally, we can appreciate the complex play of volumes in the stepped base, where the gently sloping bodies display various projecting moldings that we will soon see crystallized into the superposed "apron" moldings typical of this architecture. The influence that this building apparently exerted in its time can be perceived not only in the neighboring city of Tikal *(plate 101)*, but in sites as far away as Acancéh, in northwestern Yucatán, whose Pyramid of the Masks offers a clear similarity to E-VII-sub.

We might also mention that the construction that ultimately covered over the latter, together with the three buildings that rose to the east, constituted one of those architectural groups frequently used by the Maya as an astronomical observatory or, more precisely, as points for determining solstices and equinoxes. They comprised a series of visual references whereby a man standing at a specified point at the foot of Pyramid E-VII, looking past the axis of the building perpendicular to it and over the outer angles of the other two buildings, would be able to observe the principal visible declinations of the sun on the horizon *(plate 100)*.

In Proskouriakoff's detailed reconstruction we can study five of the eight remodeling phases that, in the space of five centuries, went into what today we call Complex A-5 at Uaxactún. We refer to roughly the period between the early fourth and the early ninth century A.D., spanning almost the entire Classic period. Here we see a simple, well-balanced complex of three small temples—perhaps the Maya equivalent of Teotihuacán's "triple complexes"—gradually invaded by new shrines, elongated palace-type buildings, platforms, and stairs, to the point where two of the original three temples are

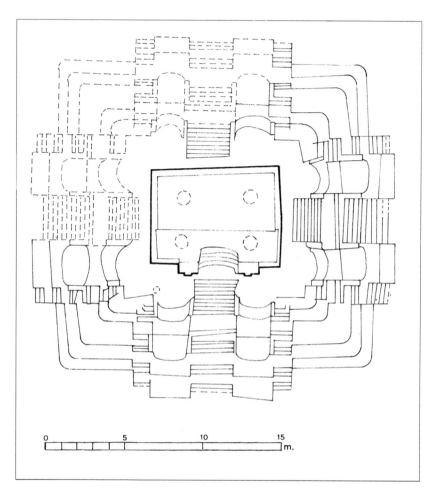

0   5   10   15
m.

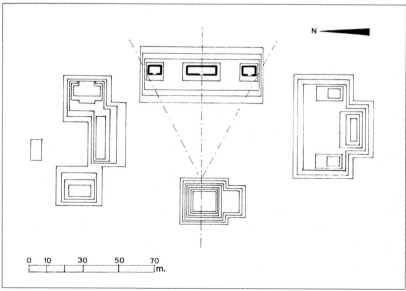

0   10   30   50   70
m.

101. *Tikal: Building 5-D-sub-1-1°*

102. *Sketch of various cross sections of corbel vaults found in the Maya area.*
   A. Building E-X in Uaxactún   B. Building 1 in Tikal
   C. Temple of the Frescoes in Tulum   D. Building A-5 in
   Uaxactún   E. Arch at Labná   F. ball court at Copán
   G. secret crypt at Palenque   H. House A of the Palace at
   Palenque   I. Governor's Palace at Uxmal

103. *Tikal: Temple 23 of the North Acropolis ▷*

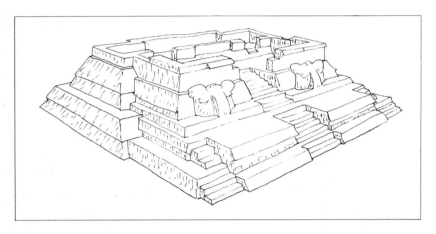

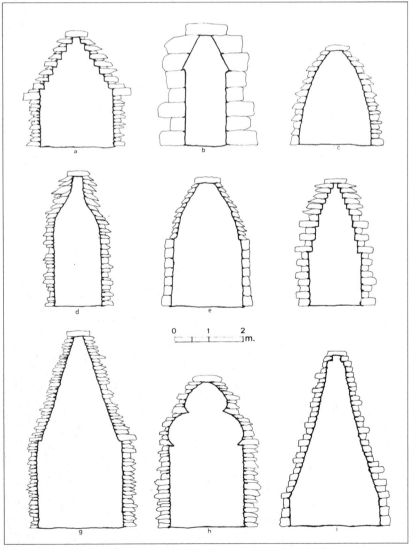

absorbed and the third virtually engulfed by a compact mass of structures. Yet despite the length of time required for this metamorphosis, the architectural style seems to have changed little. The conspicuous regional constants are retained: massive yet lofty roof combs crowning the temples, with slightly inclined friezes underlined by a thick frame topping the roof of the elongated temple; and heavy superposed "apron" molding that creates the projecting and receding planes so common in the bases and platforms of this area.

These examples offer a kaleidoscopic view of the evolution of particular architectural complex over a span of some 500 years of continuous remodeling and amplification; and so we turn to Tikal a neighboring town, for a more detailed study. The largest city of the central Maya area during the Classic period, Tikal was recently the object of a long and minute exploration—including the partial reconstruction of many of its buildings—under the auspices of the University Museum of the University of Pennsylvania (headed by William Coe) and of the Instituto de Antropología e Historia of Guatemala. At its apogee, this great Maya urban center—with its five imposing pyramid-temples, its palaces and sanctuaries and ball courts, its ceremonial platforms, terraces, patios, steam baths, and thousands of other structures—occupied ridges of a terrain that stretched from the Great Central Plaza toward all four cardinal points of the compass. Each of its earthen strips—7 1/2 miles (12 km.) long and 1,625 feet (500 m.) wide,[11] and covered with buildings—was separated from the others by deep hollows and *aguadas* (natural water reservoirs). Their orientation shows that the Maya, like all Mesoamericans, were ever mindful of the cosmos and its association with man and his work.

Tikal

In Tikal, a true urban center, we find a rare instance of a Maya city departing from the usual settlement pattern of its region. Among the Maya, in general, each great city was a true ceremonial center dedicated to religious observance and to the administration of the community's property by ruler-priests. Here lived only the members of the elite class; the general populace inhabited the surrounding villages supporting the center—unlike the settlement pattern of the Mexican plateau, where temples, palaces, multiple dwellings, offices schools, and craft workshops formed part of the city proper.

Under the several feet of fill and superposed layers of floors and buildings that comprise Tikal's North Acropolis (*plate 106*), excavators discovered the structure designated 5-D-sub-1-1°—the city's oldest known building to date (*plate 101*). Built before the Christian

104. *Tikal: colossal mask inside Temple 33-sub*
105. *Tikal: detail at the base of Temple 32* ▷

106. *Tikal: plan indicating two phases of the development of the North Acropolis in the years 1 A.D. (a) and 800 A.D. (b)*

107. *Tikal: rear view of Temple I*

108. *Tikal: partial aerial view of the center of the city, showing the North Acropolis and the Great Plaza with Temples I and II ▷*

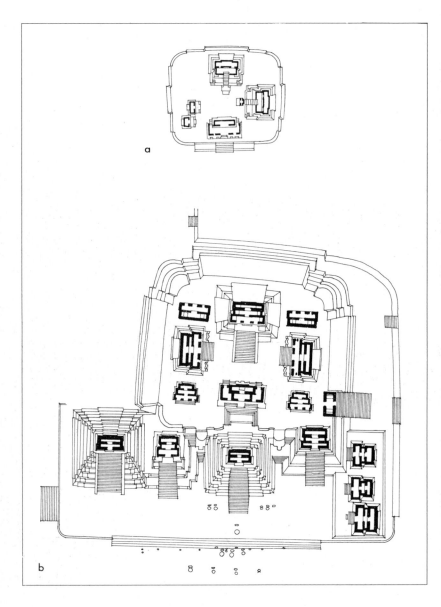

era, it retains some of the early characteristics we saw in Pyramid E-VII-sub at Uaxactún (such as the main stairway set into the body of the base, and the small stairs near its foot); but we find here, for the first time, slender masonry walls (perforated by small ventilation holes in their lower portions), which probably supported a roof of wood and palm fronds.

There is a marked differentiation between the two levels of the sanctuary, clearly reflected on the exterior by a skillful play of volumes in which the projecting and receding planes and the heavy superposed moldings point to the special character of the two interior spaces. These particular elements continued to evolve for more than 800 years; and to them we will see added principles that were to be decisive in Maya architecture—the corbel vault, for example, and the roof-comb.

The first three centuries of the Christian era (or the end of the Proto-Classic period) mark the appearance in this area of cultural elements destined to profoundly influence the Classic development of Maya architecture. Now, the Maya began to build commemorative monuments (mostly stelae), dating from the inauguration of the initial series. Tikal's Stele 29, the oldest of its kind known, bears the date 292 A.D. Early examples of the corbel vault are found in funerary architecture, and arose from the need to roof over tombs; later, the vault appears in temples, palaces, and other structures. In the course of two or three centuries, its popularity spread throughout the region of Maya influence, although almost never beyond it. For this reason, the corbel vault, so basic to the development of Maya architecture, is usually known—in this part of the world, at least—as the "Maya arch," or sometimes, unjustly, as the "false arch" *(plate 102)*.

Another definitive architectural element whose appearance in this area seems to coincide with that of the corbel vault is the roof-comb, or *cresteria*. This soaring structure usually rises from the rear of the temple, growing progressively smaller toward its top, far above the temple roof. The roof-comb lends the temples of the Petén region an unmistakable silhouette and almost always entails a mode of construction in which solid walls predominate over interior space.

With the birth and refinement of these elements, Maya architecture finally evolved a basic style toward the third century A.D. (around the time, for example, when Teotihuacán witnessed the construction of the Pyramid of Quetzalcóatl). From El Petén, strong cultural currents radiated in all directions, borne by a common cultural vocabulary apparent throughout the Maya zone—an idiom whose principal feature was clearly an ingenious and exact system of vigesimal numeration and glyphic writing, capable of registering with

precision not only astronomical observations and computations but dates, historical occurrences, and other material. On the other hand, while contemporaneous Mesoamerican peoples such as the Zapotecs and those in Teotihuacán were using flat roofs atop wooden beams (which in turn were supported by walls and pillars or columns), the Maya's exclusive use of the corbel vault fatally limited flexibility in the arrangement and size of interior space. In some parts of the Maya area, as we shall see, ways were found to overcome the limitations inherent in the principle of the corbel vault; but in El Petén, as in most other sectors, interior space was considered secondary to the matter of emphasizing large open spaces, and to the exterior appearance of buildings. Indeed, even though temples were becoming larger, there was less and less space inside them *(plate 109).*

Few Mesoamerican temples express as eloquently as those in Tikal the essential role of the temple as a reliquary, or tabernacle, built to house an effigy of some deity. The priests officiated from the summit of the pyramidal base, thus stressing their supremacy over the mass of worshipers to whom access to the sanctuary was normally forbidden and who could observe religious ceremonies only from below, standing in the plazas at the foot of the pyramids, on platforms and steps provided for that purpose. Pre-Hispanic worship was, above all, an open-air proceeding, the temple having acquired a symbolic value rather than being thought of as a space for intimate communication between man and his gods.

This concept of the temple as a raised reliquary, inaccessible to mortal man, impressive in its aura of mystery and veiled in clouds of incense, helps us understand the symbolic function that the roof-combs served in Maya religious architecture. In Tikal, where that element seems to have originated, it was so closely tied to the structural system and to formal usage that it cannot be viewed as simply ornamental and symbolic in nature—as a mere architectural finial. To understand the slow and somewhat rigid evolution of architectural elements during the entire Classic period (that is, from the third to the ninth century A.D.), it is important to visualize all these elements simultaneously.

Temple 23 of the North Acropolis offers one of the best early examples of Classic architecture in Tikal *(plate 103).* There are superposed moldings, along with the marked differentiation of levels we have already discussed. Furthermore, the roof-comb was conceived as a great pile of masonry, substantially lightened by interior arches and rising from the rear of the temple; the sense of verticality is intensified by a deep central panel that creates a strong play of light and shadow. The impression is that the roof-comb grows directly out of the temple floor *(plate 107),* an impression heightened by the "spinal column" effect of the vertical panel on the rear wall and by the way the different levels of the inner sanctuary are unified. These last two elements appear in the oldest phases of this architecture, and lead us to suppose that the principle of the *cresteria* might have been in use from the beginning of the Christian era, along with the first masonry walls—but executed in part, perhaps, in perishable materials. This might explain why so early an example as Temple 23 shows such a firm sense of confidence in the complex combination of its volumes. We can observe the continuity of some of the architectural elements, such as a peculiar thickening of the back wall, which rises up from the floor level like a spinal column, and soars uninterruptedly skyward past the wide cornice. The evolution of this typical "backbone" in Tikal can be followed over five centuries. We can also trace other, equally characteristic elements, such as the graded panels on the sides of the comb and a progressive decrease in the size of the upper (usually more ornate) elements that face forward.

In Tikal, the items of interest tend to be found on the front of the temple. The broad frieze crowning the roof above the sanctuary; the elaborate sections of the front of the roof-comb; the delicately carved lintels of wood *(plate 111)*—all carried a profusion of ornamentation, little of which remains today. Through a millennium of total abandonment, the fertile jungle reclaimed its own; some of the temples in this and other Maya cities sit engulfed by trees up to their very roof-combs. We gain a sketchy idea of the former splendor of this *cresteria* when we take a close look at one of Tikal's most heavily ornamented buildings, Temple II *(plate 110),* where the remaining traces of a set of elaborately carved ear-hoops suggest the one-time existence of an enormous central mask, while smaller masks adorn the upper section of the roof and flank the access stairway to the sanctuary. When we compare the remains of the openwork at the top of this structure with similar elements still visible on Temple IV and others, we suspect that Temple II is missing a quarter of the original height of its comb—which, even as it stands in fragmentary form, almost equals twice the height of the temple itself.

From the standpoint of form, the roof-comb served as a finial that enhanced the sense of vertical thrust so characteristic of the temples of this region. Notwithstanding the ponderousness this feature engendered—in some cases it reduced the interior space almost to the point of absurdity *(plate 113, lower right)*—we can appreciate the powerful impetus that the *cresteria* gave to the temple's upward striving *(plates 108, 109).*

In dramatic contrast to contemporaneous Teotihuacán (where

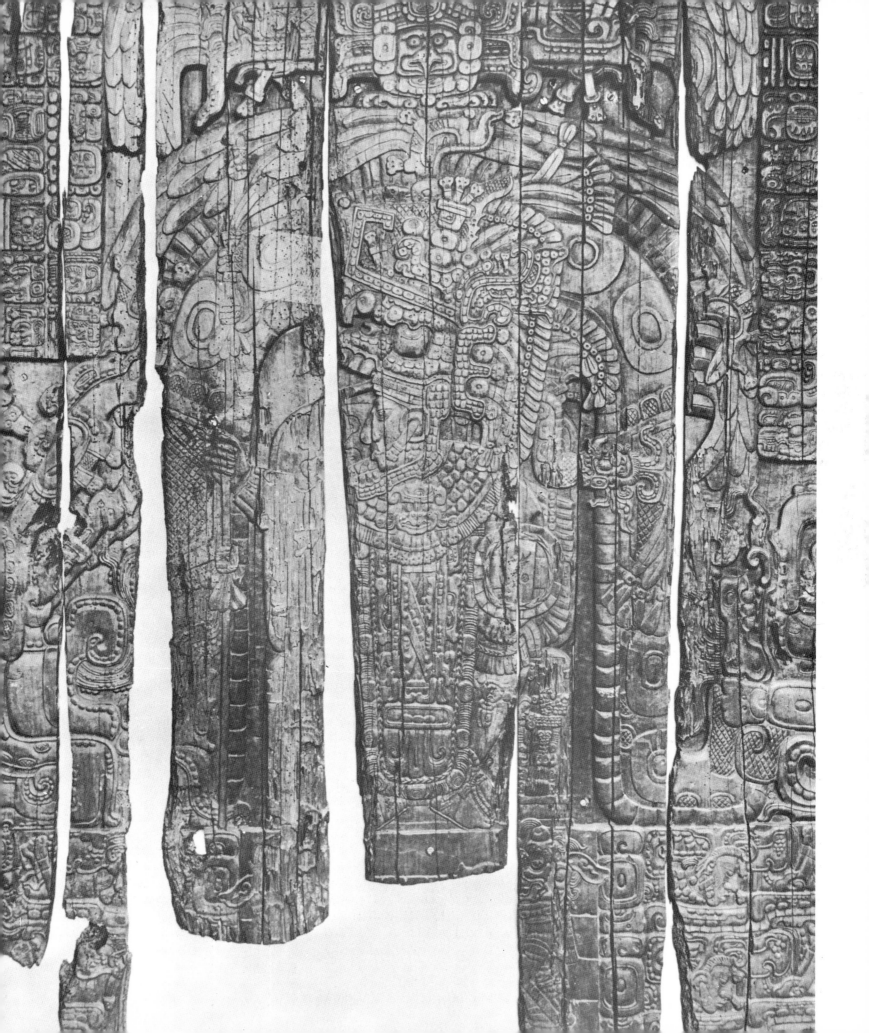

a basic feeling for the horizontal was accentuated by the ever-present *tablero*), the Maya of Tikal clearly oriented their architecture to make another kind of statement, drawing on every architectural device at their command to give their temples a feeling of verticality. Thus, even the heavy projecting "apron" moldings superposed on bases seem to point to the sky in a subtle play of protruding and receding planes *(plates 105, 108)*; and along with colossal masks in stone and stucco *(plate 104)*, such elements are an almost inseparable aspect of Tikal's architecture.

A most imposing embodiment of this regional style appears in the magnificent building designated Temple IV, 230 feet (70 m.) high; but unquestionably the purest example, even at only 164 feet (50 m.), is the beautiful Temple I, or Temple of the Giant Jaguar, which bounds the eastern side of the Great Plaza at Tikal *(plates 108, 113)*. Everything here contributes to the underscoring of this marked vertical orientation: the unusually slender proportions of the stepped bodies comprising the base (there are nine—a magic number for the Maya); the rhythmical arrangement of moldings and central panels with their characteristic cut-away angles, their alternately projecting and receding planes becoming smaller toward the top; the steep stairway, unprotected by *alfardas,* leading to the sanctuary; and, finally, the prolongation of the skyward sweep of the temple in a high roof-comb with characteristic set-in panels and inclined planes. The true culmination of architectural trends born several centuries earlier, the Temple of the Giant Jaguar, with its well-balanced proportions, becomes something of a prototype in Tikal. Its slender yet sturdy outline stands silhouetted against the dense tropical forest that, for a few centuries at least, was virtually dominated by the splendid buildings of Maya culture. But of all the cities of the Maya only Tikal—her temple-crests sparkling above the treetops—ever really conquered the forest.

And so the North Acropolis, its sixteen temples visible on the surface and the remains of a hundred other buildings buried under the mass of fill—the product of some eleven centuries of constant remodeling—comprises, together with Temples I and II, both the original nucleus and the ceremonial heart of Tikal. Offsetting these markedly religious structures is the Central Acropolis, across the Great Plaza, which offers buildings of a residential and administrative character (as we saw in Teotihuacán, in the mega-complex formed by the Citadel and the Great Compound). In contrast to the crowded placement of the temples forming the North Acropolis, the more elongated buildings of the Central Acropolis are usually grouped around plazas or courts on different levels and dominate the Great

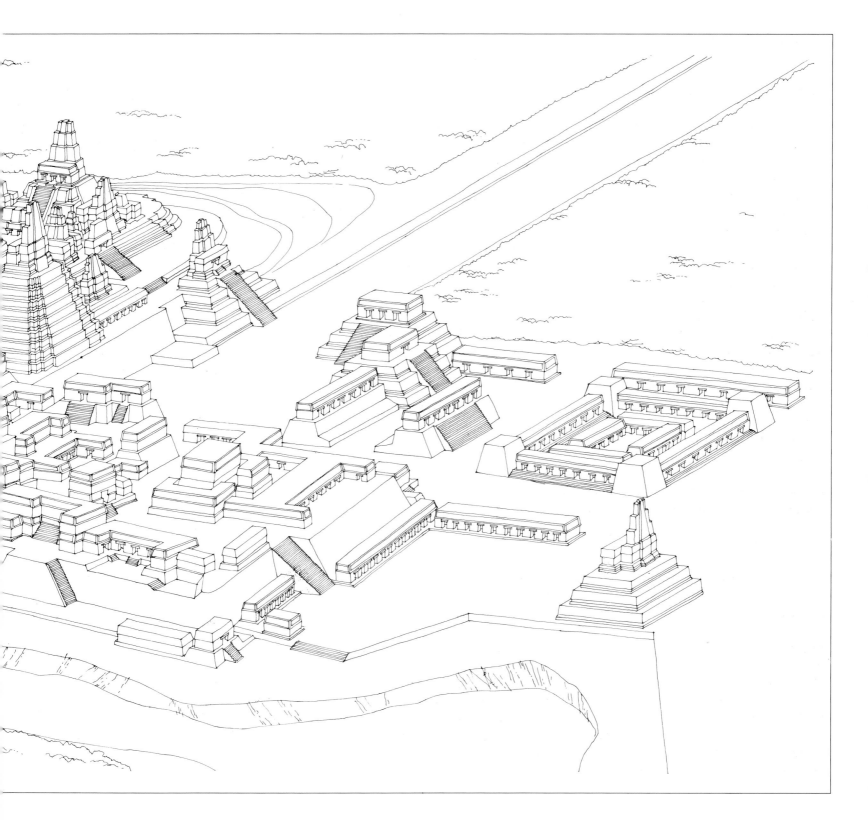

Plaza from an average height of 33 feet (10 m.) *(plates 106, 112)*. Except for the unusual finials on the roof of Building 5-D-63, the type of long galleries that predominate (at times consisting of two and three stories) and the absence of *cresterías* suggest that this part of the ceremonial center had some kind of distinct and special function. The ample dimensions of the interior spaces *(plate 115)* and the presence of several wider-than-usual apertures indicate that these buildings may have served as habitations of either a permanent or temporary sort.

With its two levels—the upper one opening out toward the opposite side—its two low, slightly extended wings, its raised base, and a continuous frieze (decorated above each door only), the Maler Palace offers one of the clearest examples of this type of residential architecture. Only a few fragments remain of the rich relief ornamentation that once embellished the friezes of certain buildings. However, we do find well-preserved galleries with vaulted ceilings—often crossed by wooden braces; lintels of sapodilla wood; built-in benches; and the stucco rounded off to avoid sharp angles *(plate 115)*.

These buildings reveal the typical arrangement of interior space in elongated galleries, sometimes forming three or four parallel rows occupying two or three stories, but seldom provided with any means for easy or flexible intercommunication *(plate 114)*. There were probably exceptions; but due largely to the limited dimensions permitted by this mode of construction, the interior spaces tend to be narrow, dark, and quite damp—"unsuitable for prolonged habitation," Hardoy feels, adding that it is "hard to believe that these 'palaces' were permanent residences. But they may have been occupied by novices and priests during the relatively protracted period imposed by the long vigils that preceded important ceremonies."[12] Whatever their function, and however they may have been occupied, few of the structures could be called appealing as architectural approaches to the use of space—especially when compared to the lightness and spatial flexibility to be found in far-away Teotihuacán, with which Tikal and other Maya cities shared cultural and commercial ties.

Between the third and seventh century, the influences that Teotihuacán seems to have exerted in the Maya area were many and subtle. Tikal, perhaps the largest and most important Maya city of this epoch (its 45,000 inhabitants occupying some 75 square miles, or 123 sq. km.),[13] reflects the impact of the City of the Gods in many ways, including its ceramics—often inspired by Teotihuacán forms or themes—and its sculpture, as in Stele 31, for example, wherein some important personage is seen escorted by two warriors dressed in the Teotihuacán manner.

Although in general local styles dictated quite otherwise, the architecture of Tikal includes some curious bases obviously modeled after the typical Teotihuacán *talud-tablero,* two of them appearing in the middle of a plaza—not a customary placement in Tikal; a third example can be seen in the small building to the north, at the foot of the Central Acropolis (in front of the ball court of the east plaza near the Great Market). Built of large limestone blocks in accordance with local practice, this base displays a coarse imitation of the Teotihuacán *tablero,* crowned by a beveled cornice—apparently an inverted version of the *talud*—resulting in an appearance totally distinct from the far-away original *(plate 116),* despite decorative motifs adopted equally from the Teotihuacán style.

But these few cases aside, we find little of Teotihuacán in the architecture of Tikal; indeed, its buildings reflect a highly individual regional stamp. Its own basic tendency seems to have been to deliberately cut itself off from the structural possibilities offered by the flat-roof approach of its contemporaries. The sole feature around which Tikal developed its architecture was the corbel vault.

To conclude our study of Tikal, we should mention the "twin complex"—an element created here toward the end of the Classic period (between the seventh and ninth century A.D.), and almost always local in its application. Several examples have been found at Tikal *(plates 117, 118)*. William Coe suggests that they were erected to commemorate the end of a *katún,* or period of 7, 200 days.[14] These consist of an artificial esplanade with rounded corners, supporting two identical stepped bases rising at the east and west ends *(plate 117)*. The bases have four stairways, but there is no trace of a temple on the upper platforms; so it is possible that they served some other type of function—sacrifices, perhaps, or ritual dancing, or theatrical performances. In front of the western base we usually find nine stele-altar pairs devoid of any relief decoration *(plate 118)*. On one side of this same esplanade we see a long building with nine doors that look across onto a precinct that opens to the exterior only through an unusual doorway shaped like a Maya arch, cut through the thickness of the wall. Within the precinct stands the only stele-altar combination carved in bas-relief; and here we find inscribed the date on which this enormous ceremonial complex was solemnly inaugurated *(plate 119)*.

We should note the characteristic form these monoliths almost always took in Tikal, and in the Petén region in general. The stele, its front face slightly wider and more rounded toward the top usually portrays a richly attired priest carrying an elaborate cere-

114. *Tikal: plan of Building 51 of the South Acropolis*

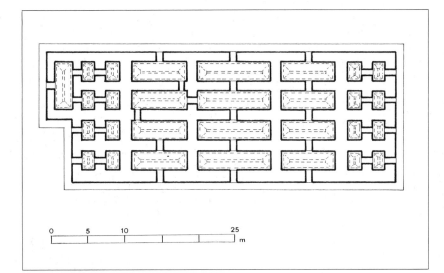

115. *Tikal: interior of a gallery of a five-storied palace in the Central Acropolis*

116. *Tikal: base showing the Teotihuacán influence, situated at the foot of the Central Acropolis* ▷

0 5 10 25
m

117. *Tikal: aerial view of one of the twin complexes*
118. *Tikal: one of the two twin stepped bases of Complex Q*

119. *Tikal: precinct located north of the twin complexes, with an entrance i
the form of a Maya arch and a pair of carved monoliths (stele-altar)*

monial rod in his two hands; the altar looks like a thick stone dru
(plate 120). The sculptures have the dual purpose of commemoratir
a specific period in time and, as Westheim puts it, the "glorificatic
of the *halach uinic* or all-powerful priest."[15] They are often associate
with the construction of new buildings, denoting the principal ax
of the urban plan *(plate 121)*.

A millennium ago the forest of El Petén, its lush vegetation no
completely grown back, was densely populated. But can we speak
true urban planning at that time? William Bullard, who mapped o
these ridges and swampy reaches in order to study the settlement pa
terns of the ancient Maya, mentions the difficulty of trying to d
lineate the areas that were clearly urban in each city, scattered as th
were through the dense forest like an archipelago in the sea. Tl
peripheral nuclei of farm dwellings, at a ratio of five or six inhabitar
per every two and one-half acre, seemed so widely spread that "
a quick first glance it appears that they are practically everywhere."

This impression grows as, following the thousand pathways ar
wide causeways, or *sacbé-oob*, that cut through the forest, one a
proaches the ceremonial and administrative center, where the vario
buildings—temples, palaces, steam baths, ball courts, and markets
are grouped around plazas and esplanades on large artificial platform
near rain-storage reservoirs created from natural depressions in t
land. In the last analysis, the function of the broad causeways th
interconnect the most important architectural complexes was esse
tially ceremonial *(plate 112)*. As Hardoy remarks, "It is possible th
Maya architects used these causeways to dramatize the approach
to the temples and principal complexes. In Tikal, we invariab
find that some of the visual corridors created by the few causewa
we know of are closed off by a temple."[17] He then adds a particular
evocative comment, postulating "a fifth- or sixth-century mercha
from Teotihuacán visiting some of the centers we have mentione
to trade articles made in the central part of the Valley of Mexico f
products from the tropical forest. He would find it difficult to app
the term 'city' to the harmonious complex of temples built around
plaza, its dwellings scattered about in the cleared portions of cultiva
ed fields. . . . But as the visitor became familiar with various aspec
of life in Tikal, he would realize that he was in a place unlike any
might have encountered in the forest. He would note the unusu
architectural scale . . . a detail and harmony in the friezes connotir
the hands of almost unsurpassed artists . . . more stelae than usu
and ceremonies more elaborate, and attended by greater numbe
of people."[18]

In spite of its informal pattern of growth and its enforced adapt

tion to a difficult landscape, the heart of Tikal reveals a conceptu
grandeur wherein, in place of an undesired and in any case almo
impossible symmetry, the architects managed to create a sequence
ever-changing impressions along the principal access roads leading
the ceremonial center—roads whose once lengthy vistas are obscur
today by the insurgent forest, so that only with the aid of a map ca
they be fully appreciated. We will have other opportunities to observ
the skillful, and at times subtle, devices of Maya architects, wh
found in the very ruggedness of the topography ways to add grande
and drama to their ceremonial complexes.

It is interesting, and perhaps even surprising, to learn that th
area of El Petén contains some urban layouts that seem least to be th
products of random growth: Ixkún and Nakum, for example, ar
Yaxhá *(plates 122–125).* The first two centers suggest a quite ca
culated alignment of buildings along established axes, the symmetr
at times achieving an almost Teotihuacán rigidity. In Yaxhá, who
important and dense structural groups lie on the banks of the lake
the same name, we find a layout that seems freer and more like th
of Tikal—including a twin complex of the same type. A painstakin
study by Nicholas Hellmuth established the existence of a local varia
of the *talud-tablero,* and of structures in the centers of plazas an
patios—a device common in Teotihuacán, but infrequent in th
cities of this region.[19] Even more significant is the finding of urba
elements midway in style between the Teotihuacán avenue and th
typical Maya causeway. These *vías,* as Hellmuth calls them, appe
more rigid, with ninety-degree intersections; they are usually bo
dered by more buildings than are the *sacbé-oob,* whose main purpo
was to connect major building groups that were set out in no pa
ticular pattern *(plate 124).*

Except for such aspects of the urban plan and some local varia
tions in the style and disposition of the buildings, the cities of I
Petén are similar to those of Tikal. The stylistic influence of this regic
is known to have spread to far-distant sites such as Cobá, northea
of the Yucatán peninsula, where El Petén's typical indented corne
are transformed into something much more rounded *(plate 126).*

THE USUMACINTA RIVER BASIN

Piedras Negras

The dense forest of El Petén extends westward through the Usuma
cinta River basin into more rugged terrain—the setting for man
other Maya cities that competed in the arts of sculpture and architec
ture during the Classic period.

One of the most important was Piedras Negras, on the Guate

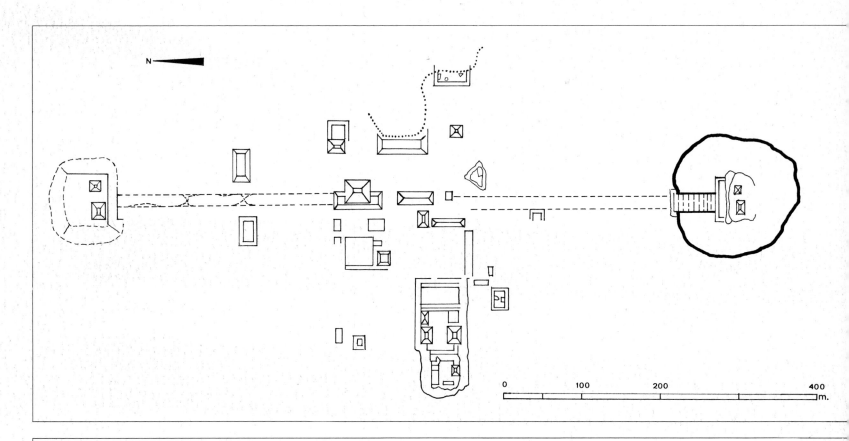

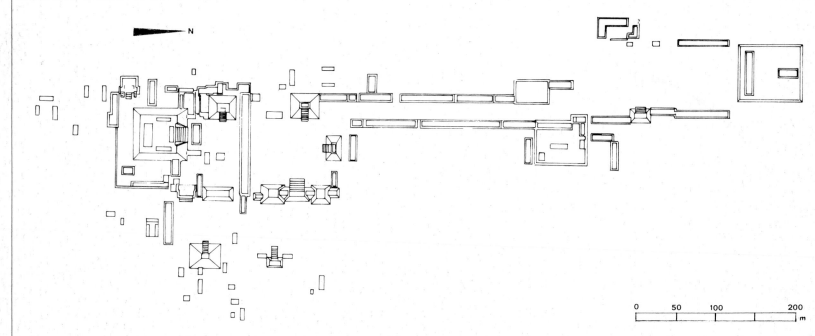

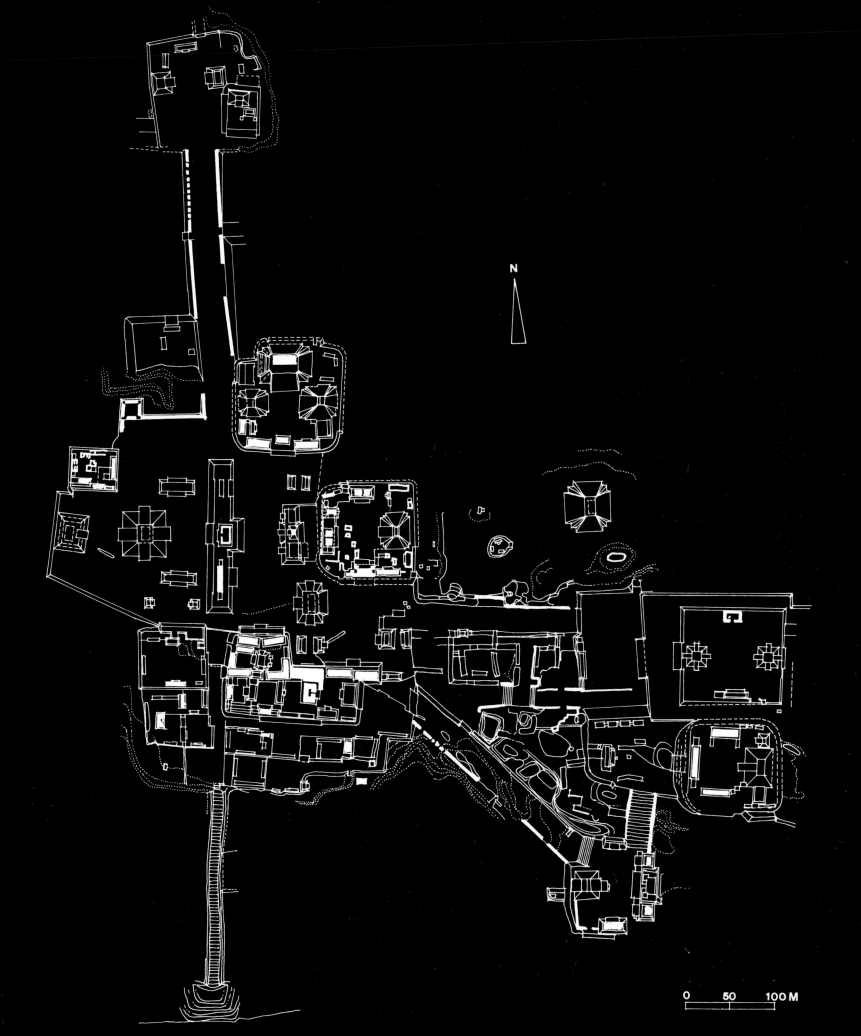

0   50   100 M

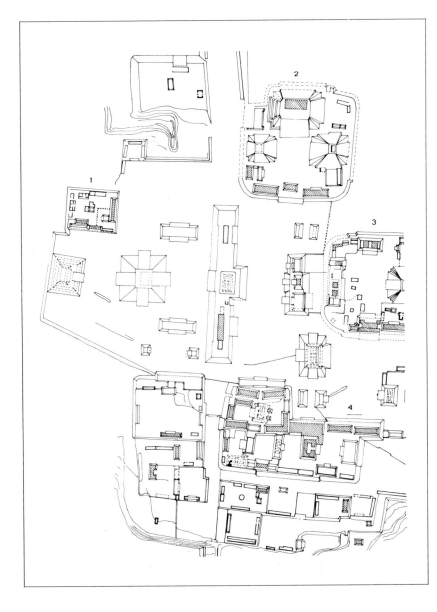

malan side of the Usumacinta River *(plate 127)*. Here we find a series
of skillfully laid out buildings and esplanades, giving the appearance
of freedom—yet not without a sense of plan—and spreading out over
the hills and along artificial plateaus created on the slopes *(plate 128)*.
The complex, today all but destroyed and totally overgrown, must
have been imposing in its time of splendor, judging by Tatiana Proskouriakoff's reconstruction of the Acropolis in the northwestern
sector *(plate 129)*.

Apart from the virtues of its location and the way its builders
utilized the unevenness of the terrain to terrace various buildings and
alternate pyramidal bases with patios and long galleries, our first
impression of this complex is that it resembles some of those we saw
in Tikal. Like Tikal's temples, some of the principal sanctuaries in
Piedras Negras are crowned by heavy *cresterías,* rising in similar
fashion above the rear wall. Too, the stepped bodies of the base are
outlined with the same type of projecting and receding planes and the
same superposed moldings, though more obviously rounded at the
corners. But the feeling is less vertical here, and the more elongated
sanctuary has three doorways *(plate 129, Temple J-4 at right)* instead of
the one that is more frequent in Tikal. This local style is seen not only
in temples of the Late Classic period—such as J-4 or K-5—but in
much earlier buildings in this city, as in the initial phase of Temple
K-5. This, like the oldest known structure in Tikal (Building 5-D-
sub-1-1°), offers a spaciousness incomparably greater than its later
version—the former's slim masonry walls having been designed to
support only a light roof of wooden beams and palm fronds.

The influence of El Petén emerges, in certain of these temples, a
a marked decrease in the amount of interior space, necessitated by the
adoption of the heavy roof-combs (in the style of Tikal). However,
some buildings in Piedras Negras managed to reassert the dominance
of space over solid walls. The builders of the latter were most likely
swayed by Palenque, the city that, as we shall see, seems to have
achieved the most notable architectural advances in this region of the
Usumacinta.

In contrast to the El Petén style of sanctuaries, we find others
that, as in Palenque, bear a light *crestería* supported by the central
part of the roof, a solution that permits a thinner wall and the gaining
of space with greater flexibility. Such is the case in Temple J-24.
Recalling the covered galleries that surround the Palace at Palenque,
we find here halls that allow a relatively fluid communication between
the facades. In some of the elongated buildings of the Acropolis
multiple apertures almost reduce the exterior walls to simple pillars
(plate 129)—a revolutionary departure from the normally cumber-

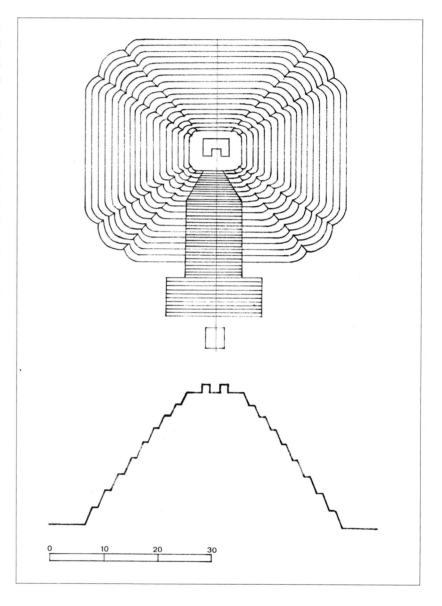

me quality of central Maya architecture. Finally, we should
ention—as exemplifying this surprising structural lightness—the
acious and attractive Building P-7, largest of the eight steam
aths in Piedras Negras, and displaying a rare combination of the
orbel vault and a flat roof.

Along with its architecture, representing a compromise between
e influence of Tikal and that of Palenque, and explained in part by
e fact that it was situated midway between these two strong poles,
iedras Negras' stone sculpture looms large in Maya art—as much
r its quantity as for its novelty of expression, which avoided the
revailing forms. In this rich repertory of sculptural themes, we
ould point out four outstanding examples, beginning with Throne
, which was placed inside a kind of niche in the shape of a Maya
ch in Building J-6. On the back we see an enormous mask of the
in god, Chac; two great holes represent the eyes, out of which
nerge two personages whose gesturing hands suggest that they are
aving a conversation *(plate 130)*. Of the numerous carved stelae,
veral deserve special mention. In one we see a seated figure in a niche,
irved in high relief, with glyphic inscriptions and other motifs in
very delicate bas-relief *(plate 131)*. But perhaps the most beautiful
ele in Piedras Negras, in composition and execution, is Stele 12
late 132), dominated by the elegant figure of a *halach uinic*, who is
ated with one leg drawn up, leaning forward, spear in hand, to hear
plea by the chief of a group of bound captives guarded by two
med soldiers. We can see how the artist was able to draw attention
the upper part, emphasizing the social hierarchy by changing
radually from low to high relief. But the most surprising *tour de
rce* in this city's sculpture is undoubtedly Lintel 3. Although badly
amaged, it reveals the entire sculptural repertory from the delicate
ching of glyphic inscriptions to parts carved in the round, and
compassing all degrees of relief from the shallowest to the deepest
between *(plate 133)*.

axchilán

tuated up-river on the Mexican side, Yaxchilán's principal building
roups lie along slender man-made esplanades set into the banks of
e Usumacinta River, with certain edifices that complete the cere-
onial center placed on the sides of the adjacent hills *(plate 134)*.
lthough its position is more southerly, Yaxchilán's architecture
ems less influenced by the El Petén region than by Palenque,
espite the eclecticism of many of its buildings. Few Maya cities, in
ct, display such diversity in their conception of certain architec-
ral elements. Here, for example, we find doors of different shapes,

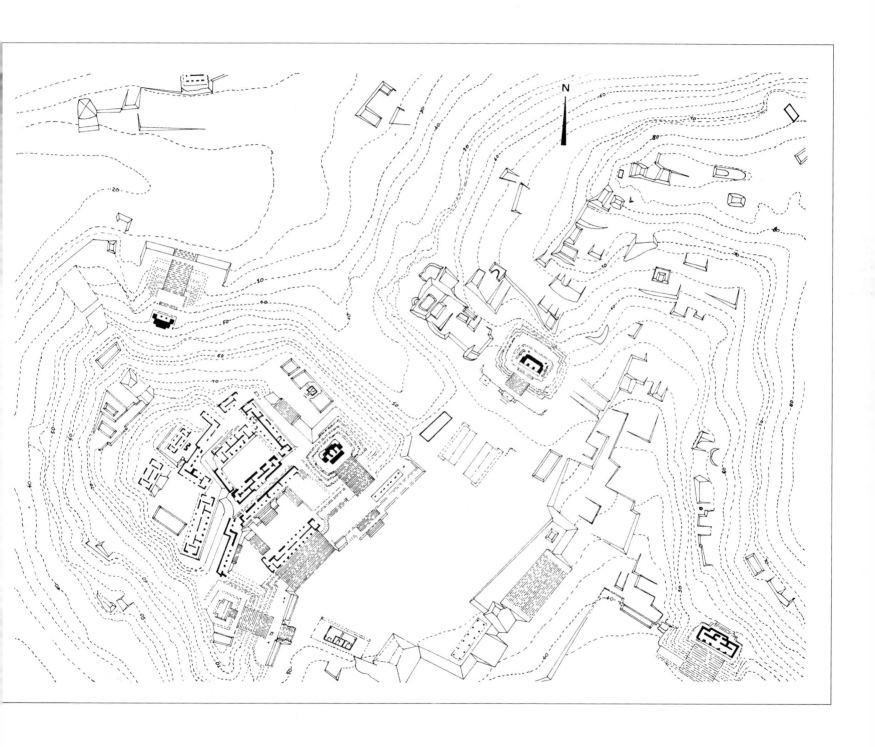

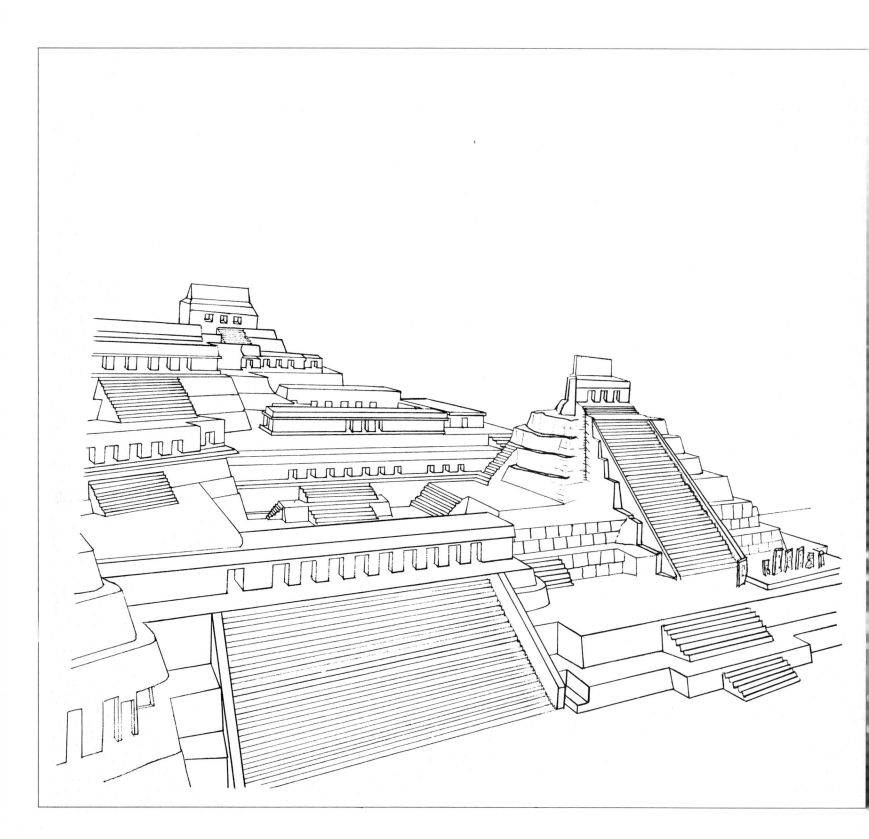

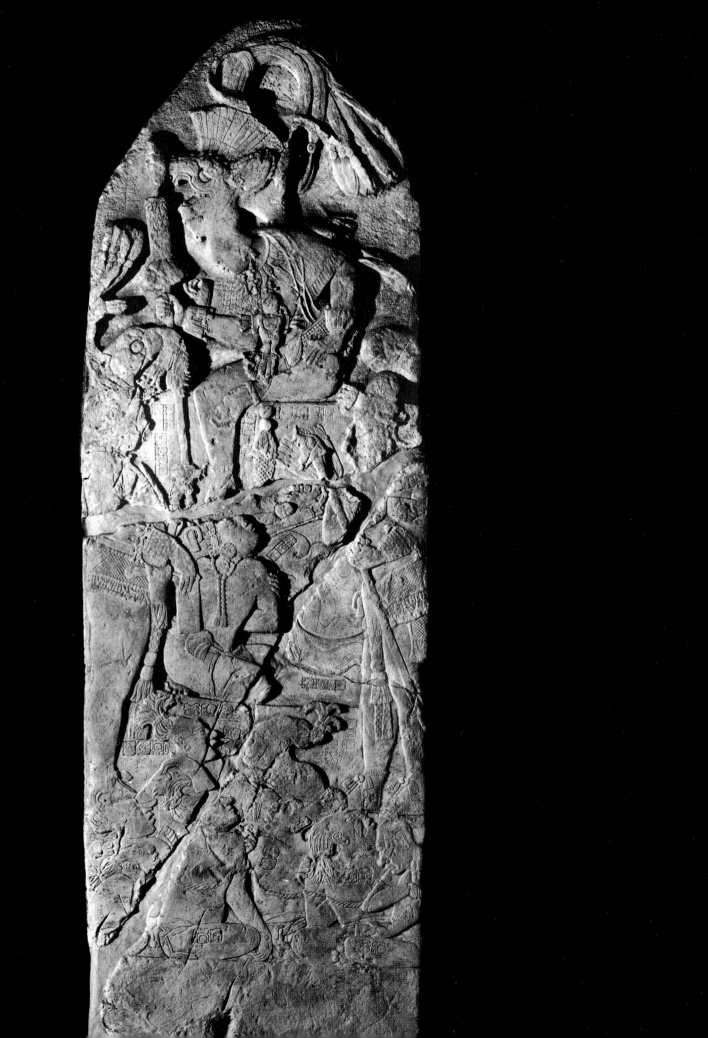

and variants of the *cresteria,* which—unlike those of Tikal—do not rise from the rear of the building, but are based on different principles. The least common of these involves setting the roof-comb directly above the main facade (we see this variation in certain regional styles of the Yucatán peninsula). Another, similar to the hollow *cresteria* of Palenque, consists of two openwork walls fastened together, tilted slightly to the rear; but this roof-comb is taller and wider than that at Palenque, and each of its two walls rests on one of the interior walls of the building, which in this case consists of three parallel galleries. The effect produced by this colossal superstructure is overwhelming, as we can see in Building 6 (the Red Temple of the Shore), part of whose rich sculptural decoration can be observed in its frieze *(plates 135, 137).*

The most frequent type of roof-comb found in Yaxchilán is more in tune with the elongated proportions of the galleries and with the particularly wide frieze that adorns the upper part of the facades. It consists of a thick, high, openwork wall that usually grows thinner toward the top and that rests on the central part of the roof—though at times it may crown a building with one gallery only, as in Building 33, the prototype of this local style *(plates 136, 138).* We note here the richness of ornamentation and the vigorous chiaroscuro to be found in its wide, inclined frieze, as well as the monumental character of the roof-comb, with the remains of a large sculpture in strong relief standing out in the center. The interior of the sanctuary shows a lovely variant of the corbel vault, with a multilobed appearance that will occur again in Palenque *(plate 139).*

Among Yaxchilán's sculptures, we should mention especially the richly carved monolithic lintels that adorned the doors of many of the buildings. Whereas Tikal bequeathed us beautiful specimens carved in hard sapodilla wood, Yaxchilán's were of limestone. In Lintel 26 we can admire the exquisite and minute detail with which the hair style, costume, and even the expressiveness of the hands are rendered; and, in Lintel 25, the linear fluency of a composition showing a god armed with a spear and shield, emerging from the jaws of a fantastic serpent while a priestess raises her face in ecstasy *(plate 140).*

Bonampak

In speaking of the Usumacinta River basin, we cannot ignore Bonampak, a ceremonial center located in the same region as Yaxchilán. Though small in size, it occupies a preponderant place in Maya art on the strength of its painted murals, still the loveliest we know in the Classic Maya world (and, indeed, in Mesoamerica). We are mindful, also, of their great documentary value in reflecting diverse aspects of

35. *Yaxchilán: Building 6 (Red Temple of the Shore)*

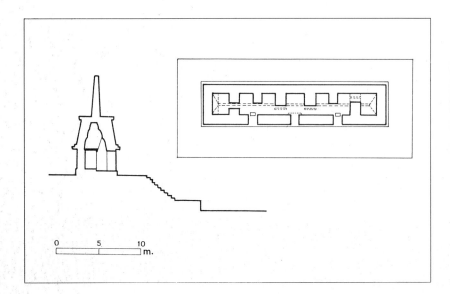

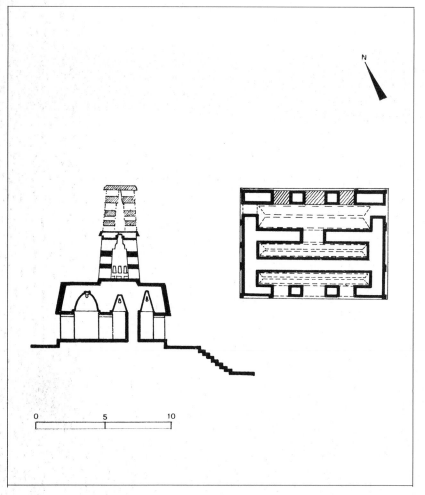

Maya life up to the end of the eighth century A.D.

We need only glance at the work of the Master of Bonampak to appreciate the freedom and sureness of line and the keen sense of composition that place this painter on a par with the great masters of other civilizations. The central part of the scene known as the *Torture of the Captives* shows a dying prisoner sprawled on the stairs of the stepped base at the feet of triumphant warriors. With spare but sure strokes, the artist depicts the agony of the victim, his body draped diagonally, his head thrown back, breathing with difficulty, his right hand clenched and his left hanging limp. While one of his companions in misfortune reaches out to him in compassion, another, his face filled with horror, tries to staunch the flow of blood from his own wounded hands.

Palenque

We now turn to Palenque, regarded by many authors, and with good reason, as the jewel of this region. It seems to have been in many respects the headquarters of a school of art, which is why we choose this site as a vertex of the Classic Maya "triangle." Everything in Palenque fascinates, beginning with the city's very location. Its buildings rise on the harmonious series of artificial terraces situated on the nearer spurs of the Chiapas Mountains, and from here they dominate the lowlands to the north, protected to the south and southeast by high mountains covered with a dense, eternally green forest. Between these mountains flow the crystalline waters of the Otolum River, a small tributary of the Usumacinta that in its passage through the ceremonial center was channeled, in Maya fashion, through a tunnel roofed with a corbel vault. Another stretch of the same tributary was crossed by a broad stone bridge based on the same principle. On the steep slope that abruptly bounds the city to the north, we find what is left of some retaining walls whose apertures, combined with narrow flights of stairs, suggest that their purpose was defensive. All these features together afforded Palenque a most privileged position—strategic in the eventuality of attack and, above all, the probable civic and religious center of the broad and fertile region fanning out at its feet.

Apart from its excellent location, and the skillful use of topography that we have already observed in other Maya cities, Palenque offers a composition utilizing the ridges themselves—along with artificial platforms, buildings, and stairways—to create an array whose balance and harmony are rare in Maya architecture. In the central area we find the Palace, from whose sprawling mass there rises an asymmetrically sited tower of several stories; balancing it to the southwest is the massive Temple of the Inscriptions *(plate 142)*. To the southeast, on higher ground, appears a lovely trio: the Temples of the Sun, the Cross, and the Foliated Cross *(plate 141)*. But even the monumentality of this spatial symphony—its perspectives constantly changing, its buildings silhouetted against the sky or the green of the forest—pales before the grandeur of nature's setting.

Prominent on its artificial base, the complex known as the Palace reflects the work of many epochs. "Cellar" chambers have been found partially hidden in the bulk of its base *(plates 143, 146)*. Its various surface buildings, only portions of which exist today, are arranged around a series of more or less regular patios *(plate 155)*, and include the unique and famous tower that commanded a view of the open reaches to the north and that probably served as both astronomical observatory and watchtower. The tower makes the Palace one of the best-known buildings in Maya architecture; but we find other unusual features as well. On at least three of the outer facades there is a series of galleries built in different stages; they eventually girded the structure with an almost continuous "arcade" offering sheltered access to each of the interior patios *(plates 143, 144)*. The feeling of lightness in the structures arises from the many openings that tended to reduce their outer walls to mere pillars such as we saw in some of the buildings at Piedras Negras.

In Palenque, this relative delicacy of structure is the first thing that catches our eye. The principal buildings here date, however, from the beginnings of the seventh century A.D. (that is, the middle of the Classic period), a hundred years or more before Tikal erected her higher temples. It would seem that the architects of Palenque—a city of relatively recent vintage—found, despite certain limitations, ways to employ to maximum advantage techniques that had been created several centuries earlier by their neighbors in El Petén (the latter, as we know, never having managed to escape entirely from the ponderousness of their original style).

One of Palenque's great innovations was to reduce the weight of the roof through the simultaneous use of two techniques: leaving niches in the *intrados* of the vaults over the middle wall—thus eliminating some of the dead weight *(plate 150)*—and slanting the upper part of the facade as though the outer wall itself were following the line of the corbel vault *(plate 147)*. There was also a conspicuous outer cornice with an ingenious drainage system for rain water, and an exceptionally light roof-comb that rested on the central part of the structure. All of this permitted Palenque's architects to reduce the thickness of the walls, creating additional interior space and increasing the number of openings. These truly revolutionary features would

141. *Palenque, Chiapas, Mexico: aerial view from the northeast. In the foreground, the Palace; to the right, the Temple of the Inscriptions; to the left, the Temple of the Cross, Temple of the Foliated Cross, and Temple of the Sun*

142. *Palenque: aerial view from the north. In the foreground, the Palace; in the background, the Temple of the Inscriptions*

soon be accompanied by a refinement of proportions to produce a style of singular elegance *(plates 145, 146).*

Innumerable details add enchantment to the Palenque ruins. There are stucco medallions, masks, and other adornments on the interior walls. There is the trilobate shape of the arch giving access to House A of the Palace *(plate 151).* There is the sudden view, as one passes under this arch, of the harmonious west patio leading to the front of House C, behind which we see the profile of the guard-tower *(plate 147).* There is the subtle richness of House C's base, with its glyphic inscriptions in the center of the steps *(plate 156),* its *alfardas* representing kneeling figures, and the decorations on the sides of the base, where groups of four glyphs alternate with projecting vertical panels carved in relief and portraying individuals *(plate 148).* There is, finally, the small T-shaped window cutting through the central wall of House B, highlighted by whimsical motifs in stucco that still show signs of the original polychrome *(plate 149).*

Noteworthy at Palenque is the bas-relief sculpture, whether carved in very fine limestone or modeled in stucco. We must admire the great stone tablets embedded in the walls of some of the rooms, which in Palenque replaced the stelae of other Maya cities. In the center detail of the exquisitely executed Tablet of the Slaves, for example *(plate 152),* we recognize the theme—so frequent in Maya art—of a *halach uinic* accepting offerings from a man and a woman sitting on either side of him. Seated on a thick cushion carried by two slaves, the principal personage here impresses us by the simplicity and nobility of his silhouette, and by the somewhat mannered hand gestures, which—in the Usumacinta mode—are always so expressive. This "idealization of the Maya man" described by Beatriz de la Fuente finds one of its greatest exponents in the Tablet of the Scribes, in which the purity and harmony of the contours of the human body attest to an art fully mature.[20]

Similar qualities of expression are to be found in the many remaining examples of rich ornamentation, modeled in stucco and then painted, that once covered the facade and some of the interior walls of Palenque's buildings. Some better-preserved fragments are still to be admired in the west facade of the Palace *(plates 153, 154),* embellishing the slim walls that, pillar-like, supported the roofs of the wide galleries surrounding the building. On these piers we find various scenes, apparently liturgical in nature, in which the artist was able to give his human subjects a particular freedom of action, framing each scene with ornamental bands and garlands—veritable arabesques in which elegant and imaginative plant motifs were combined with small masks and the heads of various deities from the Maya pantheon.

144. *Palenque: general plan of the Palace*

145. *Palenque: plan and longitudinal section of House A of the Palace*

146. *Palenque: cross-section of House H and of the "cellar" chambers of the Palace*

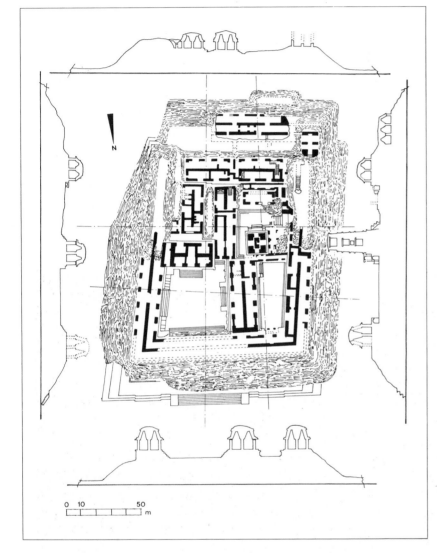

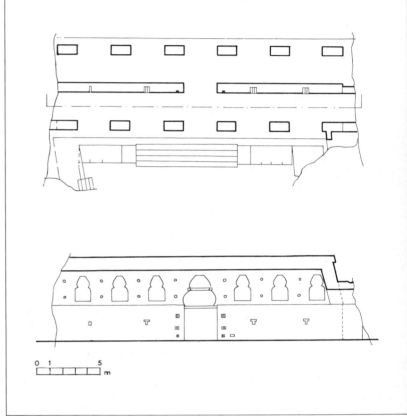

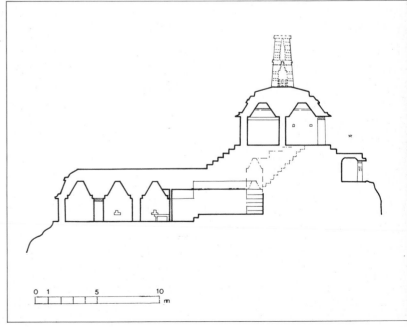

48. *Palenque: detail of the base of House C*
49. *Palenque: interior of House B. Detail of the decoration around a
    T-shaped wall opening*

Let us now analyze Palenque's principal temples, selecting as a prototype the Temple of the Sun, which retains the greatest number of its original features *(plates 157–159)*. We note first a delicacy of proportion that, perhaps along with an only slightly elevated base, makes the building seem almost small. This impression lasts only until we see the width of the access portico, as drawn by the English artist Frederick Catherwood, who visited these ruins in 1844 in the company of the famous North American explorer John Stephens. The lower part of the facade has few remains of its stucco decoration; but the frieze on the upper part shows a number of fragments carved in high relief. The ornamentation must have continued up the roof-comb itself, judging by some white patches of stucco that still adhere to this lightweight skeleton and that suggest decorative riches we can only imagine today *(plate 159)*.

Compared to the imposing and ponderous *cresterías* of Tikal, the type developed in Palenque displays an almost incredible lightness in both senses of the word. Formed by two thin walls of deep open-work, joined together and diminishing in size toward the top, Palenque's *crestería* suggests an ornate Spanish comb for a mantilla. Unlike the Petén version, it rests not on the rear wall but on the building's roof, its weight bearing directly down over the central wall that separates the front and rear galleries *(plate 157)*, and so presenting no impediment to the creation of a spacious interior. It seems that the architects of Palenque, outstripping their mentors in Tikal, were able to carry the basic elements of Maya architecture toward a greater purity. We need only compare characteristic buildings in each city to see how totally changed were the proportions between solid walls and openings, almost to the point of complete reversal *(plates 109, 159)*.

What Tikal gained in breath-taking monumentality was almost always at the cost of interior space; Palenque, on the other hand, created an architecture that instead of overwhelming the viewer was in keeping with the human condition, and yet still majestic. Inside, in the width of its portico, and outside, in its sober elegance of line, we find a more human, gentler feeling. Whereas Tikal placed all the emphasis on the front of the sanctuary, Palenque's temples, through the central position and linear symmetry of their outer bodies, were endowed with a more harmonious silhouette from any angle. Palenque's completely new approach to traditional architectural elements, in the middle of the Classic period, seems to have had repercussions over a wide area, even including Piedras Negras, despite the latter's dependence on Tikal in architectural matters. From Comalcalco, at the western boundary of the Maya zone, to Toniná and Agua

2. *Palenque: central detail of the Tablet of the Slaves. Palenque Museum*

153, 154. *Palenque: stucco decorations on one of the piers of the western facade of the Palace*

condida, more to the south, and in such sites as Bonampak and axchilán to the southeast, we find the same laudable tendency toward riness in architectural spaces.

We do not, as yet, understand the symbolic role of the *cresteria* the architecture of Palenque; however, the use of the roof-comb es not seem to have been limited to religious purposes, for traces f it appear on buildings that seem more likely to have been residen- al, such as the Palace. The temples of this city do, on the other hand, ive a distinctive feature that confirms their role as sanctuaries: a nall roofed shrine usually placed in the central chamber, against the ear wall, and apparently the *sanctum sanctorum* of almost every religious ructure in Palenque. We find it, quite well preserved, in the Temples f the Sun *(plate 157)* and of the Cross *(plates 162, 163)*. The latter, s roof-comb almost intact despite the collapse of the better part of s main facade *(plate 162)*, is the subject of a lovely reconstruction by atiana Proskouriakoff illustrating the "tabernacle" quality of this nall interior sanctuary, whose central feature was invariably one of 1ose great tablets, richly carved in bas-relief and embedded in the ack wall, that are so typical of this city *(plates 160, 161, 164)*. It is y the central theme of its panels, and the name it suggested, that we now each of these sanctuaries today.

We will mention, finally, the Temple of the Inscriptions, one of 1e most imposing of Palenque's monuments in terms of its dimen- ons and its partially restored stepped base *(plate 165)*. But what 1akes this building one of the most fascinating in Mesoamerica is s famous tomb, discovered in 1952 by Alberto Ruz-Lhuillier. To 1is day, it serves as a most extraordinary exception to the seeming 1le in Mesoamerica that a pyramid is nothing more than a base to 1hance the temple. In this case, the building seems intended es- 2ntially to hide the tomb of someone whose existence must have een of prime importance in the history of Palenque. Unlike several urial chambers introduced *a posteriori* into the bases of other re-Columbian buildings, we have here a tomb carefully planned to 2main forever hidden under the temple's enormous mass. The subter- anean passages that lead to it were found to be completely ob- :ructed by rubble, and the access to these passages, through the floor 1side the temple, was sealed off by a thick stone slab, leaving only a 1all tube running up one side of the stairs as a magical contact with 1e outside world. As it appears today, its debris cleared away, the 1terior stairway (roofed by short sections of corbel vaulting) goes :raight down to a landing where two wide ventilation galleries nce connected with a small sunken patio. It then continues in the pposite direction, to a level lower than the building's base. There,

157. *Palenque: section and plan of the Temple of the Sun*
158. *Palenque: Temple of the Sun seen from the level of the Temple of the Cross* ▷

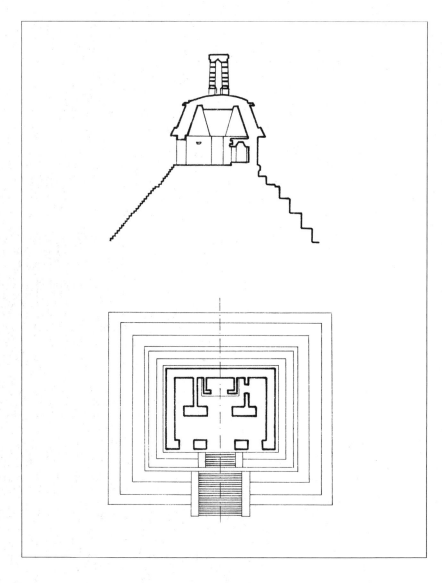

159. Palenque: Temple of the Sun
160, 161. Palenque: Temple XIV. Stone bas-relief with scene of
an offering

◁ 162. *Palenque: Temple of the Cross*
163. *Palenque: Temple of the Cross. Detail of the Maya "false" arch and interior shrine*

164. *Palenque: detail of one of the personages represented on a tablet in the Temple of the Foliated Cross*

165. *Palenque: Temple of the Inscriptions seen from the northwest* ▷

166. *Palenque: Temple of the Inscriptions. Interior of the secret crypt with sepulchral slab*

the very core of the pyramidal base, lay the secret crypt—perpendicular to the axis of the stairway, its entrance sealed by a thick trapezoidal slab at the high point of the ceiling *(plate 167)*.

The interior dimensions of this sepulchral chamber—23 feet (7 m.) long, 23 high, and 12′4″ (3.75 m.) across at the widest point—constitute in themselves a technical triumph, in view of the limitations of Maya construction techniques and the enormous pressure of the pyramid's weight. But what makes this crypt a truly unique find is the sarcophagus, carved in the shape of a uterus out of a huge monolithic block, and covered by a finely carved heavy slab, 12′6″ (3.80 m.) by 77 inches (2.20 m.) across and 10 inches (25 cm.) thick *(plate 166)*. Upon lifting this slab, Ruz-Lhuillier found the remains of a clearly august personage, his skeleton covered with beautiful jewels of jade. The immense sarcophagus sits on thick stone supports covered with bas-reliefs, and fills almost the entire chamber. On the walls of the crypt we see nine figures modeled in stucco, symbolizing perhaps the Bolontikú, or Nine Lords of Night of Maya mythology; and on the floor, apparently as final offerings, lie two stucco heads. These, together with the bas-reliefs and other fragments, make Palenque one of those Maya cities in which modeling in stucco reached its purest form.

Comalcalco

We will close this analysis of the architecture of the Usumacinta River basin with a mention of Comalcalco, one of the cities located in the western confines of the vast Maya zone, within Palenque's sphere of influence. What we find most interesting at this site is the use of great flat bricks joined by lime mortar, a rarity in Mesoamerican architecture in general, and among the Maya in particular *(plate 168)*. The charming designs carved on the bricks before baking look like the work of the architect himself—scribbled calculations, made with the material still in his hand. Or, perhaps the brick-makers amused themselves by doodling while waiting for the oven to heat.

Apart from these brick walls and vaults, which follow a pattern similar to those of Palenque, Comalcalco has some good examples of stucco relief, including an impressive mask set in the center of the access stairway to a temple *(plate 170)*.

THE MOTAGUA RIVER BASIN

Copán

Southeast of the central Maya zone, at the other end of the Classic Maya "triangle," is a section of the Motagua River that today con-

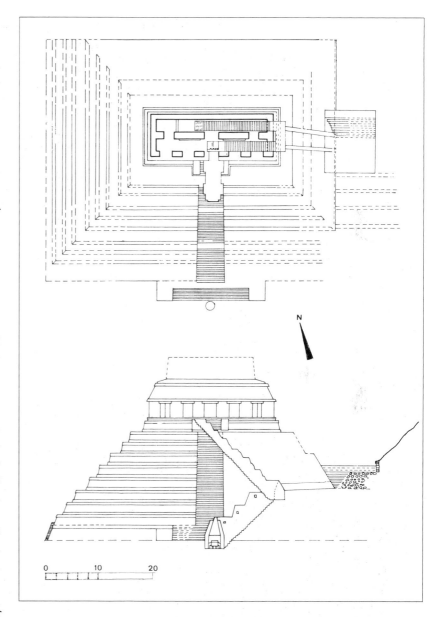

168. *Comalcalco, Tabasco: detail of a structure constructed with flat bricks*
169. *Copán, Honduras: Altar Q (Altar of the Astronomers), with relief representing a gathering of astronomers*
170. *Comalcalco: stucco mask on a temple stairway* ▷

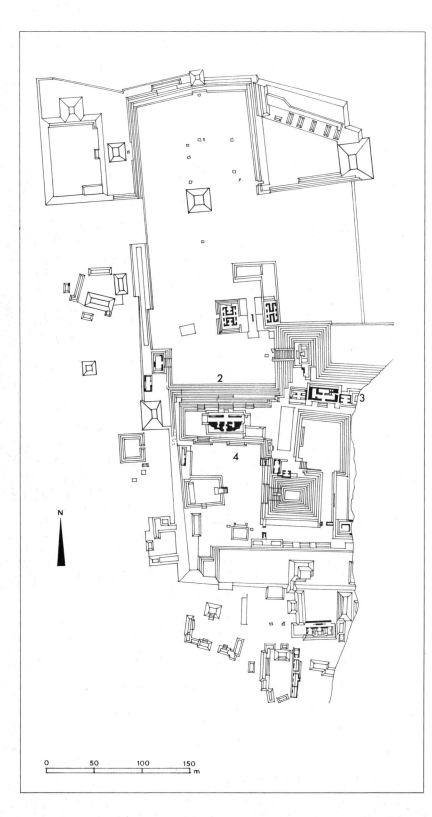

171.

stitutes part of the border between Guatemala and Honduras. Thi
region—relatively small, and quite far from El Petén—created
style unto itself in both sculpture and architecture, and made notabl
contributions to Maya astronomy.

Copán, undoubtedly the key exponent of this regional style, wa
the site of important assemblies attended by renowned astronomer
priests who came from all over the Maya world to compare thei
most recent sidereal computations, thus perfecting the complicate
Maya calendar *(plate 169)*. By the end of the seventh century A.D
(at the beginning of the Late Classic period), the calculations of th
tropical Maya year as made in Copán anticipated our own wit
incredible exactitude, deviating by an error of three ten thousandth
of a day per year, and surpassing in accuracy all solar calendars create
up to that time.

Proskouriakoff's reconstruction of the ceremonial center c
Copán reveals a flexible urban layout, one "with greater dynamisı
than that found in Monte Albán," observes Raúl Flores Guerrerc
and with some subtle reminders of its overall lines of compositio
(plate 171).[21] The Great Plaza, laid out along a north-south axis,
divided into sections by various major elements. The far norther
end became an immense amphitheater, clearly ceremonial in charac
ter, with tiers of steps that enclose three sides of the plaza. A pla
form, or altar, bounded the other side, and rows of stelae and alta
underscored some of the principal axes. The marked regional style c
these carved monoliths appears not only in their sheer size *(plate 173
but even more in the depth of their relief carving, in their form–
which is both freer and more capricious—and in their generally le
static and more baroque appearance *(plates 172, 174)*.

The central part of the Great Plaza is a sober series of esplanad
situated at different levels, leading out to the rest of the city. Th
section at the far south ends at the imposing front of the Acropoli
whose unusually wide stairway must have provided another immens
tribune, as well as offering access to the platforms on the upper lev
and to Temple 11, which rises majestically on the plaza's axis. (Th
city's astronomers carved a glyphic inscription on the temple wa
announcing the number of eclipses the planet Venus would underg
in the course of a million years.) This face of the Acropolis, elongate
to the east and northeast by other structures placed at about the sam
level, had the effect of minimizing the increased elevation of the ea
and west courts, which were situated on higher terrain—perhaps t
protect them from the possibility of flooding. Passing through th
sector of the city in a menacing curve, the Copán River, over a peric
of a thousand years of total abandonment, ultimately undermine

and destroyed almost all of the eastern part of the ceremonial center.

Returning to the Great Plaza, we note that its south side is bounded primarily by the platforms and buildings of the Acropolis. Into the center of the plaza there juts out a small ball court, together with its L-shaped annex *(plate 175)*. Despite its modest size, the court is notable for its significant placement and for the quality of its sculptures, especially its six *marcadores* (markers) in the form of macaw heads *(plate 176)*. We can peer through the openings in the half-ruined facade of one of the two adjacent temples and observe the intersection of two corbel vaults—a beautiful stepped variant of the basic architectural principle of the Maya *(plate 177)*. And we might note, in passing, the strange disposition of interior space in the two small temples that form part of the ball-court complex *(plate 171)*.

Here we find one of the most famous buildings in Copán, its pyramidal base touching one end of the ball court. The extraordinarily rich sculptural detail on its front has earned it the name of the Temple of the Hieroglyphic Stairway *(plate 178)*. On the risers of its steps are a series of over 2,500 Maya glyphs—giving us the longest inscription in this culture known to date. Further embellishment is seen on the broad *alfardas* that border the stairway, presenting a succession of sculptures in strong relief, including some outstanding stylized masks of birds. Emerging from the center line of the stairway are large sculptures in the round, some of which represent enthroned personages, richly dressed in the local style. Little is left of the temple that stood on the upper platform, but its rubble has yielded some of the most beautiful examples of Maya statuary, such as a face that seems to portray the young maize god and here serves as the prototype of classic Maya beauty *(plates 179, 180)*. A reconstruction (again by Tatiana Proskouriakoff) lets us imagine more easily the baroque splendor of this building, which in its heyday must have had a richness seldom found in the panorama of Maya architecture, testifying to a genuine feeling for the integration of sculpture with construction.

The special talent that Copán's builders used to incorporate sculpture (both in relief and in the round) into their principal buildings is seen in perhaps its most flamboyant and rococo expression in the Hieroglyphic Stairway. But many other architectural complexes also show the impressive remains of integrated sculpture—sometimes quite subtle, and always displaying fresh principles of composition. Let us take for an example the small Tribune of the Spectators *(plates 171, 183)*. Sometimes called the Reviewing Stand, it looks toward the west court from its position near the foot of one corner of Temple 11's stepped base. The front of the tribune is gently delineated by

176. *Copán: a marker for the ball game in the form of a macaw head*
177. *Copán: semi-destroyed facade of one of the buildings bordering the ball court*
178. *Copán: Hieroglyphic Stairway* ▷

179, 180. *Copán: head of the young maize god, from Temple 26.*
Washington, D.C., Dumbarton Oaks, Bliss Collection

carved stone slabs erected on the court floor; the rear is embellished with enormous seashells carved in stone and a series of deep niches that, like simulated doorways, enliven the sides of the stepped base. The tribune proper is formed by steps joined to the foot of this base and is flanked at its upper corners by two large figures—carved almost totally in the round—that rise up from its sides. One of the figures wears a grotesque mask and waves a timbrel with his left hand *(plate 184)*. These compositional features are united by a string of glyphs running along the last step of the tribune. The step is decorated in the center by a mask in relief, and it ends at the foot of each of the impressive "guard" statues in a kind of "dado" emerging from the step above, from which yet another step descends, like an embroidered border falling at the sides *(plate 183)*.

More subtle still is the composition of another of Copán's many tribunes, known as the Jaguar Stairway, whose tiers span an entire side of the eastern court. The steps are flanked by elongated and slightly sloping panels, which are bordered at the top by the thick cornice typical of the region *(plate 181)*. On the sides of the wide access stairway, ornamentation (in particularly deep relief) is limited to two rampant jaguars, reminiscent of a European heraldic device; the animals' large spots are suggested by deep cavities *(plate 182)*. On the top, there is an enormous mask of the sun god (or planet Venus?) between two narrow flights of steps *(plates 181, 185)*. Two small glyphs on the sides of one of the access stairway steps, as well as stone slabs embedded in the plaza floor—like those in the Tribune of the Spectators and in the ball court—complete the sober decoration.

In the northeast corner of the plaza, the broad Jaguar Stairway runs into the access stairs of Temple 22, which, along with Temple 11, is one of the best-preserved and most representative of Copán's sanctuaries *(plate 186)*. The temple proper stands on a platform that projects forward at both ends and is bordered by the heavy molding typical of the region. On the corners of the building, we see great masks of Chac, the Maya rain god, with his characteristic hook-shaped nose *(plate 190)*—a motif common in the architecture of the Yucatán, as we shall see later. As for the frieze that once crowned the facade, some fragments remain of those enchanting deities misnamed the "singing maidens," who appear to be associated with the young maize god *(plate 191)*. The wide entrance door retains enough sculptured material for us to identify enormous monster jaws similar to those we will see again in the Río Bec, Chenes, and Puuc styles in the Yucatán *(plate 189)*. Today there remains only the lower part of the imposing entrance decoration—including, toward the front on the

181. *Copán: Jaguar Stairway*
182. *Copán: Jaguar Stairway. Detail showing a rampant feline creature*

183. *Copán: Tribune of the Spectators*
184. *Copán: Tribune of the Spectators. Detail showing a grotesque figure with timbrel*
185. *Copán: Jaguar Stairway. Detail showing a mask of the sun god (or planet Venus?)* ▷

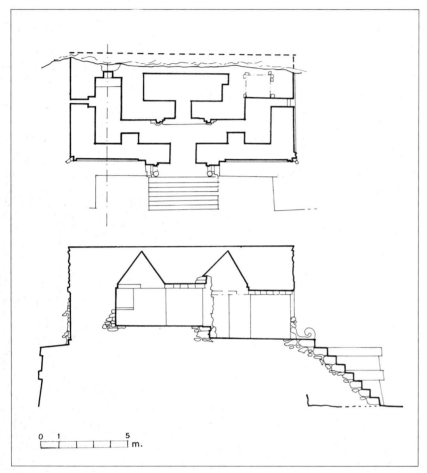

access platform, the two tips of a serpent's forked tongue (or fangs?).

But what captures our attention, once we cross the threshold, is the interior portal on both sides of the middle doorway that embellishes the central wall *(plates 187, 188)*. Unique for its lavish ornamentation, the portal is outlined by a row of glyphs that border a thick molding; around it is the heavy baroque frame that makes this interior doorway one of the masterpieces of Copán's sculptural art. Here, carved in particularly vigorous relief, we see two corpulent atlantes seated on enormous skulls and leaning on the edge of the molding. They appear to be holding aloft the whole upper section of the sculpted frame—among whose fantastic volutes we find those frolicking gnomes who symbolize the "maize spirits."

This peculiar sense of sculptural integration, markedly baroque in style, constitutes the essence of Copán's architecture. The city is unique, among those in the Maya sphere of influence, for its apparent absence of *cresterías* and for its preference for sculpture in the round as an artistic expression, rather than the bas-relief and mural painting that have predominated in other Mesoamerican sites. But over and above these regional aspects, Copán breathes a spiritual intensity that we associate with only a few Mesoamerican centers, such as Monte Albán and Palenque.

Quiriguá

Northwest of Copán, the ceremonial center of Quiriguá shows the direct influence of the former on its urban layout. The general lines of its architecture are also similar to Copán's—except for one temple that may have possessed a roof-comb in the style of El Petén. But the importance of Quiriguá lies in its outstanding monolithic sculpture, and particularly in the outsized dimensions and imaginative conception of some of its stelae and altars *(plates 192–195)*. We might mention the glyphic inscription displayed on one side of Stele F, whose glyphs, representing personages carved in the round, are considered the most beautiful in all Maya writing. Then there are colossal sculptures such as Stele E, whose 36-foot height (10.67 m.) makes it the largest in Maya art; and the strange "tropical fantasies" such as Zoomorph B *(plate 195)* or P, the latter 11 1/2 feet (3.50 m.) wide and possessing an especially intricate composition.

SOME ARCHITECTURAL ASPECTS OF THE YUCATÁN PENINSULA

Dzibilchaltún

We will continue our survey of Classic Maya architecture with a look at the northern zone—the area comprising the greater part of the

197. *Kohunlich, Quintana Roo, Mexico: mask on a temple facade*
198. *Fragment of a facade in painted stucco, perhaps from the south of Quintana Roo or Campeche. Mexico City, National Museum of Anthropology*

Yucatán peninsula. We have already mentioned the importance her of such sites as Dzibilchaltún, which by the Early Classic period ha grown to be one of the largest in the area.

The heart of this ceremonial center shows evidence of a larg central causeway around which groups of buildings were placed. On of these complexes was deliberately positioned in the middle of th causeway, which at this point becomes a wide ceremonial plaza whos secondary buildings surround the unique Temple of the Seven Dol *(plate 196)*. In this latter building, we find at least two features com pletely new in Maya architecture. The windows opening on i front and back facades have dimensions that in general seem larg compared with the occasional narrow apertures seen in other May buildings. And a curious blind central tower rises from the roof not a true roof-comb, but presumably meant to lend dramati visual impact to the building from all angles.

The Temple of the Seven Dolls, still possessed of the stone skele tons of its great masks and the remains of its stucco decoration, wa built around 500 A.D., during the Middle Classic period. The revo lutionary elements we see here could well have marked a turning poir in the development of Maya architecture; nevertheless, their influenc seems to have been confined to the city of Dzibilchaltún itself.

In the architecture of the Yucatán peninsula, we find man atypical structures that seem to elude attempts at classification int any of the various great regional styles. These include the grea Pyramid of Izamal and the Palace of the Stuccoes at Acancéh—whos upper frieze displays zoomorphic motifs rare in Maya architectur Acancéh's Pyramid of the Masks clearly reflects the influence of th Proto-Classic architecture of El Petén. And Cobá, in the eastern par of the peninsula, shows obvious sculptural affinities with the style c the Usumacinta River basin, while its architecture is more reminiscer of that of El Petén.

The Stucco Masks of Belice and Quintana Roo
Although we can as yet draw no general conclusions as to the evolu tion of architecture in this vast zone, which still remains only partiall explored, certain regional characteristics are beginning to emerg The area on the eastern and northeastern edge of El Petén, fc example, in what is modern-day Belice, and in the southern part c Quintana Roo, seems outstanding for facades richly ornamented i polychrome stucco. Here we find great masks of Maya deities; an sites such as Altún Há and Benque Viejo, also in Belice, illustrate thi same tendency.

One of the temples in Kohunlich, in Quintana Roo, retains a

most intact the sloping walls of its main facade, whose dominant theme is the mask of the Maya sun god that stands out in strong relief amid other mythological references *(plate 197)*. Judging by another richly ornamented mask found at a still unidentified site—which portrays the sun god flanked by two ancient fire gods of apparent Teotihuacán inspiration *(plate 198)*—we might consider the possibility of outside influences (Teotihuacán or Zapotec) in certain architectural elements of this zone.

The Río Bec Region

Let us turn now to a study of the Classic architecture of various areas from the center to the northwest of the Yucatán peninsula—areas whose respective styles show so many similarities that we often find it hard to distinguish between the structures involved. This applies to the zones we now call Río Bec, Chenes, and Puuc, which, during the Late Classic period (the seventh through the tenth century A.D.), produced the peninsula's most characteristic architecture. We will try here to bring out some of the stylistic highlights, indicating which elements reflect local approaches and which arise from a common vocabulary of forms.

In Río Bec's architecture, the predominant characteristic is the use of heavy masonry towers that simulated pyramids and temples in the fashion of El Petén, which lay some 74 1/2 to 100 miles (120 to 160 km.) south of this region. These ornamental structures are usually found rising in pairs at each end of the main facade of an elongated building—not only in Río Bec itself, but in Chicanná, Becán, and Hormiguero as well. Occasionally they appear in sets of three, as in the main building at Xpuhil.

Xpuhil

Tatiana Proskouriakoff's beautiful reconstruction of this latter building *(plate 199)* gives us an opportunity to study these strange towers, with their rounded corners and simulated stairs along whose axes large masks appear. Reinforcing the illusion that we are looking at some of El Petén's sanctuaries is the presence of the temple—also simulated—complete with a roof-comb and a false door. The facade is of a type common in the area for its ornamental opulence. There is a "dragon-mouth" entrance, echoing the theme of Copán's Temple 22. Combined here, over the lintel of the door, are the features of a mask, facing forward, with two enormous serpent's jaws seen in profile. The jaws seem to close around both sides of the door, transforming it into the all-engulfing mouth of a monster associated, perhaps, with Itzamná, the Maya god of creation, who is, as Jack Eaton suggests,

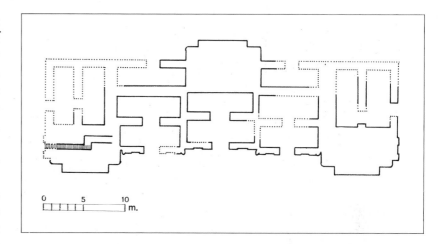

"displayed here in reptilian form, with possibly both celestial and terrestrial attributes."[22]

Uniting and complementing Xpuhil's three-towered structure is a low building—the only truly functional one—whose main facade is clearly divided into three parts, a characteristic identified by Pollock and others as a basic principle of architectural composition in these areas.[23] The upper frieze of each of the three parts, slightly inclined and projecting, displays a mask seen frontally; the walls of the lower part bear, as their only decoration, wide vertical strips of bas-relief—an equally common motif in the Río Bec and Chenes areas. Finally another original trait can be seen in the simulated columns, embedded in the corners, which project from the two bodies that stand away from the front. The columns serve to reinforce the resemblance of these low buildings to the simple wooden palm-thatched huts that still characterize the typical dwellings of the Yucatán peninsula.

Chicanná

Lateral towers in the shape of a temple-pyramid might be called distinctive features of the Río Bec style. With this exception, the elements we have just discussed appear in many buildings of the region. In Chicanná, which was recently explored, a lovely temple on a pyramidal base displays vertical panels in relief like those at Xpuhil. Along with these panels is found an element we saw at Copán which will appear again in all these areas—namely, the superposition of masks of Chac, the Maya rain god, with his typically prominent nose *(plate 200)*.

One of the better-preserved examples of an entrance in the shape of monster jaws has just been found at this site. Here we see the prominent fangs of the large upper mask jutting out sharply over the lintel of the doorway; a wide access stairway in front shows the remains of other fangs, which vigorously dramatized the similarity to a monster's mouth *(plate 201)*. Once more, we see the facade as a tripartite conception whose lateral doors are crowned with an imitation palm roof, the wide aperture suggesting the entrance to a Maya house. In the middle of the roof we find the remains of an openwork *crestería*—an architectural element always present in these regions but less frequent here than in El Petén or the Usumacinta River basin.

Becán

It would be wrong to confine a description of Río Bec's architectural repertory to those few elements mentioned above. Aesthetically, the ornamental tower—a prototype of the area—seems a pale reflection of those imposing sanctuaries in the forests of the south (for example

204. *Nocuchich, Campeche: tower with colossal mask in stucco*
205. *Hochob: plan of the main building*
206. *Edzná, Campeche: five-storied building* ▷

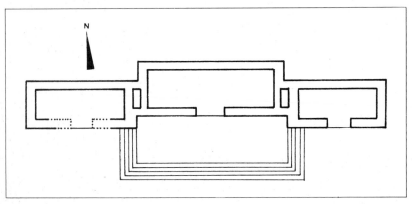

in Tikal), but a more detailed study of the buildings on a site such as Becán reveals the "variety and complexity" cited in David Potter's recent work.[24] We note in passing that the ceremonial center of Becán is totally enclosed within one of the oldest known defensive systems in Mesoamerica. It consists of a deep, dry moat, complete with raised terracing works. Furthermore, the cylindrical construction found on the Puerto Rico site suggests similarities to the *chulpas,* or stone burial towers, of the Andean region.

The Chenes Region

Located more to the northwest, the neighboring region of the Chenes shares with Río Bec a large number of architectural elements. Although it did not build huge symbolic towers—exclusively a Río Bec characteristic—we find here and there strange masonry towers of medium size that may have been incorporated into larger buildings and that show the remains of a rich stucco decoration, as we see at Chanchén and Nocuchich *(plate 204).* These towers do not, however, seem to be imitations of temple-pyramids, as in Río Bec, nor are they so frequent as to be considered a distinctive regional feature.

Hochob

One of the sites most representative of the Chenes style is Hochob, whose main plaza has an interesting array of buildings grouped around it, ranging from a simple temple with pure lines, unadorned walls, and an openwork *cresteria* to some large and imposing buildings whose facades are covered in an assortment of ornamentation that Marta Foncerrada de Molina terms "the most baroque phase of Maya art."[25] Within this group, and outstanding for its opulent decoration and harmonious play of volumes, is one of the most interesting variants of the "tripartite rule"[26]—a building whose central body, crowned by an enormous roof-comb decorated with human figures, rises from a higher base than do the two lateral bodies that project slightly toward the front *(plates 202, 205).* Its decoration, heavily applied, consists essentially of a typical dragon-mouth entrance, bordered in this case by elongated geometric motifs inspired by Maya huts. On the one hand, this ornamental avalanche pleasingly offsets the ethereal effect of the openwork *cresteria;* on the other, it contrasts with the smooth walls of the lateral bodies—decorated, on their upper parts, solely by an enormous mask and on the corners by rows of small masks of Chac.

El Tabasqueño

We see the motif of Chac's mask again on the corners of a small temple in El Tabasqueño, a building that likewise illustrates the

markedly baroque character of architecture in this region *(plate 203)*.

In comparing these elements at El Tabasqueño (and also at Hochob or at Dzibilnocac) with those we saw in another small temple at Chicanná *(plate 201)*, we find a similarity that makes it difficult to distinguish clearly between the Río Bec and Chenes styles—and sometimes, as we shall see, between these and the style of Puuc.

THE PUUC REGION

Edzná

The Puuc style developed in a hillier region, northwest of the Chenes and Río Bec zones, and probably was strongly influenced by these two sites. Edzná, a city located west of the Chenes region and southwest of the Puuc, in the state of Campeche, may have been another transitional site. As we will now see, many elements perhaps born in the areas that separate the central Maya zone from the Puuc region seem to come together here, evolving during the last centuries of the Classic period into one of the most outstanding architectural styles in Mesoamerica.

The five-story building at Edzná that rises amid an imposing complex of structures—forming the artificial "acropolis" so popular in Maya city planning—presents various solutions new to this architecture. The high stepped base that supports the temple on the top level is girded by narrow galleries, so that each of the five stories forming the base presents a row of chambers that rest on the fill of the floor below, while its roof serves as a terrace for the floor above *(plate 206)*. In addition, a very rare feature in Maya architecture appears here: the short column, with pronounced entasis, provided with a quadrangular capital and designed essentially to emphasize the apertures of one of the facades *(plate 207)*. Finally, we note how the wide stairway manages to free some of the layers of the facade through corbel vaults that act like flying buttresses *(plate 206)*. The ornamentation of the facades consists of simple moldings, while the temple on the upper level is crowned with a high roof-comb *(plate 208)*.

We will find these innovations again in various buildings in the Puuc zone, especially in a broader utilization of the corbel vault system and in the use of columns as a decorative feature on facades. We should remember that the pillar and the column, whether of masonry or monolithic stone, were architectural elements that had been in common use by other Mesoamerican peoples from Pre-Classic times. Throughout the central Maya area, where the prevailing mode of construction was based on the corbel vault, columns were almost nonexistent. (The finding of one building with columns at Tikal, and another in Yaxhá, is merely an exception confirming the

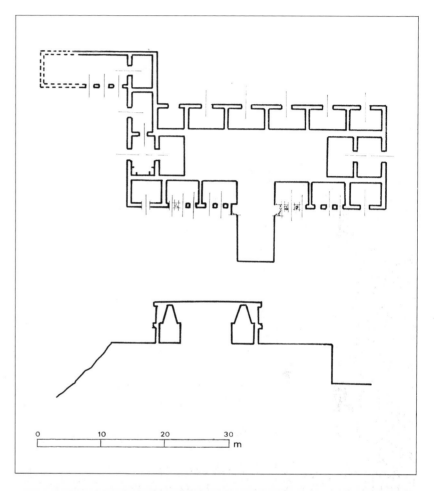

rule.) The architecture of the Yucatán peninsula, on the other hand seems to have been less resistant to the idea. Apart from the example mentioned at Edzná, we can add others, on such sites as Pechal, Channá and Peor es Nada in the Río Bec zone; and there is a quite exceptional representative of the sculptured column with glyphic inscription in a place southwest of the Puuc area known as Xcalumkín Holactún. We will see this element used with greater frequency in Puuc architecture, beginning with one of the great masterpieces of this style—the three-storied Palace of Sayil *(plate 209)*.

Sayil

Its three successive stories mounted on a pyramidal base (as at Edzná) the Palace of Sayil shows an entirely different treatment on each level. The lowest floor is still in ruins and partially buried in rubble, while the upper one displays simple, smooth walls whose sobriety only emphasizes the richness and balanced composition of the level in between *(plate 209)*. We can note, in the classical harmony of this facade, how the single openings alternate with the wide apertures sectioned off by pairs of columns, and how the tops of the jambs end in a projection that balances the effect of the capitals. In both single and triple openings, the jambs show a slight inclination—an evident attempt at subtle optical correction.

The decoration of the middle sections includes simulated vertical rows of *junquillos con ataduras* ("reeds with knots"), a design that imitates in stone a common wooden brace consisting of short trunks secured with couplings (still visible *in situ* as reinforcing beams in the interior of some buildings: *plate 115*). On the upper part of this facade we find vertical rows of *junquillos,* or plain colonnettes alternating with those of the lower story. Other ornamental elements are harmoniously placed on both sides of a broad central motif consisting of a mask in strong relief, its great jutting fangs suggesting the influence of Chenes or Río Bec. The motif between the central mask and that of the corner—the latter with the hook-shaped nose of Chac that is a familiar sight in this region—consists of two fantastic serpents flanking the grotesque figure of a "descending" deity. Looking at the unit formed by this serpent motif and the section just below it—a single doorway with *junquillos con ataduras* on each side—we might again think we were gazing at a Maya hut equipped with a richly ornamented roof.

The facade of the top level also observes the tripartite rule common in these regions. It shows, between the two cornices that gird the upper wall, large jutting stones that seem to have served as supports for the decorative panels that may have risen above the level of the roof; this is demonstrated in a reconstruction by Proskouriakoff.

215. *Labná: detail of the junquillos con ataduras and fantastic mask at
    a corner of the Palace*
216. *Labná: facade of a building of the Palace*

217. *Labná: northwest facade of the Arch*
218. *Labná: southeast facade of the Arch*

In a small building on the neighboring site of Xlabpak we can still find decorative finials *in situ (plate 210)*. We will see them again at Uxmal, in one of the buildings that form the so-called Nunnery Quadrangle *(plate 237)*.

This first contact with the architecture of the Puuc region allows us to note some of the characteristics of its style: a cleanness of line, a great clarity in the composition of elements, and a true feeling for balance in the use of its varied ornamental motifs. As in other Maya regions, Puuc's architecture occasionally surprises us with evidence of the contrast between a gigantic expenditure of materials and labor and the ostensibly nonfunctional results. We find a ready example in the buildings at Chacmultún, with their impressive land-fill works and terracing *(plate 211)*. We are fascinated too by the ever-new appearance of these buildings, despite the relatively limited range of elements employed in their composition. Stucco plays a minor role here, and is less often used than in buildings elsewhere; but the work in stone is impeccable, and it seems almost incredible that these precise and delicate carvings were made by artisans totally ignorant of the use of metals.

Labná

Rather than attempting to compile an exhaustive list of the ornamental repertory of the Puuc region, we will try to show some representative motifs, beginning with the simple medallions adorning the upper frieze of a building at Kichmool *(plate 212)*. Although such was not the rule—as we shall see—some of the lower sections of the facade are carved in diverse motifs, as in the three examples at Labná, which include a variant of *junquillos con ataduras (plates 213–215)*. The mask, one of the favorite iconographic themes of the region, appears in the city of Labná in a number of different forms—sometimes equipped with prominent fangs and flanked by the remains of small statues similar perhaps to the atlantes sketched by Frederick Catherwood at Chunhuhú, and sometimes armed with huge gaping jaws out of which a deity's face emerges *(plate 216)*. But what makes Labná another of the most outstanding sites of the Puuc region is unquestionably its monumental Arch *(plates 217, 218)*, which connects two groups of buildings, today in ruins, and which embodies an architectural concept exclusive to this region and quite revolutionary within the Classic Maya framework.

Up to now, we have seen the Maya arch used solely as structural device, providing a roof over interior space; and except perhaps, for archways used as entrances—as in the precincts of the twin complexes at Tikal *(plate 119)*—this element has been visible

from the outside, only through the openings in some half-ruine
facade *(plate 162)*. At Labná, however, the corbel vault was employe
for its own aesthetic value, running through the facade from front
back and clearly meant to be seen from the outside. Its shape—th
upper part gently concave, its curve rising cleanly over the walls
the facade—is quite novel. And its solitary silhouette is set off by
sharply contrasting ornamentation, completely different on each side.

On one facade all is sobriety: essentially, large stepped frets i
strong relief over a frieze of *junquillos (plate 218)*. The ornamentatio
becomes much more complex on the other side of the Arch *(plate 217*
obviously intended to be the front—as indicated by its customar
tripartite division and by the two small lateral doors of slightl
trapezoidal shape whose purpose is to enhance the monument
feeling of the central archway.

The Arch cuts through the middle of the facade, and it is almo
unadorned. The lateral bodies are ornamented by a lovely stylizatio
of a Maya hut, which stands out against a background of lattic
work motifs—a facsimile in stone of a wooden or palm-frond scree
One of the corners displays a mask of Chac and an embedded colum
—an element we saw at Xpuhil. Fine beveled cornices, typical of th
region, complete the decoration, limiting and defining the con
positional elements, outlining the principal contours, and establishin
clear lines of shadow. Finally, elegant stepped openwork *cresterí*
give the building a feeling of lightness.

Kabáh

Contrasting markedly with the ornamental richness of Labná's arc
the isolated arch that heralds the entrance to the neighboring city
Kabáh—at the end of a wide *sacbé-oob,* or "white road," coming fro
Uxmal—is devoid of decoration *(plate 220)*. Here, among half-ruine
buildings, we find a perfect example of a "flying" stairway *(plate 219*
forming a sort of vault-supported arch. Built on the principle of th
corbel vault, it constitutes another regional variant of the Maya arc
as did the one we saw at Edzná.

But the most interesting structure at Kabáh is the so-called Cod:
Poop, rising, along with other constructions, on an enormous art
ficial platform and crowned by an elongated roof-comb decorate
in stepped frets. Something of an anomaly in Puuc's architectu
(which usually maintains a balance between plain and decorated panels
this building is covered entirely with sculptures in strong relie
their quality of execution fully justifies the name of Kabáh, which
the Maya language means "the hand that chisels." Except for th
doorway openings and the cornices that divide the facade in
long horizontal strips, this sculptural ornamentation consists of

222. *Kabáh: Codz-Poop. Detail of the facade*

223. *Kabáh: Codz-Poop. Detail of a corner of the facade*
224. *Kabáh: Codz-Poop. Detail showing the protruding hooked noses* ▷

223. *Kabáh: Codz-Poop. Detail of a corner of the facade*

uninterrupted series—both vertical and horizontal—of hook-nosed masks of Chac, the god of rain. Over and over, like a litany, the same fervent theme repeats itself. What surprises us, in this elaborate building, is the harmony of the composition, which takes a feature that might have been monotonous and makes it fascinating *(plates 221–227)*.

Let us try to imagine the extraordinary play of volumes and of chiaroscuro that these facades must have offered, with their almost surrealistic efflorescence of great hooked noses, only one of which remains intact today *(plates 223, 224)*. The same noses—broader, and resting on the floor outside—became steps rising up to the full height of each door *(plate 227)*; inside the rooms, they connected the two different levels of the building (as did the great mask, with its broad, thick nose, which earned this structure the name of Codz-Poop, or "rolled mat").

Uxmal

One of the most important and best-known cities of the Puuc region is Uxmal, whose plan shows, in a relatively free layout, the raised artificial platforms and quadrangular placement of buildings that are typical of this area *(plate 228)*. In the middle of the complex, we find some high bases, among them the so-called Pyramid of the Magician, which looms large on a rectangular base rounded at the sides *(plate 231)*. Careful exploration reveals that its present aspect is the result of five stages of building that probably took place between the sixth and tenth century A.D. *(plate 229)*. To one of the last of these phases belongs a stairway whose lowest portion partially cleared the facade of the older building *(plate 232)*. Impressive in its simplicity, the stairway ascends steeply, subtly divided into three flights. A stepped series of masks of Chac flanks the sides of the level that constitutes the deepest recess, establishing an interesting play of radiating lines and adding a dramatic touch to an already strong upward thrust. This stairway leads to Temple IV, whose facade, in the form of monster jaws, shows a marked influence from Chenes, in contrast to the facade of Temple V, which stands on the top level and reflects the purest style of Puuc *(plate 235)*.

Let us turn now to the Nunnery—one of the typical quadrangles located near the Pyramid of the Magician. This architectural complex is much less compact than the acropolis-type groupings of the central geographic areas. The elongated buildings are arranged around a spacious patio, with the corners left open; and they rise from different levels, perhaps for hierarchical reasons. From the level of the buildings

227. *Kabáh: Codz-Poop. Detail of masks at a doorway*

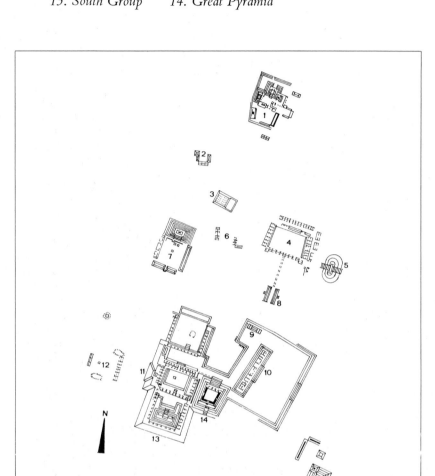

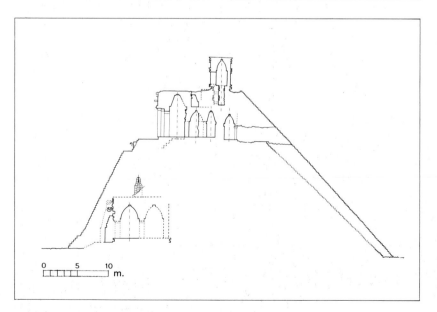

236. *Uxmal: Nunnery Quadrangle. Facade of the east building*

237. *Uxmal: Nunnery Quadrangle. Details of the cornices of the east and south buildings*

238. *Uxmal: Nunnery Quadrangle. Detail of the east building showing masks of the rain god Chac above the central doorway*

241. *Uxmal: Nunnery Quadrangle. A lower room of the north building, showing the corbel vault typical of Maya building technique*
242. *Uxmal: Nunnery Quadrangle. Corner of the north building*
243. *Uxmal: House of the Doves (Dovecote)* ▷

244. *Uxmal: House of the Turtles. Lateral facade*
245. *Uxmal: House of the Turtles. Half-ruined facade showing stonework technique*
246. *Uxmal: House of the Doves (Dovecote). One of the doorways in the shape of a Maya arch* ▷

247. *Uxmal: Governor's Palace. Interior of the central chamber*

248. *Uxmal: Governor's Palace. Plan and elevation*
249. *Uxmal: Governor's Palace. Main facade*
250. *Uxmal: Governor's Palace. Detail of the main facade* ▷
251. *Uxmal: Governor's Palace. Doorway with a Maya arch in the shape of an arrowhead* ▷
252. *Uxmal: Governor's Palace. Detail of a corner showing masks of the rain god Chac* ▷

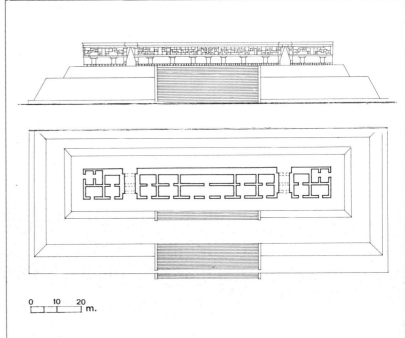

located toward the south (the Governor's Palace, for example), we see the south building of the Nunnery Quadrangle in the foreground, with one of the region's typical great open archways leading to the outside. Our line of sight ends with the front of the north building in the background.

Some elements of Puuc's architecture are apparent in Uxmal in an especially pure form. The east building of the Nunnery Quadrangle *(plates 236, 238)* has a facade clearly divided into vertical strips. There is a slightly projecting socle, soberly adorned with rows of short *junquillos,* and a wall whose lower part has smooth panels and wide openings subtly outlined by a set-in frame that adds a note of lightness. Enclosed between two moldings with *ataduras,* the upper section of the facade stands uncompromisingly vertical, being adorned, in this case, with vertical rows of masks of Chac in its center and on its corners *(plate 237)*. Over the secondary doorways, we find an elegant trapezoidal design formed by stylized double-headed serpents, out of which emerges the head of an owl god of Teotihuacán inspiration. The same double-headed serpent motif embellishes the central part of the cornice, on top of the main doorway, while on the rest of the facade it appears against a latticework background *(plate 236)*. The two cornices outlining this upper strip are entirely in the style of Puuc: they are composed of two beveled moldings, seemingly almost crushed beneath the pressure of a central listel adorned with small shields and terminating at each corner in a mythological animal's head.

The clarity of the elements composing the facade and the particularly clean silhouette created by these impeccably executed cornices are outstanding qualities always evident in the architecture of this region. At the foot of the east building we find a stairway conceived with such surprising complexity as to suggest a role in ceremonies involving elaborate and pompous protocol.

The north building of the Nunnery Quadrangle, in contrast to the massive sobriety that predominates in Uxmal, is conspicuous for its high placement and for its more elaborate appearance *(plates 239, 240)*. Its broad access stairway is flanked by two small, impressively simple buildings whose delicate friezes are supported by heavy monolithic pillars, subtly lightened by a wide central groove tracing thin vertical lines of shadow. On its main facade, above a frieze offering alternating motifs of stepped frets, latticework, and stylized Maya huts, we see various types of finials rising above the roof—the culmination of a style we encountered in such sites as Sayil and Kabah.

palm roof; this tone of naive realism departs from the customary geometric rigidity of Uxmal's ornamentation. And at this point we should mention the so-called House of the Doves, or Dovecote, located to the south of the city, where it formed part of another important quadrangle *(plate 243)*. From a distance, this elegant structure—featuring an interesting example of the long roof-comb frequent in the region—indeed deserves its appellation. It stands almost intact, on top of a building whose facades lie in total ruins and whose center is penetrated by the usual passageway in the form of a Maya arch. Composed largely of openwork, this *cresteria* consists of a series of stepped elements in the same style as its counterpart on the famous Arch at Labná *(plate 218)*. These elements rise above a section of wall similarly perforated, from which protrude stones that originally supported a rich sculptural decoration *(plate 246)*.

Among Uxmal's architectural diversity, the House of the Turtle —named for the large turtles, carved in the round, that adorn the listel of its upper cornice—is distinguished by its sober ornamentation and classic purity of proportions, exemplifying in its highest form that cleanness of line so characteristic of the style of Puuc *(plates 244, 245)*. Its simple frieze, composed entirely of smooth *junquillos,* provides a subtle contrast to the horizontal lines of shadow that outline its typical cornices with *ataduras (plate 244)*. Unadorned save for the sculptured turtles that emerge from the centers of the generally wider upper segments, these beveled cornices clearly were copied from the ties used to fasten palm roofs—a technique we still see used in many Maya peasant houses.

Of all the styles to be found in the Maya area, it is the architecture of Uxmal that most graphically expresses the practice of paralleling in stone the traditional building elements of the time-honored Maya hut. If the corbel vault—represented here in a highly developed form *(plates 241, 247)*—indeed owes its character to the interior contours of the hut, elements such as the *junquillos*—left either plain or decorated with *ataduras*—the cornices, and even latticework, all seem like stone versions of such perishable materials as wood, palm, and braided fiber cord or ropes. We should bear in mind the importance of stylizations of Maya huts as a decorative motif in Yucatán's architecture.

We will conclude this discussion of Uxmal's architecture with a brief analysis of the Governor's Palace, considered by many authors to have been the finest in this region and in fact one of the most outstanding structures of all Mesoamerica *(plates 247–252)*. This building, about 328 feet (100 m.) long and standing on immense

Probably derivations of the "flying" *cresterias* frequent in Yucatán architecture, these interesting roof-combs emerge on the Nunnery's exuberant facade in three different aspects *(plates 239, 240, 242)*. The smallest, rising over four of the intermediate doorways, breaks the continuity of the upper cornice with an elaborate mask silhouetted just above the level of the roof. The other two variants, larger and more prominent, ascend from the middle cornice and consist of vertical rows of masks, including four of Chac, on the corner combs. On the seven remaining wider cornices we find the same four masks, this time crowned with a fifth. The latter represents Tláloc, Teotihuacán's counterpart of Chac; it underscores once more the importance to Maya culture of that metropolis on the Mexican plateau.

Not far from the Nunnery Quadrangle we find the well-advanced ruins of a small building decorated with doves perched on a artificial platforms, appears divided into three principal bodies by two inner passageways roofed by high archways that, as we can see, were covered over in later times. In the management of structural masses and in the balancing of their proportions we detect a sure hand at work; the many elements comprising this composition were modulated and disposed with a precision that gave to the whole a nobility and equilibrium rarely achieved in Mesoamerican architecture. As in other buildings at Uxmal, visual interest is drawn to the central part by the presence there of a wider door and by the modification of the intervals between the adjoining doors. The latter are outlined by set-in frames that add a feeling of lightness to the walls.

Above the central door is an enormous trapezoidal motif in strong relief, similar to but more elaborate than those we saw in the east building of the Nunnery Quadrangle. All the ornamental elements flow from this central motif *(plate 249)*, underlined by a skillful interplay of the different planes in the relief: great step-and-fret elements alternate at forty-five-degree angles with planes of lattice-work *(plate 250)*. To break the monotony of this long border there is interwoven in the design an uninterrupted string of masks of Chac—a serpentine form that crosses the long stretch between the central motif and the upper cornice and descends diagonally, forming steps, to run along the middle of the cornice. From there, it climbs again to embellish a stretch under the upper cornice, and descends to terminate just before the corner, sharply outlined by a vertical row of masks *(plate 252)*.

Except for the upper cornice, which girds the entire building and whose listel is adorned with an undulating serpentine motif, the ornamentation of the three principal bodies of the Governor's Palace stops abruptly at these corners, establishing a dramatic contrast to the immense cut-out arches, which originally were open from end to end but which today are partially obstructed by later additions *(plate 251)*. We must admire the elegance of these daring arches, not only among the loftiest in Maya architecture, but unique in their mildly convex configuration.

Sabacché

The above analysis of Classic Puuc architecture allows us to appreciate the impressive range of workable solutions that its creators could elicit from a relatively limited repertory of ornamental elements. Notable are those innovations in technique and style introduced by the use of columns on the facade, and a broader utilization of the Maya arch in both "flying" stairways and archways. We might also note some new features, such as the stone imitations of wooden *ataduras,* which, as we see at Sabacché, replaced the typical beveled cornices *(plate 253)*.

Chichén Itzá

Puuc's architecture owes some of its traits to the influence of the neighboring Chenes and Río Bec areas; but it toned down the baroque exuberance of these styles, creating clean-lined structures embellished with a rich but balanced ornamentation, more geometric in nature, and so intimately a part of the walls of the buildings that, as Marta Foncerrada de Molina observes, it cannot be considered a superimposed element.[27]

The influence of the style of Puuc seems to have spread to cities as distant as Chichén Itzá, located much more toward the northeast of the Yucatán peninsula, where an architectural style developed that is similar in many aspects. Let us take the Nunnery Annex and the so-called Church *(plates 254, 255)*, two buildings whose complicated moldings (either very wide or broken above the doorways) seem to represent early phases of the local style. The Church has a "flying" *cresteria*—a relatively common type of roof decoration in the Puuc and neighboring areas—that rises up over the principal facade. We should also mention the Chichanchob, or Red House; it is the only structure known to date that bears two parallel combs—one "flying," the other resting on the central wall. In the buildings just mentioned, we find certain local characteristics; others, such as the Temple of the Three Lintels *(plate 257)*, could easily pass as the purest examples of the Puuc style.

As we noted at the beginning of this chapter, the years between the ninth and tenth century A.D. saw the almost total collapse of Classic Maya culture. Soon Chichén Itzá would be dominated by an important Toltec group coming from the Mexican plateau. And, as we shall see, a new Maya-Toltec phase would begin, with its seat in a new Chichén Itzá. As successive migratory bands passed over various Maya regions—hastening the eclipse of this lively world and the abandonment of almost all of its cities—they left their traces in areas such as the Pasión River, in the southern part of El Petén. The last stelae carved toward the end of the Classic period in Seibal *(plate 258)* reflect a gradual metamorphosis probably brought about by the presence of new dominant groups from other regions of Mesoamerica who, after more or less successful attempts at acculturation, ultimately provoked a total rupture of the already precarious Classic balance.

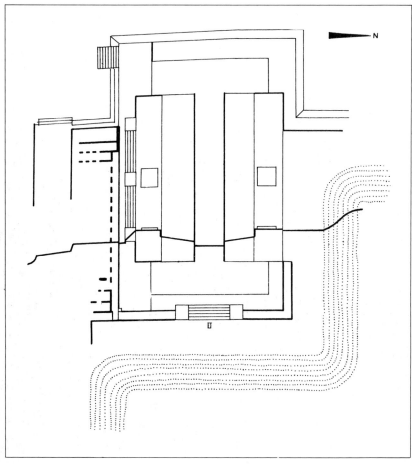

At Teotihuacán, every mural or decorated vessel is a prayer exalting the elements of nature, unlike El Tajín, where the pictorial system centers upon the ball game, or Monte Albán, where public sculpture commemorates conquests and great captains, as do Late Classic Maya art and Post-Classic art throughout Mesoamerica. . . . Teotihuacán is perhaps the terminal expression of an old theocratic system represented also by late Olmec art and by Early Classic Maya art. The few traits it shares with Late Classic Maya dynastic art belong mainly to Teotihuacán IV. Personal glorification, the cult of war, and the appearance of dynastic lineages are the traits of the new, emerging society of the centuries after 500 A.D.[1]

Thus George Kubler indicates the characteristics and changes in Mesoamerican cultures—from the point of view of artistic expression—toward the end of the Classic period. Society in general was changing from a theocratic to a militaristic base, although the seeds of the latter were to be found early in the former, and vice versa. Economic factors probably influenced the development of these varied types of society, making them not so different from one another after all.

But change there was—especially in the great Classic centers, many of which almost completely ceased to function, while the rural areas around them continued to prosper. As we have mentioned before, this is clearly seen in Teotihuacán: the population of the valley continued to be dense, but the ceremonial and political center was reduced to minimum activity. It would seem that while the elite lost its former power, the general populace gained in strength. Nevertheless, when one great center suffered an upheaval and abandonment, another came into prominence in its place, usually nearby. In the case of Teotihuacán, its power gave way to that of Xochicalco, Cholula, El Tajín, and later Tula. Thus one elite perished and another came into being. Some centers were never abandoned, but continued either without change or with increased prestige and wealth. Among these were Cholula in the central Mexican highlands and Cobá and Dzibilchaltún in the Maya region.

Xochicalco

Just over the edge of Mexico's central plateau, to the south, is the state of Morelos, and a little farther south, Guerrero. These two states are lower in altitude and warmer in climate than Teotihuacán or Cholula. Durán, the sixteenth-century chronicler, said of the Morelos region, called the Marquesado in his day, "This is certainly one of the most beautiful lands in the world, and if it were not for the great heat

259. *Xochicalco, Morelos, Mexico: plan and section of the ball court*
260. *Xochicalco: view of the ball court and base of La Malinche from the northeast*

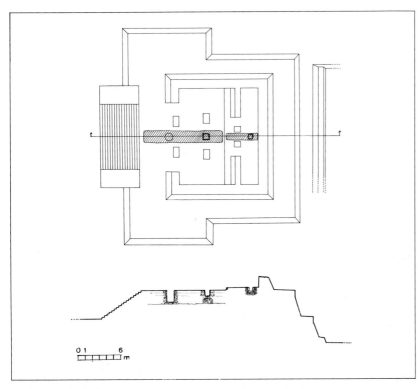

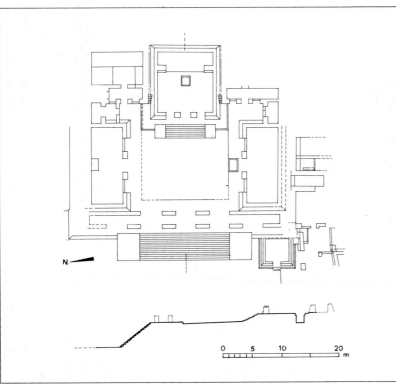

it would be another Garden of Eden. There are delightful springs, wide rivers full of fish, the freshest of woods, and orchards of many kinds of fruits. . . . This place is very rich in cotton and trade in this product is carried on here by people from all over the country."[2]

Morelos is important archaeologically, although some of its most striking ruins are without architecture—the Pre-Classic rock carving at Chalcatzingo, for example. Guerrero, too, has its share of exciting remains from early cultures in the form of cave paintings at Juxtlahuaca, Oxtotitlan, Colotlipa, and Acatlán.[3] These two states have been little explored, although at the present time great strides are being made in unearthing more of the secrets in this south-central Mexican region. Chimalacatlán, on the Morelos-Guerrero border, whose architecture is of large worked stone, probably was an important trade center during the Pre-Classic and Early Classic periods.[4] In Guerrero, Xochipala has produced beautiful clay sculpture and displays Maya influence in the form of corbeled arches.[5]

The main site in this area is that of the House of Flowers in Xochicalco, just southwest of the capital of Morelos, in Cuernavaca. Xochicalco was a great trading city and a center of calendrical-mathematical knowledge, which grew prominent as Teotihuacán declined, probably at the expense of the City of the Gods. Xochicalco was situated in a rich cotton-growing region (cotton was the luxury cloth of pre-Hispanic Mesoamerica), strategically located on the trade route that connected the basin of Mexico and the Balsas River to the west and south. Along this route came and went cacao, cotton, fine green stones, feathers, and obsidian. This Mexican highlands-Maya route prospered before the surge of Teotihuacán, and after the latter's decline Xochicalco assumed command of trade and made its influence felt south to Oaxaca and the Maya lands, east to the Gulf Coast, and north to the rich obsidian mines near Huapalcalco and Tula.

About Xochicalco's rise toward the end of the Classic period, Litvak reports:

. . . since Xochicalco does not have many features that connect it to Teotihuacán, but rather to the Maya area, Oaxaca, and the Gulf Coast, its role could very well have been that of a rival instead of a satellite, of the great Classic site, reducing its zone of effective power in the south by stopping, or at least slowing, the flow between the Valley of Mexico and a region that corresponds somewhat to the states of Morelos, Guerrero, and the Balsas River basin, traditional suppliers of cotton, cacao and green stones in pre-Hispanic Mexico. The effect of Xochicalco's existence along with that of a powerful Classic Cholula, by

264. *Xochicalco: Stele 1. Frontal view. Mexico City, National Museum of Anthropology*

265. *Xochicalco: Stele 1. Rear view. Mexico City, National Museum of Anthropology*

266. *Xochicalco: Temple of the Plumed Serpents. Detail of a lateral facade* ▷

Tajín, and a nascent Tula, would have been the reduction of Teotihuacán's domain, from a pan-Mesoamerican power, to the control of, roughly, the Valley of Mexico. . . . As a consequence, its power would be drastically reduced and its decline and final fall would ensue. . . . Its decline would produce a release, at the regional level, of its components, that would then be realigned to cope with the new situation. The effect would be a strengthening of regional networks and some shifts within them to different pattern centers that could explain some of the phenomena in the Classic-Post-Classic transition.[6]

The Maya-influenced site of Xochicalco has a ball court similar to that of Copán, a small pyramid covered with elaborate relief carvings of serpents, Maya personages and glyphs, and stelae showing multiple outside influences. These stelae are carved with hieroglyphs and numerals from the Náhuatl, Maya, and Zapotec cultures. Objects from Veracruz found at the site show Gulf Coast influence.

The monuments at Xochicalco were dedicated essentially to calendar corrections. Around 650 A.D., a congress, attended by representatives of all Mesoamerican groups, evidently was convened here for the purpose of adopting a new calendar.[7] When the data carved on the stelae was no longer considered useful, these monuments were painted red—the color of death—and then broken (ceremonially "killed" in order to avoid their continuing to exert influence), and were finally buried.

Lying in the midst of a semiarid region, Xochicalco's imposing ruins cover a number of hills of varying size, some of which seem to have been connected by broad causeways. The principal complex, organized in the fashion of an enormous acropolis, consists of a series of stepped terraces that span some 3,900 feet (1,200 m.) from north to south and 2,280 feet (700 m.) from east to west. It includes the hill of La Malinche, which rises to the west with its voluminous truncated base and wide causeway, bordered on one side by a row of strange round platforms that join this pyramid to the ball-court complex (*plate 260*). At the foot of the acropolis we find the remains of roadways that must have led to other cities; the center's main access routes, to the south and east, seem to have been fortified.

Leading up into Xochicalco from the south is a straight road that, after wending its way over various levels, reaches a small plaza, "the 'antechamber' of the main plaza, which is the final element of the complex," in the words of Hardoy, who goes on to emphasize the basic role this element played in the composition, "since it not only directed pedestrian traffic . . . but gave a sense of access, drawing

attention to the principal complex."[8] Unlike the enclosed vistas created by the architects of Monte Albán *(plates 80, 82),* Xochicalco's builders "utilized the hillsides to introduce changing views, as well as a series of sequences leading to the main plaza. Almost all the structures were set back toward the interiors of the artificial esplanades . . . leaving what amounted to balconies, from which one could enjoy the exceptional panorama of the other sectors of the city and the valleys below."[9] Such is the view we get of La Malinche and of the monumental ball court from the northeast *(plate 260).*

Along with Manzanilla, Xochicalco seems to have been one of the first cities of the central plateau to have built an I-shaped ball court *(plate 259).* This was a common shape from Pre-Classic times onward in other regions of Mesoamerica; but courts of this type have not as yet been found in Teotihuacán, the Mexican plateau's Classic metropolis. Xochicalco, which maintained cultural ties with the Maya zone from the end of the Pre-Classic period, may well have been inspired to build similar courts but of different dimensions, as did Piedras Negras and Copán. We might also note that although Xochicalco's ball court has a pair of rings as opposed to the beautifully carved macaw heads that served as markers in Copán, an equally masterly macaw head found in Xochicalco might signify a relationship with those in Copán.

Aside from a simple astronomical observatory and some palaces around La Malinche's enormous base (one of which contains interesting remains of a public steam bath, or *temazcalli),* a number of Xochicalco's temples have been explored and partially restored. Like Building C *(plate 261),* they generally present a simple truncated pyramidal base, sloping on the lower part and nearly vertical on the top, beginning near that point where the stairway of the base intersects *(plate 263).* The temple designated Building D has a wide portico that opens to the outside through great spaces interrupted by masonry pillars. Though only the lower part of the facade remains, we see that its sloping walls echo those of the base. Stylized representations of temples, carved on some of Xochicalco's monuments, permit us to re-create the appearance of the city's temples more fully.

Larger, more complex in the disposition of its elements, and built around a raised patio that opens out through a portico supported on pillars, the Temple of the Stelae *(plate 262)* has a sanctuary set on a base whose moldings apparently derived from forms frequent in Monte Albán *(plate 92).* These moldings seem to be transitions between the "scapulary" *tablero* of Classic Zapotec architecture and a variant that—as we shall see would prevail in Toltec and Maya-

Toltec architecture of the early Post-Classic period *(plates 266, 267).*

In the strange meeting ground of diverse cultures that is Xochicalco, a prominent position is occupied by the stelae *(plates 264, 265)—* a common element among the Maya, one frequently found in Oaxaca, yet practically nonexistent in Teotihuacán. Three stelae that figure among the most richly carved in Xochicalco were found buried in a trench in the floor of the building thereafter called the Temple of the Stelae. They illustrate Xochicalco's probable role as the cultural link between the late Classic and the early Post-Classic worlds. On the one hand, we find masks of gods and other symbols that recur in the Classic iconography of Teotihuacán or in Maya and Zapotec inscriptions; on the other, we see glyphs and signs already clearly part of the Post-Classic repertory of the peoples of the Mexican plateau, of Oaxaca, and of the lands along the Gulf of Mexico.[10]

We come finally to the Temple of the Plumed Serpents, unquestionably the most interesting sanctuary in Xochicalco and one of the finest jewels of pre-Columbian architecture on the entire Mexican plateau. The structure occupies a key position in the principal plaza, which stands on one of the higher elevations. Converging on it are not only all lines of sight on these levels but, in subtle ways, some of the elements of the urban layout in general.

Unique in Xochicalco—and in Mesoamerica—the temple combines an especially high *talud* with a heavy *tablero*-like molding, crowned by an elegant beveled cornice. As in other temples in this city, its outer walls are sloped. While this particular play of volumes gives the building an unmistakable silhouette, the important remains of sculptural ornamentation in high relief (once polychromed) enliven the outer walls with the rhythm of great plumed serpents, their bodies undulating along the *taludes* in the company of priest-astronomers, glyphic inscriptions, and symbols of the New Fire *(plates 266–269).*

It seems probable that this fascinating building was erected to commemorate the New Fire ceremony, at the close of one of the fifty-two-year cycles that marked the coincidence of the two Mesoamerican calendars—the solar version, with 365 days, and the ritual calendar of 260 days. This jubilant occasion ushered in a new life cycle in that difficult universe in which the community's exhausting task was to keep the gods happy and fed with an endless round of penances and sacrifices—all designed to avert an ever-possible final cataclysm. Indications are that to honor this new cycle, Xochicalco's rulers may have organized an important congress of astronomers attended by many prominent Maya. We see, on the one hand, the conspicuous

position these personages occupied in the composition of the panels. On the other hand, one of the panels of the principal facade displays an apparent calendric rectification—a suggestion that in the wake of this congress a significant revision was made in the calendars used in this region.

The Toltecs

Before the year 900 A.D. a group of seminomadic Toltecs, led by Mixcóatl—the cloud serpent—swept into the Valley of Mexico and helped destroy the already dying Classic cultures. In his incursions into the central area, legend tells us, Mixcóatl penetrated into the Morelos Valley, where one day he came upon a young woman. He shot arrows at her, but she turned them aside with her hand, therefore earning the name Chimalma, "Shield Hand." Struck by her magic powers, Mixcóatl married Chimalma, but she died in childbirth months later. Mixcoatl too died, killed by a usurper. Their son—called Ce Acatl (One Reed; date of his birth) Topiltzin (Our Prince) Quetzalcóatl (as high priest in the cult of the god Quetzalcóatl, which he later became)—was brought up by his grandparents in Tepoztlán, but studied with the priests in nearby Xochicalco. As a young man Topiltzin avenged his father's death by killing Ihuitimal the usurper, and by re-burying Mixcóatl's remains on the sacred hill at Culhuacán. Thus deified, Mixcóatl became a hunting god. Topiltzin, then leader of the Toltecs, changed the capital of his people from Culhuacán to Tulancingo and then to Tula.

The group called the Toltecs came into the Valley of Mexico about the time the astronomers held their congress at Xochicalco. They were then the Toltecs-Chichimecs, which means "nomads," and they probably lived side by side with the Teotihuacanos during the decadence of this great city. They acquired the name Toltec—Artisan—after having absorbed the arts of their neighbors. Thus the term which describes skills became the name of an entire ethnic group.

The Toltecs brought with them a knowledge of metals, a warrior caste, and a militaristic society. They worshiped the god Tezcatlipoca, a war god, who "brought vice and sin . . . [and] all evils which came to men . . ."[11] But Topiltzin, educated in the advanced Valley of Morelos, was the living representative of Quetzalcóatl, the plumed serpent, a god of peace and creation (who legend says had given maize to mankind and had taught people arts and agriculture), the god of the region where he was reared.

This difference of ideals caused the expulsion of Topiltzin-Quetzalcóatl from Tula and the triumph of the militaristic faction.

Again, legend tells us that Quetzalcóatl prohibited human sacrifice and led his people in an industrious, religious-oriented existence. But his enemy, Tezcatlipoca, one day came to the palace disguised as a merchant and showed Quetzalcóatl a mirror. Topiltzin, like Nanahuatzin in Teotihuacán, was covered with sores. He was shocked when he saw his likeness and accepted a cup of *pulque,* a centuryplant liquor, which Tezcatlipoca claimed would cure him. But the "cure" was drunkenness, and when Topiltzin-Quetzalcóatl awoke the next morning he discovered that he had broken his celibate vows by having called a priestess to his chambers and ignoring his sacred duties. Feeling he should no longer be Tula's leader, Quetzalcóatl left Tula with a group of followers in 987 A.D., going to Tlillan Tlapallan ("Place of Black and Red," or "Place of Writing"), identified with Cholula or with the Maya region. He promised to return from the east, a prophecy which was in part responsible for the downfall of the later Aztecs, inasmuch as the Spanish came from the east and by chance arrived in Mexico in a Ce Acatl year, the precise day and year of Quetzalcóatl's birth and also the year of his supposed return. Thus Cortés was thought to be the long-awaited god. Another source tells us that Quetzalcóatl went east, sacrificed himself in the fire, and became the morning star. As this star Quetzalcóatl occupies the most important position architecturally in Tula (under the name of Tlahuizcalpantecuhtli, lord of the dawn) in the great pyramid dedicated to this deity.

The last great Toltec leader in Tula was Huémac, or "Big Hand" (the story is that he liked women who measured at least four hands across the hips). Around the middle of the twelfth century drought and then famine hit the region. The chronicles say that the Tlaloques, the little rain gods, played ball with Huémac and the ruler won, but he insisted on being given as prize jades and precious feathers instead of the green corn and ripe corn leaves the Tlaloques offered him. The Toltecs, it would seem, received rich tribute but were forced to go hungry.

Some of the population deserted and went south and east. Huémac himself was ousted in 1168 A.D. and fled to Chapultepec, now part of Mexico City, where he died not much later. Meanwhile Tula fell prey to groups of barbarians, called Chichimecs because the name is equivalent to nomads. One of these groups was the Mexica or Aztecs, who arrived around 1200 A.D.

Kirchhoff[12] believes that Quetzalcóatl and Huémac were contemporaneous, Quetzalcóatl the religious leader of Tula and Huémac the secular ruler. Eventually the two disagreed on both political and religious points and left the metropolis at the same time, in the twelfth

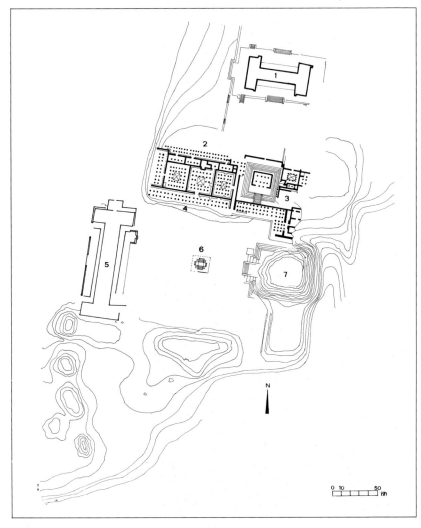

270. *Tula, Hidalgo, Mexico: plan of the ceremonial center.* 1. Ball Court 1 2. Burnt Palace 3. Building B 4. Colonnade 5. Ball Court 2 6. Central Altar 7. Building C

271. *Tula: atlantes and pillars of the Temple of Tlahuizcalpantecuhtli* ▷

272. *Tula: one of the four atlantes of the Temple of Tlahuizcalpantecuhtli*

273. *Tula: partial view of the Burnt Palace and Colonnade*
274. *Tula: aerial view of Ball Court 1, seen from the northwest*
275. *Tula: partial aerial view of the Great Plaza. In the foreground, the Burnt Palace and the Colonnade; in the center, the Temple of Tlahuizcalpantecuhtli; to the right, the Temple of the Sun ▷*
276. *Tula: Temple of Tlahuizcalpantecuhtli as seen from the Temple of the Sun ▷*

century. As Weaver points out,[13] Quetzalcóatl's abandonment of Tula in 978 A.D. is more logical, inasmuch as a Toltec or Putún-Maya (Mexicanized) group reached Tabasco or Campeche around this time, led by Kulkulkán, which means Quetzalcóatl or Plumed Serpent in the Maya tongue.

Tula

Scholars have long pointed to similarities between Tula and Chichén Itzá (in Yucatán) as evidence of this migration of Quetzalcóatl and his followers as well as a later Toltec migration. Kubler, however, feels that the current ran the opposite way:

> A question concerning the direction of these influences is relevant. . . . The north pyramid and colonnade at Tula resemble the Temple of the Warriors; another building encloses a colonnaded courtyard like the Mercado. Chacmool as well as serpent figures and Atlantean columns have also been found, but there is nothing at Tula corresponding to the first periods of Toltec art at Chichén. Tula therefore suggests a colonial outpost of Chichén rather than the reverse.
>
> The conventional view today is still that an alien art was imposed upon the Maya artisans of Chichén Itzá. However, the formative stages of that art are lacking at Tula. They are fully accounted for only at Chichén. At Chichén, alien rulers brought ideas rather than objects and artisans and eventually acquired an art from their Maya subjects. Thus Mexican ideas, clothed in Maya forms, were eventually implanted at Tula. . . .
>
> In the Mexican highlands, feathered serpent forms appeared at Teotihuacán long before their Toltec revival. The interpenetration of Mexican ideas and Maya forms is at least as old as the Early Classic art of Kaminaljuyú. At Xochicalco, the Late Classic investiture of Mexican symbols with Maya figural forms was another forerunner of the Toltec-Maya union of highland symbol and lowland art.[14]

In view of Maya influence in Guerrero and Morelos during the Classic period, it would seem plausible that this influence continued north to Tula when this center became dominant at the beginning of the Post-Classic, thus introducing new architectural forms to the Toltec site not only through trade but perhaps through groups of Toltecs who lived in the Maya zone and then returned north. Recent excavations in Tula carried out by Richard A. Diehl have shown that this center was probably occupied from the Early Post-Classic until after the Spanish Conquest and, indeed, continuously after that up to the present time.[15] Although the Toltecs were frankly militaristic, their city of about 6 square miles (10 sq. km.) was unfortified. The multi-family residences common at Teotihuacán were also popular in Tula, and constituted a type of defense in themselves.

Much of Tula's wealth must have come from the numerous obsidian mines in the region, especially since the volcanic glass mined here was the fine translucent green obsidian so popular in the pre-Hispanic world. This obsidian was a source of local taxes and long-distance trade.[16] The large quantity of spindle whorls found in Tula suggests an active textile industry, while evidence of trade goods from many corners of Mesoamerica indicates great activity in commerce and perhaps tribute. The Aztecs may well have learned some of their trading customs while living in Tula. A *temazcalli* or public steam bath of Aztec manufacture, placed directly in an earlier Toltec ball court, is one evidence of their occupation of Tula.[17]

The Architecture of Tula

There are many chronicles that link the beginning of great cultural advances on the Mexican plateau with the founding of Tula—leaving the Classic splendor of Teotihuacán and all the formative phases of the Pre-Classic period buried in oblivion. And yet, the heart of the Toltec ceremonial center, today partially reconstructed, seems a rather modest architectural grouping (plate 270) compared to what had existed two or three centuries earlier in the City of the Gods (plate 39). Except for some important innovations in building techniques and design, the legendary capital of the new Toltec empire displays a certain poverty of execution, explained perhaps by the recent barbarian origin of its founders and by the marked cultural slump that was provoked in these regions by the crumbling of what Jiménez Moreno calls the *Pax Teotihuacana*.[18]

The first thing we notice when studying Tula's main plaza is the importance, for the first time in Mesoamerica, of great colonnades (plates 273, 275, 276). As we saw in previous chapters, the independent support (column or pillar) existed in the area of Oaxaca from Pre-Classic times, and had been in common use during the Classic era in Oaxaca itself, in Teotihuacán, in the Gulf Coast area, and even in many Maya cities on the Yucatán peninsula. Except for such special cases as the monumental porticoes that marked the access to Monte Albán's north platform or to the Building of the Columns at El Tajín, this architectural element was used primarily to dramatize a facade (as in the Yucatán) or placed in pairs—and in formations of one, two, or three pairs deep—to support the roof of a portico or of a broad interior space (frequent, for example, in Teotihuacán). Here in Tula, on the contrary, we see compact rows of columns and masonry pillars: starting from one side of the Temple of the Sun, they round a corner of the plaza and continue along the foot of the Temple of Tlahuizcalpantecuhtli to cover one whole end of the plaza, blending in with the other interior colonnades that, separated by walls and banquettes, make up the various sections of the Burnt Palace. The latter was named for the charred remains of the calcined wooden beams that had once supported a flat roof over its semiopen spaces. These remains are confirmation of the fire that occurred around 1168 A.D.—the work, perhaps, of Toltec dissidents, or of the Chichimec invaders headed by Xólotl.

In their time of glory, these great halls of the Burnt Palace—bounded only by walls with banquettes against them, and open in the middle to form a kind of *impluvium*—must have seemed novel indeed. The great colonnaded exterior, connecting the halls and the adjacent temples, provided open views of the rest of the plaza and of the other buildings surrounding it. In addition to its role as a link between all these elements, the broad covered space must have served ceremonial purposes and various civic functions as well.

Atop the pyramidal base of the Temple of Tlahuizcalpantecuhtli stand the pillars and columns that once supported the temple roof. Among these loom the four famed atlantes of Tula *(plates 271, 272)*, with their heroic proportions and warriors' gear. Arrayed and armed in Toltec style, these imposing figures clearly embody the militaristic spirit that indeed prevailed from then on in Mesoamerica. Each atlas, 15 feet (4.60 m.) high, is made up of four great blocks of hard, well-carved stone, perfectly engaged by means of dowel holes and tenons—a principle that in Teotihuacán appears only in smaller sculpture. We find it here in the ruins of the serpent-shaped columns that once supported the door lintel. Of the decorations on the temple's base, there remain only some fragments toward the rear, where we can appreciate the new and complex Toltec version of the *tablero*, perhaps derived from certain forms found in Monte Albán and Xochicalco. This style of *tablero* rises above a simple, smooth *talud* to unfold on two levels and on different planes *(plate 276)*; the upper level contains an uninterrupted frieze portraying walking jaguars and coyotes; on the middle level we see pairs of eagles devouring human hearts and alternating with the effigy of the god Tlahuizcalpantecuhtli (god of the planet Venus or the Morning Star), whose mask emerges from the fangs of a crouched jaguar adorned with feathers and equipped with a forked serpent's tongue.

Completing the complex of the Temple of Tlahuizcalpantecuhtli is the *Coatepantli,* or "Serpent Wall," which partially sur-

278. *Tenayuca, Mexico: model of the pyramid in its penultimate phase of construction. Mexico City, National Museum of Anthropology*

279. *Tenayuca: pyramid. Detail showing the various phases of construction*

rounds the pyramidal base on the sides and back, set off from the body of the pyramid. This wall (like a symbolic cordon, it may have served to isolate the sacred area from the rest of the city) was crowned by conch-shaped merlons—stone imitations of a seashell, which was the symbol of Quetzalcóatl in his role as the wind god. Its central theme, set between two rows of step motifs, shows a group of serpents pursuing and devouring half-flayed human beings in a memorable *danse macabre*.

To these carved structures, we may add many other sculptural elements that here are often found out of their original context (in far-away Chichén Itzá they can usually be seen in more appropriate surroundings, as we shall see later). Among them, as part of the typically Toltec repertory, we might mention the monolithic columns of atlantes, smaller than their gigantic counterparts in the principal temple; the small statues of atlantes with upraised arms that must have been altar supports; the standard-bearers that sometimes topped the *alfardas;* and the curious *chac-mool,* a personage invariably depicted partially reclining on his back with his head turned to one side.

Our study of Tula's main plaza ends with an examination of the central platform—provided with four stairways and bordered by the remains of the local style of *tablero*—and of the immense Ball Court 1 *(plate 274),* whose 380-foot (116-m.) length earns it second place in importance in Mesoamerica, after the main court at Chichén Itzá (with which it shares a number of characteristics). A smaller ball court, behind the Temple of Tlahuizcalpantecuhtli, presents many affinities—both in its proportions and in the placement of almost all its elements—with the court we saw at Xochicalco. This tends to confirm the role of the latter city as a "cultural bridge" during the beginnings of the Post-Classic era. Finally, we wish to point out the semicircular base located some distance from the heart of the ancient city, on a site now called El Corral—undoubtedly once a sector of Tula. Apart from some remains of a small *Tzompantli,* or altar of skulls, adorned by a frieze of skulls alternating with crossed tibias and found to one side of its stairway, the architectural importance of this structure lies in the unusual shape of its base, which combines both truncated-pyramidal and truncated-conical elements *(plate 277).*

During the Classic period, the round "pyramids" such as the one at Cuicuilco *(plate 18)* yielded to forms based almost entirely on right angles. It is interesting to note that a new tendency involving composite forms emerged at the beginning of the Post-Classic period. This may have originated in Tula; at any rate, it continued its development in a variety of regional styles until the arrival of the Spaniards.

LATE POST-CLASSIC ARCHITECTURE OF THE CENTRAL PLATEAU OF MEXICO

Tenayuca

After the Chichimec hordes from the north destroyed Tula around 1168 A.D., the Post-Classic world's fragile equilibrium was shattered once again. For some time, the scene was dominated by the Chichimecs, who, having absorbed the culture of the conquered, established their first capital at Tenayuca around 1224. The seat of the Chichimec kingdom was later moved to Texcoco, the birthplace of the sage and poet-king Nezahualcóyotl.

Tenayuca's principal temple seems to have been the first of its kind to show, even in its earliest building phases, a new architectural style that involved placing two temples, instead of a single structure, on a pyramidal base provided with twin stairways (*plates 278–281*). It was a style that would soon be adopted by the Aztecs and other peoples, spreading during these last centuries of pre-Hispanic life to regions as distant as Guatemala (where it illustrates the degree of "mexicanization" reflected by the last Maya cities of the Guatemala highlands).

Like Teotihuacán's Pyramid of the Sun, the pyramid at Tenayuca is oriented toward the point where the setting sun last touches the horizon, on the day it reaches its zenith over the city. On each side of the pyramid stand two sculptures of Xiuhcóatl, the Fire Serpent (*plate 284*), each endowed with a nose crest covered with stars. The sculptures confirm the distinct solar character of this pyramid by marking the point at which the sun sets during the solstices. There are also numerous sculptures of serpents surrounding three sides of the pyramid (*plates 282, 283*). In addition—and this is the only really proven case to date—it seems that each of the six or seven stages of amplification and superpositioning undergone by this building coincides with the end of a fifty-two-year cycle and its corresponding New Fire celebration.

We have no clear evidence of what the twin sanctuaries built in each of these stages may have looked like, but the small pyramid standing on the outskirts of Tenayuca—in Santa Cecilia Acatitlán, an ancient quarter of this city—suggests a sanctuary with slightly inclined walls, its elevated roof adorned with relief sculptures—"nailheads," skulls, or vertical strips—and crowned with the typical Mexican-style roof (*plate 285*). The overall reconstruction of the small sanctuary of Santa Cecilia Acatitlán was in fact based on different sources—including a temple from Quauhtochco in Veracruz, which still retains a good part of its roof; descriptions and plans found in chronicles

243

286. *Calixtlahuaca, Mexico: semicircular base (Temple of Quetzalcóatl-Ehécatl)*

287. *Malinalco, Mexico: sculpture of an ocelot inside the monolithic temple*

from the time of the Spanish Conquest; and, above all, the many representations of contemporary sanctuaries that were modeled in clay, often with much attention to realistic detail *(plates 296–301).*

The Architecture of the Matlatzinca Region

Relatively few buildings of this period escaped, even in part, the iconoclastic fury of the Spanish conquerors. Among the survivors, we shall mention some that seem to us of particular documentary interest; they belong to the Matlatzinca region in the vicinity of Toluca. There is first the semicircular base at Calixtlahuaca *(plate 286),* which was traditionally dedicated to the wind god Quetzalcóatl-Ehécatl and whose architectural origin may, as we saw, lie in Tula. Then there are the majestic bases of Teotenango, graded on artificial terraces from which they overlook a wide valley and there are the buildings at Malinalco, partially or totally; carved into the flank of an imposing escarpment—a peculiarity that makes them, and the baths that King Nezahualcóyotl ordered cut into the Tezcutzinco hills, unique in Mesoamerica.

Carved, in its entirety, into the living rock of the mountain, the small monolithic temple of Malinalco is without doubt the one that best embodies this new breed of architecture, with its fully rounded sculptures *(plates 287, 288).* Flanked by two large figures of felines, its base emerges from the front of the rocky wall. The plateau's typical *alfardas* border a stairway that displays the remains of a central sculpture. The sanctuary door, surrounded by other sculptures, is in the shape of open jaws of a distinctly regional style totally unlike those we saw in the Yucatán. We can see that the aperture, mutilated today, was cut in the form of a semicircular arch—a shape not used in Mesoamerica, and explained here only by the unusual construction method.

Finally, inside the round sanctuary itself, we find some zoomorphic sculptures (three eagles and a feline creature—perhaps an ocelot or a jaguar) placed symmetrically around the axis of the doorway, on the temple floor, and on a horseshoe bench built into the wall.

The Mexica or Aztecs

In the thirteenth century the Mexicas arrived in the Valley of Mexico. They had been wandering for about a century and a half after having left their homeland, Aztlan ("White Place," or "Place of Herons") an island in a lake, possibly in the present-day state of Nayarit. The name Aztec means people of Aztlan. However, they referred to themselves as the Mexica, People of Mexico. The word Mexico itself poses a problem, since it could mean many things—among them "Navel of the Moon" or "Center of the Maguey Plant," signifying

289. *Huexotla, Mexico: remains of fortifications that encircled the ceremonial center*

the center of the world. The Mexica were also the People of the Sun, inasmuch as the sun was their main deity.

These Náhuatl-speaking Aztec-Mexica went from humble beginnings to the leading political, economic, and military position in ancient Mexico. Their capital, Tenochtitlan, was a splendid metropolis of about 200,000 inhabitants when the Spaniards reached it in 1519 A.D. But almost three hundred years earlier the Aztecs were nearing the end of their long pilgrimage, guided by Huitzilopochtli, who had been a tribal leader but who had died on the way from Aztlan and was deified, his ashes carried in a bundle. Supposedly he communicated with the people through his priests.

When they settled in the Valley of Mexico the Aztecs, whose custom it was to steal their neighbors' wives, attracted the antagonism of other groups. After awhile these people routed the Aztecs, who ended up in Colhuacan but who eventually were given lands in Tizapan, a barren hill overrun with poisonous snakes. After the Aztecs had lived there for some time, the Colhuacan ruler sent emissaries to see if any had survived. The Colhuacanos were amazed to see that the snakes had not killed the Aztecs but rather had been killed and eaten by them.

In 1325 Huitzilopochtli led the chosen people (as they thought of themselves) to their promised land: an island in the lake where an eagle —symbol of the sun and of Huitzilopochtli—stood upon a prickly pear cactus, with a serpent in his talons. The prickly pear, or *tenochtli*— which gave its name to the Aztec capital, Tenochtitlan—grew from the heart of Copil, Huitzilopochtli's nephew, who had tried to kill the god but who had himself been murdered by Aztec priests. Actually, the little island was wanted by no one. Azcapotzalco, the most powerful city-state in the valley at that time, owned most of the land, including the muddy island that had not even fresh water. Azcapotzalco demanded tribute from the Mexica, which was rigorously paid until these people overthrew the stronger city and assumed priority in the region.

From here on (1428) the Aztec empire expanded and reached its maximum splendor by 1502. Certain pockets in the great territorial expansion, which reached north to the limits of Mesoamerica and south to Guatemala and El Salvador, were intentionally left unconquered. The object of this was to carry on the so-called War of the Flowers (the flower in Aztec iconography symbolizes the heart and blood, and therefore is food for the sun), so that both sides—the Aztecs and the Tlaxcalans, for example—would always have prisoners to sacrifice to the sun.

The luxury and rich markets found in Tenochtitlan and Tlate-

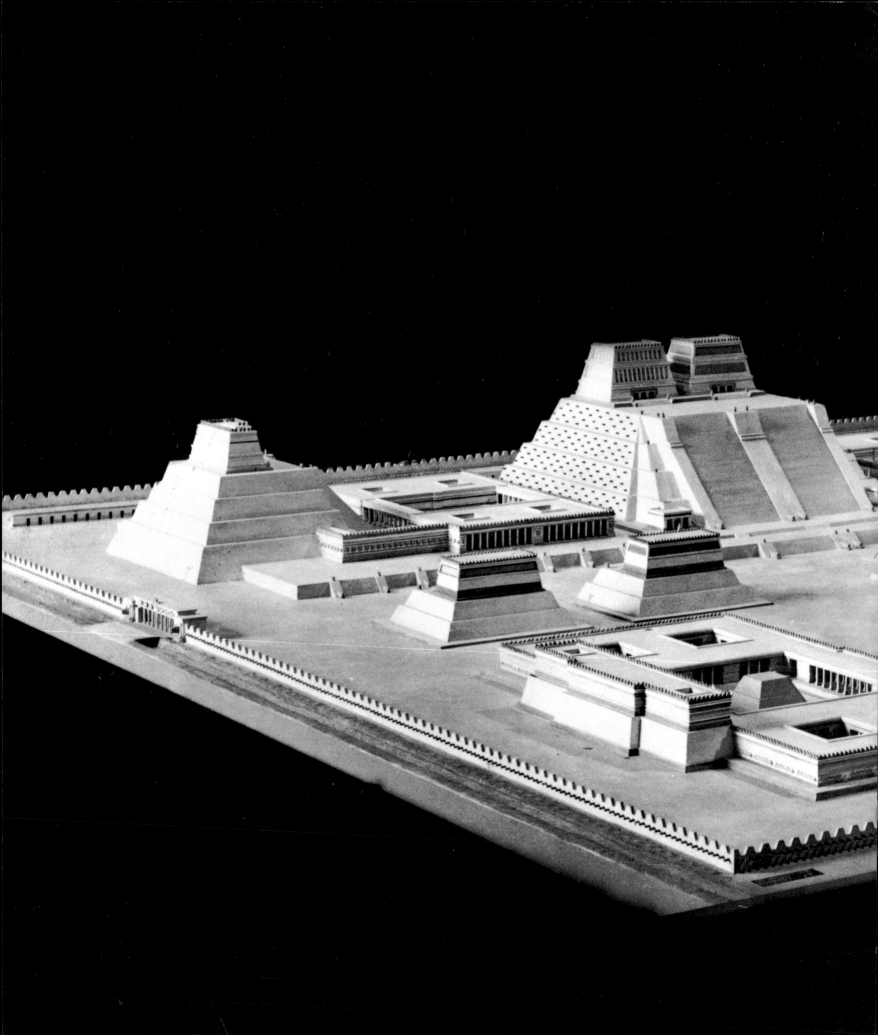

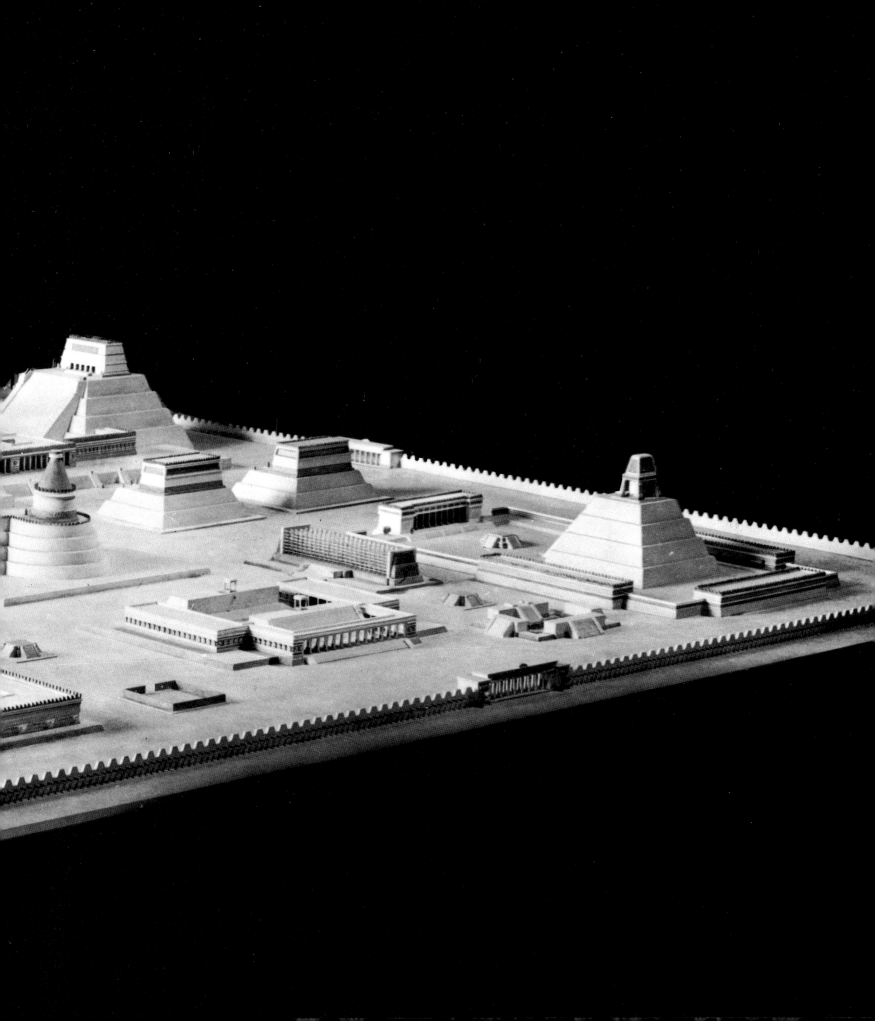

293. *Tenochtitlan: Stone of the Sun. Mexico City, National Museum of Anthropology*

294. *Tenochtitlan: colossal statue of Coatlicue, the earth goddess. Mexico City, National Museum of Anthropology* ▷

295. *Tenochtitlan: hypothetical reconstruction of the ancient Aztec capital.*
Mexico City, National Museum of Anthropology

lolco (the latter a subordinate Aztec sister-city) were the result of tribute paid by conquered peoples. According to tribute lists in the Mendoza Codex, each year Tenochtitlan received in tribute 7,000 tons of corn, more than 4,000 tons of beans, 4,000 tons of *chía* (a type of sage used for oil and for making a refreshing drink), 4,000 tons of *huauhtli* (amaranth seed), more than 21,000 kilos of cacao, more than 36,000 kilos of dried chile, 4,000 jars of honey, large quantities of salt, 2,079,200 lengths of cotton cloth, 296,000 lengths of vegetable fiber cloth, 240,000 skirts and blouses, 144,000 breech clouts, and over 100,000 kilos of raw cotton. The providing of this enormous tribute probably occupied one third of the total work time of the towns subject to Tenochtitlan.[19]

The *pochteca,* or traveling merchants, were a powerful cog in the economic wheel. They traveled all over Mesoamerica, on special roads or by waterway, staying in special houses, taking with them human carriers loaded with fine wares that were exchanged for others. The *pochteca* became wealthy and often were awarded titles of nobility—if they lived to enjoy these privileges, for they served double duty as spies, since they could see the lay of foreign lands and observe military installations. They often served a *casus belli:* if a merchant was robbed or murdered, as often happened, this served as an admirable excuse to avenge them and invade a territory.[20]

The religion of the Aztecs was polytheistic. Gods patronized every phase of life, were associated with the heavenly bodies, with the earth, with planting and sowing, and even with steam baths, gambling, haircutting, and bathing; deities themselves were seen in weaving instruments, cooking vessels, artisans' tools, agricultural implements that were carved in the image of "monkeys, dogs, or devils . . . it is such a common custom that there is not an Indian who does not use these effigies . . ."[21]

The greatest stone carvers since the Olmecs, the Aztecs left portraits of their gods that both amaze and terrify us, not only because of their masterful sculpture but because of their symbolic concepts—such as Coatlicue, the earth mother-sky goddess, whose head is a pair of snakes symbolizing blood, whose skirt is a net of twisted serpents, whose feet and hands are claws, whose necklace is of hearts and open hands, and who adorns herself with skulls. Here is life and death, earth and cosmos, the generous mother who gives life and the terrible force that takes it back *(plate 294)*. In contrast to these spectacular pieces, the Aztecs also carved figures of ordinary people, portraits of their rulers, and, with an evident love of nature, pumpkins, cacti, coyotes, dogs, jaguars, crickets, fleas, and serpents.

297. *Model of an Aztec temple dedicated to Xipe, deity of the fertility of the earth. Mexico City, National Museum of Anthropology*

Tenochtitlan and Aztec Architecture

Tenochtitlan was divided into four large quarters, probably symbolic of the four directions of the world, with the ceremonial center as the heart or fifth direction (in ancient Mesoamerica it was believed that the center held sky and earth together). The ceremonial precinct "must have been immense, for it accommodated 8,600 men dancing in a circle."[22] From this gigantic courtyard led four causeways, those to the north, west, and south leading to suburbs or smaller cities, the eastern causeway to the docks and lake (today dry). The reason for this orientation can be traced back, according to one sixteenth-century chronicler, to the creation of the Fifth Sun in Teotihuacán, when different gods faced different directions in order to see where the new sun would rise.[23]

Each quarter was subdivided into *barrios* or neighborhoods. Although each *barrio* had its own shrine and deity, as well as administrative buildings, the major temples were within the ceremonial precinct, which included not only pyramid-sanctuaries to the most revered gods but a ball court, gladiatorial stone, skull rack, ponds for ritual ablutions, schools, libraries, and residences for priests.[24] The whole precinct was surrounded by a *Coatepantli,* or "Serpent Wall," similar to that at Tenayuca. The sovereign's palace, however, outranked in authority this sacred enclosure in political, economic, and even ecclesiastical affairs.[25] As Calnek points out, although large and luxurious residential quarters adjoin religious structures at Teotihuacán, they are subordinated to an architectural design that emphasizes the mass of the temple-pyramid as its dominant component;[26] while in Tenochtitlan, there is greater independence and architectural prominence of the palace with respect to ceremonial structures. The palace of Moctezuma II occupied an estimated 2.4 hectares—"approximately double the combined areas of three closely related complexes that adjoin the Temple of Quetzalcóatl in the Ciudadela at Teotihuacán."[27]

One of the reasons that Tenochtitlan (and probably Tlatelolco too, with its great market) demanded a strong and complex administrative system is that, aside from its approximately 200,000 inhabitants, there was a large immigrant population and also a floating population of merchants and pilgrims who were constantly pouring into the city. People arrived by land and by water, since many of Tenochtitlan's streets were actually canals. The land itself was communally owned, except for property used to support the royal household, the temples and priests, or government offices. Each man had a plot of land which he could use during his lifetime and then leave the rights to his heirs. If a man failed to cultivate his land for two years he was admonished, and if he ignored the warning, a year later is plot was returned to the communal property, then assigned to a more industrious farmer.

It is unfortunate that when we want to speak of Aztec architecture, we must be guided by the old Spanish chronicles rather than by its material remains. Not a temple or palace—not even those of Cortés' Indian allies—escaped brutal and systematic destruction at the hands of the proud conquistadors or sacrifice to the missionaries' religious zeal. Fragments of the walls at Huexotla *(plate 289)*, near Texcoco, are still standing, and we find a few remains of other buildings from that era, such as part of the Great Temple of Tenochtitlan and some bases from Tlatelolco *(plate 291)*; but the great majority of the cities then flourishing had their buildings virtually razed and others substituted according to the dictates of their new Spanish masters.

This was particularly true of the ancient Aztec capital, which Cortés reduced to a heap of rubble in the course of overcoming native resistance, thus laying the foundation for a new capital several years later. In this process of evangelization and acculturation, the terrible annihilation of persons and things has generally left us with only whatever architectural evidence happened to be protected by its own debris—some small altars *(plate 290)* and statues *(plate 294)*, or simple remains of much larger buildings, among which we occasionally find rare painted sections.

And so, except for the small clay representations that we have mentioned *(plates 296–301)*, we are forced to rely on the commentaries of the conquerors themselves, with all the attendant irony of their enthusiasm. From the pen of Bernal Díaz del Castillo comes an account, occasionally somewhat wide-eyed, of the marvelous sight beheld by the Spanish on approaching the city of Iztapalapa, a vassalage of the Aztec empire that controlled access to Tenochtitlan from the south: "And when we saw so many cities and populous villages built in the water, and other great towns on solid ground, and that causeway that was so straight and level as it went toward Mexico, we were amazed . . . and some of our soldiers asked themselves if they were dreaming . . . by seeing so many things unheard-of, nor even dreamt of! And after we entered that city of Iztapalapa, the sight of the palaces in which they lodged us! How large and well-built they were, of excellent stonework, and the wood of cedars and other good sweet-smelling trees, with great courts and rooms . . . all tented in cotton. After having looked well at all that, we went to the gardens, that were a thing wonderful to see and to walk in, so that I never tired of looking at the diversity of trees and colors in each one, and beds full of roses and other flowers, and many fruit trees . . . and a pond full of sweet water. And another remarkable thing we saw

299. *Model of an Aztec temple. Mexico City, National Museum of Anthropology*

300. *Model of an Aztec temple decorated in stucco and frescoes. Mexico City, National Museum of Anthropology* ▷

were the large canoes that could enter the garden from the lake through an opening they had cut, without landing aground; and everything all very whitewashed and shining, with so many kinds of stones and paintings on them that one would never tire of gazing at them; and the different kinds and breeds of birds that came to the pond. . . . Now all is razed, lost, nothing remains!"[28]

Or, listen to Cortés, attempting to convey to Charles V, King of Spain, the splendor of Moctezuma's palaces: "As to Moctezuma's surroundings, the admirable things he had, their grandeur and condition, there is so much to write that I assure Your Majesty I know not where to begin . . . because as I have said, is there any magnificence greater than that a barbarian gentleman like this one has had copied in gold and silver and stone and feathers all the things under the heaven to be found in his domain! So natural is the work in gold and silver that there is no smith in the world who could do it better. And reason cannot comprehend with what tools they make the stonework so perfect, and the featherwork, so that it could not be done more marvelously in wax nor in any embroidery. He has his houses for lodging inside the city, so many and so marvelous, that it seemed to me almost impossible to describe the excellence and size of them . . . especially since their like does not exist in Spain."[29]

Fray Juan de Torquemada helps us to imagine what the inside of a room looked like: "all of it, every corner, very clean, polished, carpeted and tapestried with walls of cotton and feathers in many colors . . ." He notes with admiration that in the care of their palaces "these idolators were very solicitous to keep them very well whitewashed and white. And when part of the building, or some wall, lost its coating or became dull, it was immediately whitewashed and plastered again by officials in charge of this, who did nothing else nor served in any other capacity . . ." The good friar waxes ecstatic in describing the roofs of the sanctuaries, which "were of diverse and varied shapes . . . some of wood, and others of a straw like rye . . . beautifully worked, some being pyramidal, some square, some round, and some of other forms. And they made them so well that they did not seem made of actual material, but of very fine and delicate brushwork."[30]

There are of course many chronicles, and even some simple maps, describing such elements as the sacred precinct of Tenochtitlan. These documents, plus data from what excavations have been possible in the heart of Mexico City, have served as the basis of Ignacio Marquina's attempt to construct a model that could somehow illustrate those ancient accounts (plate 292). Here we see the many buildings that constituted the principal Aztec ceremonial center. These are surrounded by a *Coatepantli*, or "Serpent Wall," inspired not only

301. *Model of an Aztec temple dedicated to Quetzalcóatl-Ehécatl, the wind god. Mexico City, National Museum of Anthropology*

by Tenayuca but perhaps also by the fortifications of Huexotla *(plate 289)*. As in Tenayuca, Tenochtitlan's Great Temple stands out in the center, displaying a twin stairway and two sanctuaries. One is dedicated to the god Tláloc, the major deity of the agricultural peoples of the Mexican plateau throughout fifteen centuries, the other to Huitzilopochtli, the young and bellicose god of sun and war and the Aztec tribal deity.

In front of this twin temple rises another—that of Quetzalcóatl-Ehécatl, with its customary semicircular base. Other temples, altars, and ritual platforms complete the complex. On either side of the sacred precinct stand the two principal institutions of higher education in the Aztec world, the *Calmécac* and the *Telpochcalli*—one devoted to religion and the other to military pursuits.

And—although Bernal Díaz del Castillo laments, "Now all is razed, lost, nothing remains!"—some imposing examples of a vigorous and monumental sculpture have survived to echo the magnificence of Aztec culture, a society that not without reason considered itself Huitzilopochtli's chosen people. The· culmination and formidable synthesis of a large and fruitful cultural tradition on the Mexican plateau, Aztec sculpture ranks high in the artistic panorama of all Mesoamerica. Admirably worked in very hard stone (which in itself reflected the tenacious, fearless, and proud Aztec temperament), it broadened and enriched the Indian artistic repertory into what Miguel Covarrubias called "the last and most spectacular flash . . ."[31] As one among many first-class examples of art combined with architecture, we might cite the Stone of the Sun—a masterly synthesis of the particular cosmological ideas of the ancient Mexicans *(plate 293)*.

There exists a small map fragment in which one can see the extraordinary urban arrangement of the Aztec capital of Tenochtitlan—a unique lake city. This city plan has, in fact, been the object of many studies and hypothetical reconstructions. Let us examine an eyewitness account by the conquistadors of their first view of Tlatelolco, Tenochtitlan's ancient twin city, which the Aztecs had absorbed in their territorial expansion. (It appears to the left in *plate 295,* with its enormous *tianguis,* or open-air market, adjacent to the ceremonial center.) Cortés describes it as a plaza "as much as twice the size of Salamanca, all surrounded by entrances, where daily there are over sixty thousand creatures buying and selling. . . . Each kind of merchandise is sold in its own street, without admitting any other commodity, and this way they maintain good order."[32]

Bernal Díaz del Castillo leaves us his moving account of climbing the great *cu,* or temple, of Tlatelolco: "And after we climbed to the top of the great *cu,* on the little plaza that was higher up there . . . Moctezuma came out of a sanctuary . . . and with him came two priests who paid great homage to Cortés. . . . Then [Moctezuma] took him by the hand and bade him look at his great city and all the other cities that were there in the water and the many other towns on land all around the same lake; and said that if he had not seen the great plaza properly he would be able to do so from here. And so we looked at it, because that great and accursed temple was so high that it towered over everything. And so we saw the three causeways that enter into Mexico. . . . And we saw the sweet water coming from Chapultepec to supply the city. And on those three causeways [we saw] bridges that they had made at intervals, through which the waters of the lake passed from one part to another. And we saw in that great lake a vast array of canoes, some coming with provisions and others returning with cargoes and merchandise. And we saw that to leave any house of that great city, or those of any of these cities that were built upon the water, one could not pass from one abode to another save by wooden drawbridges or in canoes. And we saw in those cities temples and chapels built like towers and fortresses, all whitened, and things of beauty; and [we saw] houses with flat roofs, and on the causeways other little fortress-like towers and temples. And after we looked long, and considered all we had seen, we turned to view the huge plaza and the multitude of people that were there, some buying and others selling, so that just the sound, the buzzing of the voices there could be heard more than a league away. And among us were soldiers who had been in many parts of the world—in Constantinople, in Rome and in all of Italy—and they said they had never seen a plaza so well laid out, so large and in such good order, and so full of people."[33]

This glowing account continues with a description of each of the three causeways leading to dry land being "as wide as the length of two lances and very well made, so that eight horsemen abreast can ride across it. . . ." Cortés described the principal streets of the city as "very wide and straight; some of these, and all those of lesser importance, are half of land and the other half of water, and the natives traverse them in their canoes; all the streets are open at intervals, through which the water passes back and forth; and over all these openings, some of which are very wide, there are their bridges, of broad beams frequently tied together, strong and well made, so that ten horsemen abreast might pass."[34]

The immense lake city that the Spaniards saw toward the end of the year 1519 A.D. had been founded less than two centuries before, under the most precarious conditions and following a long, hazardous nomadic existence on the part of what was then merely a tribe of obscure origins. The city rose around some rocky islands that had constituted the original nucleus, "among rushes and cane-breaks, reed grass and thickets,"[35] where a prickly pear bush grew on the rocks and above it an eagle sat, devouring a serpent. Little by little the city encroached on the shallow waters of the lake by an ingenious regional system of *chinampas* formed by sinking great rafts laden with mud and securing them with cypresses planted for the purpose. By filling and consolidating these floating islands, Tenochtitlan grew according to a skillfully conceived urban plan, so that by the last decade before the Spanish Conquest the city had become the magnificent chief metropolis of an empire. Its location on a lake—the three access causeways guarded by a series of bastions and drawbridges—assured it of a practically impregnable position under the conditions prevailing at that time in the Indian world.

Confident of the glorious destiny awaiting the People of the Sun, and riding on the crest of power and riches, the Aztecs hurled their challenging chant at other peoples—unaware that all too soon there would come an abrupt halt to the rising of a star that it had seemed nothing could hold back:

> Whence the eagles alight,
> Whence the jaguars stalk,
> There the Sun is invoked.
>
> Like a sinking shield
> Is the setting Sun.
> In Mexico night is falling,
> War strikes everywhere.
> Oh, Giver of Life!
> War is coming.
>
> Proud of itself
> Stands the city of Mexico-Tenochtitlan.
> Here no one fears death in war.
> This is our glory.
> This is your command.
> Oh, Giver of Life!
>
> Bear witness, oh princes,
> Lest ye forget it.
> Who can lay siege to Tenochtitlan?
> Who can shake the foundations of Heaven?
>
> With our arrows,
> With our shields,
> The city lives.
> Mexico-Tenochtitlan endures![36]

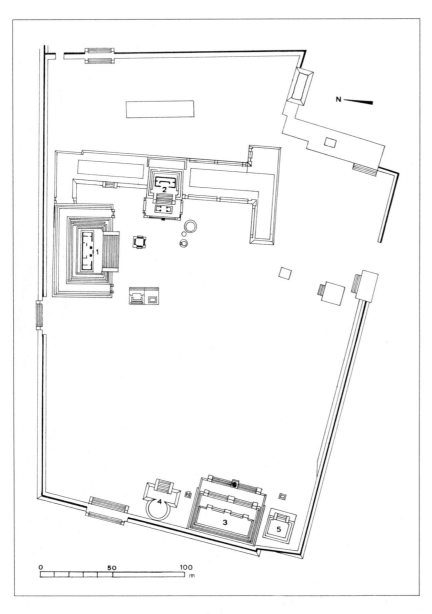

Cholula

With the decline of Teotihuacán, Cholula surged upward and in time became one of the greatest market and pilgrimage centers of Mesoamerica. In the Late Classic period (700–800 A.D.) the acropolis-pyramid ceremonial center was definitely abandoned and religious and civic structures moved to the site now occupied by the town of Cholula. As we have said before, the sanctuary of the god Quetzalcóatl stood on the site where the St. Francis monastery now stands.

Many changes can be seen through archaeological remains in the Early Post-Classic.[1] Through ceramics we see two new traditions penetrating the Puebla-Tlaxcala area: one the Xicoténcatl tradition coming from northwestern Mexico, and another the Xicalanca-Olmec, from Tabasco and the Gulf Coast, undoubtedly associated with the rich cacao trade. Changes are seen also in skeletal remains and in funerary customs; the latter include a predominance of cremated remains in jars. All these changes indicate a conquest of Cholula by the Xicalanca-Olmecs. The control of the area by these people was in turn displaced by a Toltec invasion after the fall of Tula, in the twelfth century.

By the time of the Late Post-Classic (1325–1500 A.D.) the earlier traditions had been absorbed and formed a unity, with, however, strong Mixtec and Gulf influences. Many remains of human sacrifice, including group massacres and mutilations of cadavers, correspond to this period. Ritual burial of parts of the body was common (we find this also in Tlatelolco): the cranium, hands or feet, portions of the vertebrae, or segments of the trunk were buried separately; they usually belonged to young adults between eighteen and thirty years of age.[2]

When Cortés and his men reached Cholula in 1519, en route to Tenochtitlan, they were received in a contemptuous manner. Nevertheless, the Spanish captain was finally invited into the city but was requested to leave the bulk of his troops outside. The Europeans were soon advised by the Tlaxcalans—who were by then their allies—that the invitation to Cholula was an ambush, prepared by the city fathers by order of Moctezuma. Cortés then attacked, favored by an element of surprise, and slaughtered thousands of Cholulans. Bernal Díaz del Castillo, one of Cortés' soldiers who wrote about the conquest, describes Cholula as the Spanish first saw it, before this massacre:

302. *Cempoala, Veracruz: plan of the main ceremonial precinct. 1. Great Temple   2. Temple of the "Chimneys"   3. Great Pyramid 4, 5. Buildings annexed to the Great Pyramid*

The city of Cholula much resembled Valladolid, being in a fertile plain, very thickly inhabited; it is surrounded by fields of maize, pepper, and maguey. They had an excellent manufac-

ver the country on her feast day, just as Quetzalcóatl did centuries
go.

Cempoala and Post-Classic Architecture in the Gulf of Mexico
During the Post-Classic period (900–1500 A.D.) the Gulf region be-
ame dotted with many rich cities; the largest was Cempoala. When
he Spaniards reached Veracruz, a scout saw the clean whitewashed
valls of the city and rushed back to Cortés to tell him that Cempoala
vas made of silver.[5] It was in Cempoala that Cortés met the Totonac
hieftain who complained about tribute exacted by Moctezuma, and
vho became the Spaniards' ally. It was also in Cempoala that Nar-
áez, having been sent by the governor of Cuba, Velázquez, to take
risoner the invaders of Mexico (Cortés' glory was dimming that of
'elázquez), fought with Cortés in a battle that ended in Narváez
osing one eye and all his troops, who went over to the other side.

Some ancient religious rites from this Veracruz region still sur-
ive, mainly the Flyers' Dance *(El Volador),* which was adopted by
nany regions in Mexico. This dance is executed on a tiny platform
t the summit of an extremely high pole made from the finest tree
1 the forest. Five "flyers" represent the four cardinal directions and
ne center of the earth. The person in the center dances and plays a
rum on the little platform while the other four, dressed as macaws,
ymbolic of the sun, secured to the top by ropes, hurl themselves in
ne air, face down. As they fly round and round, they play on flutes.
ach flyer makes thirteen turns around the pole as he descends, to-
aling fifty-two, equivalent to the 52-year ancient time cycle. The
ole is revered as if it were sacred, is given offerings and is deferred to
s if it were a live deity. It is called *Tota,* "Our Father." That this has
eep magic significance is shown by an accident in 1966 when two of
ne flyers in a *Volador* performance fell and were killed. The captain
f the group blamed the accident on the absence of a sacrificed hen,
vhose blood should be sprinkled on the tree's base, together with
nezcal liquor. A hen was not available and was eliminated from the
ite, with tragic results.[6]

In the Post-Classic, the Huaxtecs of the northern Gulf area con-
nued to build round structures. The people, dressed in brilliantly
olored clothing, wore spectacular jewelry and painted their hair red
r yellow. The Aztecs regarded the Huaxtecs as sensual, immoral,
iven to sexual excesses, but at the same time called their rich land
onacatlalpan, "Place of Foods." Tlazoltéotl, one of the Aztec goddesses
f love and childbirth, originally came from the Huaxtec region. And
nce the Huaxtecs kept developing an architecture of simple rec-

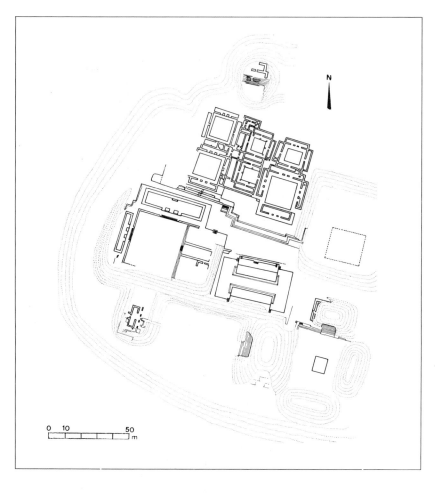

0 10   50
m

tangular or semicircular bases and generally rounded corners, E
Tajín continued its evolution up to the twelfth or thirteenth century
finally diminishing in importance and yielding its place to such citie
as Cempoala, which would witness the Spanish Conquest.

The last capital of the Totonac kingdom (and at the time
vassalage of the Aztec empire), Cempoala reveals in its architectur
the profound changes, both political and cultural, that occurred i
this region during the second half of the Post-Classic period. Far from
perpetuating the *tablero* with beveled cornices and niches or frets
which had lent such a lively note to El Tajín's buildings, the new To
tonac architecture—despite its marked regional tendencies—seem
a departure from the mainstream. The buildings in the ceremonia
center *(plate 302)* are arranged around large esplanades surrounded b
walls, erected for defensive purposes and for protection from th
rising river during the rainy season. Its bases are simple volumes
formed in general by a stepped series of sloping bodies. We note th
presence of semicircular buildings *(plates 304, 305)*—a style origi
nating perhaps with the natives of Tula and subsequently develope
by other peoples who, like the Aztecs, contributed to its wide diffusion
We also find strange circular constructions in different sizes in fron
of some of the temples *(plate 303)*—altars and ponds for ceremonia
ablutions. These, like the majority of Cempoala's buildings (including
the walls girding each ceremonial complex), are delineated at the to
by a series of stepped merlons that help give unity to the complex
Augmenting this is the texture provided by the use of boulders as
building material *(plate 305)*.

In speaking of regional characteristics, we must not overlool
the cemeteries, where, as in Quiahuiztlan—located near the beacl
where Cortés landed—we find clusters of tombs in the shape of minia
ture temples, all for the most part scarcely over 39 inches (1 m.) higl
(plate 306).

Oaxaca in the Post-Classic Period

Around 800 A.D. Monte Albán, like other great Classic centers, wen
into a decline. The Zapotec capital was moved to Zaachila and con
tinued there until the Conquest in 1521. The valley is still inhabited
by Zapotec-speaking people.

As in other parts of Mesoamerica, militarism was on the rise
The Mixtecs came down from their mountains, eventually con
quering the Zapotecs or allying themselves with them by marriage
Between 1000 and 1200 A.D. a Toltec penetration left its mark upo
the Mixtecs and perhaps was responsible for a stimulus in the arts
When the Aztecs conquered parts of Oaxaca toward the middle of th

308. *Mitla, Oaxaca: plan of the Palace of the Columns*

309. *Mitla: Palace of the Columns. Sections of the north building of the second quadrangle and of the antechamber of the Place of the Columns*

fteenth century they found that Atonal, ruler of the powerful city-ate Coixtlahuaca, still thought of himself as a Toltec ruler.[7]

The Mixtecs left their mark on Zapotec cities such as Mitla in he form of facades of stone mosaic. Other Mixtec markers are highly olished polychrome pottery with codex-type decoration, bone arving—also with codex-type themes—alabaster and rock crystal apidary, the making of codices mainly with genealogical subjects, nd exquisite metallurgy done mostly by the *cire perdue* technique. In he latter, a sun-dried mold made of clay and charcoal was covered vith a thin layer of beeswax, then with another coating of clay with small opening, in which molten gold or silver was poured. The netal melted, replaced the wax, and thus formed the piece of jewelry. he magnificent Mixtec craftsmen not only influenced the Aztecs ut probably were taken to Tenochtitlan to work there as artisans.

The social organization of the Mixtecs differed in some aspects om that of other Mesoamerican groups. Women were more power-ıl and at times ruled the city-states. They also went to war, either actual fact or as military directors, as we see in representations from he Nuttall, Selden, and Bodley codices. Sometimes transmission of ules was matrilineal, at other times the eldest son inherited from the ather and the second son was heir to his mother's territory. In the tate of Oaxaca matriarchies still exist. The Mixtecs today inhabit ome parts of the state (in the area called Ñuiñe by Paddock, for xample), and descendants of the rulers of the Yanhuitlán seignory—elated to those of Zaachila, Tilantongo, Tamazula, Cuilapan, and Chachuapan—still live in the Yanhuitlán area.[8]

Mitla and Post-Classic Architecture in Oaxaca
he brilliant cultural trajectory of Monte Albán spanned over fifteen enturies. This majestic Zapotec metropolis was finally to fall before he power of the highland Mixtecs, who continued to occupy it or a time and even buried their own dead in ancient Zapotec tombs. he famous Tomb 7 has bequeathed us an inestimable treasury of fine ewels wrought in gold, silver, rock crystal, and other precious and emiprecious materials.

The architecture that developed in the Oaxaca region, starting vith the Early Post-Classic era, begins to take on a more residential, ivic, and courtly character. In cities such as Yagul, numerous palaces re grouped around plazas and patios, often in a dense, closed pattern f quadrangles *(plate 307)*.

Mitla, the new sacred city—built in a valley rather than on a nountaintop like Monte Albán—represents the ultimate expression f the new architectural ideas, in both its characteristic distribution

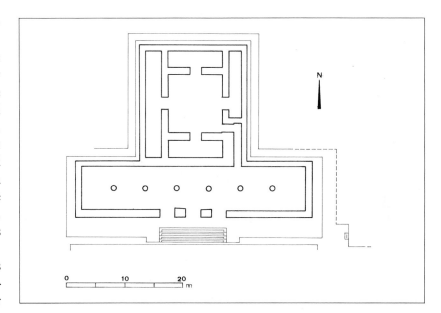

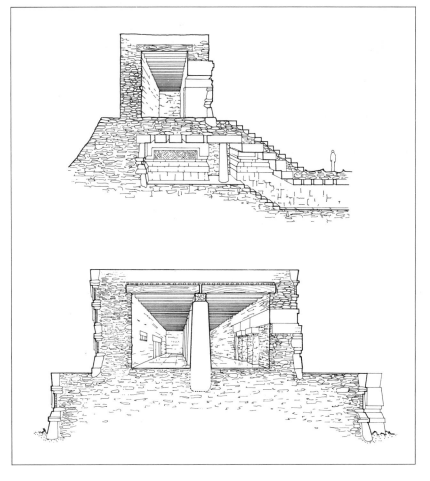

312. *Mitla: Palace of the Columns. Detail of the interior patio*
313. *Mitla: Palace of the Columns. Detail of the stepped fret wall decoration* ▷

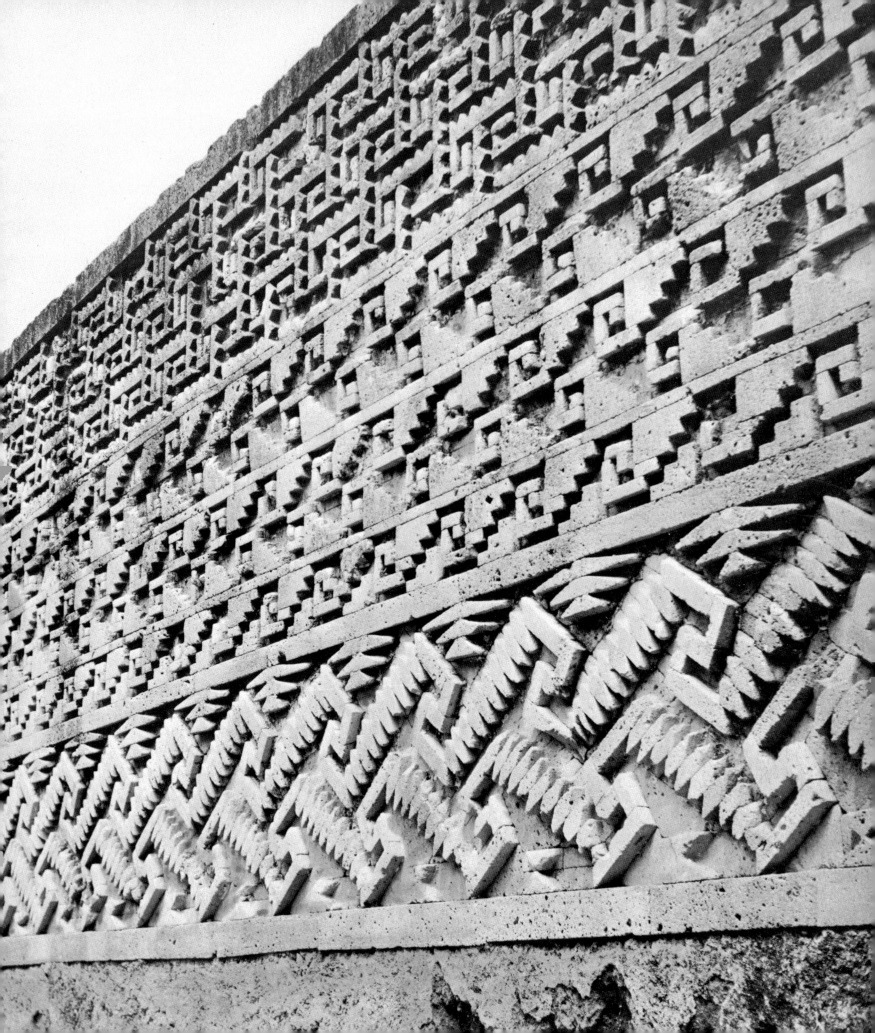

314. *Chichén Itzá, Yucatán: plan of the northern part of the city.*
1. Well of Sacrifices   2. Ball Court   3. Tzompantli
4. Platform of the Jaguars and Eagles   5. Platform of Venus
6. Temple of the Warriors   7. Castillo   8. Group of the
Thousand Columns   9. Market   10. Ball Court
11. Tomb of the High Priest   12. Red House
13. Municipal Well   14. Caracol   15. Temple of the
Painted Reliefs   16. Nunnery Quadrangle

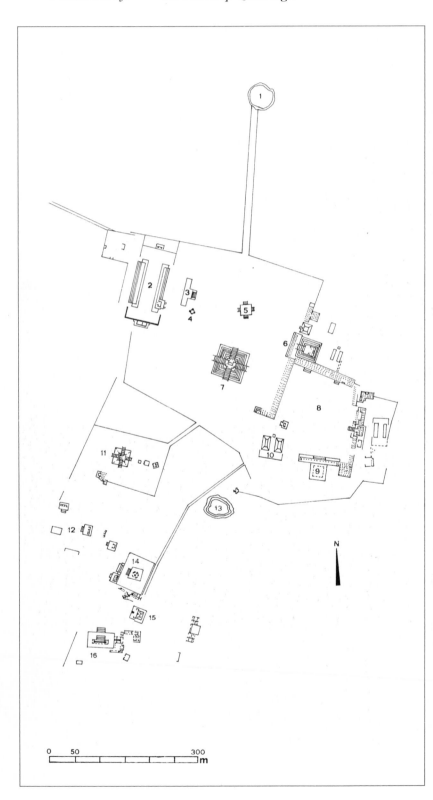

of buildings in quadrangles and in its extraordinary ornamentation of facades, found even on tombs hidden beneath some of the galleries. The best-preserved structure, and the one most clearly embodying the spirit of this architecture, is the Palace of the Columns (*plates 308–313*). Its layout gives primary importance to a broad, elongated antechamber that leads directly to the chambers in the rear, which are disposed around a patio (*plates 309, 311*).

From a constructional point of view, it is surprising to see the enormous monolithic lintels of the doors and the elegant columns (also monolithic) that help support the roof of the antechamber. Yet even more astonishing is the way the walls are made: we find here a degree of precision that is almost unbelievable, inasmuch as Mesoamerican technology knew nothing of the harder metals, having in this era just begun to work with gold, silver, and copper according to techniques possibly imported from the south.

Cut and assembled with the delicate care of a goldsmith—as became the artisans of a region so outstanding in the working of ceramics and precious metals, and the cutting of fine stones—building stone was transformed at Mitla into a kind of lacework, resulting in elongated panels in which we can see as many as fourteen versions of the stepped fret design so common in pre-Hispanic art and one of the favorite motifs in the ceramics of the region (*plate 313*).

These rich panels, worked in soft limestone, seem to reflect a Maya influence. In the interiors of the halls we see them in simple horizontal bands (*plate 312*); on the exterior facades they create an undulating rhythm, their smooth surfaces and characteristic breaks underlined by frames clearly derived from the Classic Zapotec *tablero* in its final phase (*plate 310*). We note a slight incline in the outer corners, which imparts a certain illusion of curvature somewhat similar to that found in several buildings at Tulum, although in a completely different spirit.

But what Mitla gained in sumptuousness—an ornamental richness only appreciated from a distance—it lost in monumentality and in the kind of grandeur that for so many centuries had made Monte Albán one of the loftiest spiritual sites in Mesoamerica.

Finally, we can include in this region's architectural repertory numerous representations of buildings that appear in the Mixtec codices; despite their unique style and their clearly conventional character, these reproductions give us some idea of the vast spectrum of forms employed.

The Post-Classic Maya

Toward the end of the Classic period, the Putún (Chontal Maya)

316. *Chichén Itzá: section of the Caracol*

317. *Chichén Itzá: Caracol. Plan of the observation chamber showing the spiral stairway and the three apertures oriented toward precise astronomical directions*

318. *Chichén Itzá: Castillo, or Temple of Kulkulkán, seen from the summit of the Temple of the Warriors* ▷

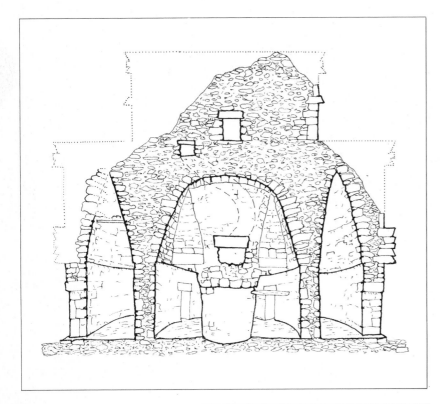

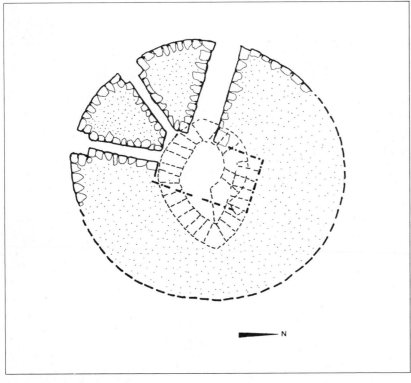

an aggressive trading group and the seafarers of Mesoamerica, brought a new element to Maya culture. The Putún culture and people were hybrid Maya-Náhuat, having received some Mexican blood and many bold habits from Náhuat-speaking (an early form of the Náhuatl language) neighbors near their original home in southern Campeche and the delta of the Usumacinta and Grijalva rivers in Tabasco. These people were traveling merchants and seem to have been little interested in art, architecture, or astronomy, in contrast to the Maya east and northeast of them.

The following data on the Putún and their tremendous impact on the Late Classic and Post-Classic Maya world was gathered by Thompson.[9] The Putún controlled the sea routes around the Yucatán peninsula. Called the Itzá in Yucatán, a branch of these people established themselves on the island of Cozumel. From here they crossed to the mainland and conquered many centers, including Chichén (in 918 A.D.). When, according to sources, the Toltec culture hero Quetzalcóatl (called Kulkulkán in the Maya tongue) fled from Tula with his followers in either the tenth or the twelfth century, these Toltecs found a central Mexican-type culture in Chichén Itzá, and brought still more Toltec-Mexican influence to Yucatán. Other Putún groups had earlier won temporary control of Yaxchilán (c. 730 A.D.) and had established a trading base at Altar de Sacrificios, a strategic point at the joining of the Pasión and Chixoy rivers. Seibal, on the Pasión, was conquered around 850, and other sites in the Belize River drainage followed. In Seibal we see non-Maya features of chieftains portrayed on the stelae.

With the end of the Classic period and the overthrow of the Maya nobility the newer Putún leaders also lost their power in this region. Some of the Putún went south of the Pasión River and gave their new land the same name as that of their homeland: *Acalan* "Land of the Canoe People." There they continued, independent until 1695, and were called the Lacandón. The Itzá, after abandoning Chichén in the twelfth century, went to Petén-Itzá in Guatemala where they were not subdued until 1697, by the Spaniards.

A good deal of the Maya region was controlled partially or absolutely by the Putún between 850 and 950 A.D., from Tabasco and Campeche in the west, to the east coast of the Yucatán peninsula from the northern tip of this peninsula, south to below the Pasión drainage in Guatemala. The most marked Putún influence is found at Chichén Itzá. Central Mexican influence is also clearly seen at Puuc sites such as Uxmal and Kabáh. The Xiuh, rulers of Uxmal, were conscious of their Toltec ancestry.

The three principal Maya cities—Chichén Itzá, Uxmal, and

319. *Chichén Itzá: Castillo*

320. *Chichén Itzá: Castillo. Detail of a plumed serpent's head at the foot of the main stairway* ▷

Mayapán—formed the so-called Triple Alliance in 1194 A.D. The alliance offered protection not only against outsiders but from each other, since all three were bellicose. Only a century or so earlier the central highland influence had brought about an artistic and commercial renaissance, with a diffusion of Toltec culture, metallurgy (probably introduced from Central America), thin orange pottery from Veracruz and Tabasco, lead-colored pottery from Guatemala, alabaster vessels from Honduras, Mixtec-inspired turquoise mosaics and codex-style murals at Tulum and Santa Rita.[10] But after the Triple Alliance Maya civilization went into a decline. Mayapán eventually assumed political control, which it retained with the help of Aztec mercenaries. Cities were fortified, human sacrifice became more and more common, the arts stagnated. Mayapán fell in 1460 A.D. With the Conquest of 1541, Montejo took T'ho (modern Mérida) for the Spaniards.

Maya-Toltec Architecture of Chichén Itzá

The architecture that developed in Chichén Itzá under Toltec rule dramatically illustrates the impact on their surroundings of this young and bellicose group from the Mexican plateau. In scene after scene—carved in relief on stone, painted in murals, or hammered in gold *repoussé* work—we see these new and zealous masters, garbed and armed in Toltec style, in the act of conquering a Maya village or, transported in boats by Maya oarsmen, preening themselves as they patrol the Yucatán coast.

It would, however, be incorrect to regard the art created under the Toltecs at Chichén Itzá merely as a replica of what was being done at that time in far-away Tula. On the contrary—and as often happens in many of the hybrid arts when the conquered peoples have a richer cultural tradition than their conquerors—Chichén Itzá emerges not simply as a "bigger and better" version of Tula, for that metropolis of the Mexican plateau seems too modest and provincial to have been able to inspire all the things that made the new Chichén Itzá such a fascinating city.

To a large extent, the elements of the new city reflect a total break with the Yucatán peninsula's Classic traditions and suggest the sudden imposition of a cultural vocabulary undeniably Mexican in origin. But we find here such a sure hand and such creativity in the handling of these elements that we are led to suspect an active local participation in the development of what is known as Toltec art. In support of this hypothesis, some authors—including George Kubler and Román Piña Chán—state that in certain buildings at Chichén Itzá we sometimes find the evolutionary phases of elements that

322, 323. *Chichén Itzá: Castillo. Section and plan*

324. *Chichén Itzá: plan of the main buildings in the ceremonial precinct.* 1. *Ball Court* 2. *Temple of the Warriors* 3. *Castillo* 4. *Group of the Thousand Columns* 5. *Market*

325. *Chichén Itzá: plan of the Temple of the Warriors*

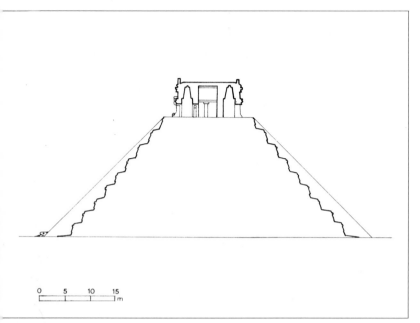

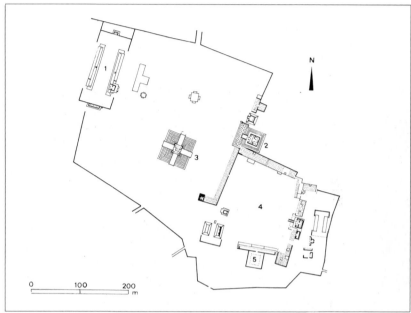

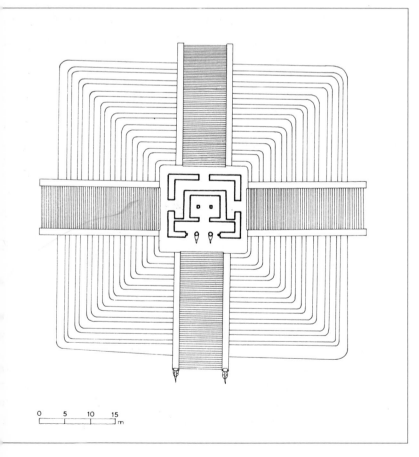

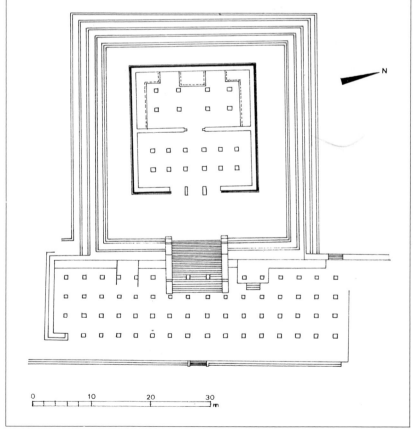

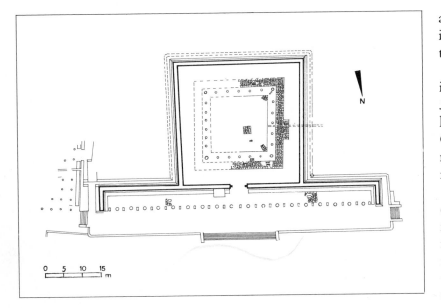

appear in Tula only in the final stage.[11] And beneath this undeniable influence of a young and vigorous tradition we can detect the master touch of the Maya craftsman.

An outstanding example of this cultural hybridization is found in the famous astronomical observatory known as the Caracol *(plates 315–317)*. The product of several construction phases, this building has an interesting circular shape—a form practically nonexistent in Classic Maya architecture (except for a cylindrical tower found recently in the Río Bec area). During this era, the form seems to have made a comeback on the Mexican plateau.

Like all of Chichén Itzá's architecture, the Caracol retains the elements of its regional stamp—an excellence in the cutting and fitting of stone; the use of the corbel vault; and the Maya decorative features of beveled moldings and masks of Chac. But we find many Toltec contributions as well: the plumed serpents that adorn the *alfardas* of the access stairway; the heads of Toltec warriors that border the upper platform; and the sculptural merlons that once crowned the observation tower. Surrounded by two circular, concentric corridors, the central body of this tower suggests a huge, thick mushroom *(plate 315)*, perforated at a point by a narrow spiral stairway (whence the name Caracol, meaning "snail"). The stairway *(plate 317)* leads to a semiruined chamber whose windows, still visible, embody a complex sequence of astronomical references, confirming fully the building's former function as an observatory.

The break with old regional traditions is seen even in the urban layout itself, with buildings departing from their usual compact placement (acropolis-type or in a quadrangle) to stand squarely in the middle of large esplanades. Their orientation is usually "Mexican" —that is, in accordance with the rules laid down in the central plateau centuries before *(plate 314)*.

In the center of Chichén Itzá's immense and irregular principal esplanade rises the most glorious fruit of this Maya-Toltec cultural fusion—the Castillo, or Temple of Kulkulkán *(plates 318, 319)*. Of relatively moderate dimensions compared with some of the bases at Teotihuacán, Cholula, Tikal, and other cities, this building is impressive well beyond its status as the largest in Chichén Itzá. Spectacular and daring in its placement, it sits apart from any other structure in the center of the gigantic esplanade *(plate 324)*. Much of its monumentality is due to the majestic proportions of the stepped base, whose ascent is subtly underlined by a succession of protruding moldings that become gradually smaller toward the top—and whose lines, inspired by the Toltec *tablero,* appear here in an infinitely softer version. We note the rounded corners and a general delicacy of shape

328. *Chichén Itzá: Temple of the Warriors. Plan indicating the superimposed structures and part of the colonnade of the Group of the Thousand Columns*

329. *Chichén Itzá: Temple of the Warriors and part of the Group of the Thousand Columns seen from the summit of the Castillo* ▷

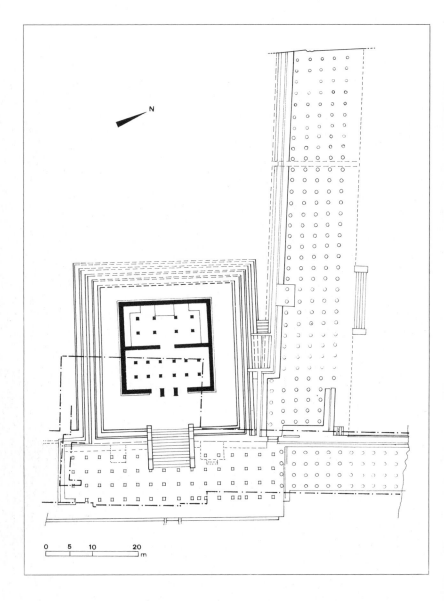

330. *Chichén Itzá:* chac-mool *statue at the entrance to the Temple of the Warriors*

331. *Chichén Itzá: Temple of the Warriors. Detail showing the pillars and the* chac-mool *statue* ▷

that is usually alien to Toltec sensibilities. Yet many elements of the building show Toltec—or perhaps more accurately, Mexican—origins, springing from the central plateau tradition. There are the serpents' heads at the foot of the principal stairway *(plate 320)*, the serpent-shaped columns that support the lintel of the entrance to the sanctuary on this same side; the *talud,* or inclined plane, that reinforces the lower part of the temple walls; and the stone sculptures in the form of cross-sectioned snails or crossed arrows, crowning the edge of the roof in the Mexican manner and definitively replacing the old Maya roof-comb.

One element that adds a particular stamp to the Castillo is the inclusion of a stairway on each of the four sides of its base *(plates 322, 323)*, unusual in Mesoamerican architecture, and here seemingly associated with some important cosmological symbolism. In fact, the sum of all the steps (91 on each stairway) amounts to 365 if we include the running stair that, like a socle, girds the base where it meets the esplanade floor. We should also mention an earlier building, although still within the Maya-Toltec period, that lies buried under the mass of the Castillo. Accessible today through a subterranean gallery, it shows the well-preserved remains of a sanctuary, including the impressive Red Jaguar Throne. More in the Maya than the Toltec style, this sculpture is beautifully highlighted with incrustations of stone and shell *(plate 321)*.

A preoccupation with interior space and with its integration into vast exterior spaces began to make itself felt in Yucatán architecture at the end of the Classic period, two or three centuries before Toltec domination. It takes on new life, with a more generalized utilization of columns, and we find groups of columns now supporting not only door lintels, but also the roofs of buildings, whether with Maya corbel vaults or flat as in the Mexican style. The walls became thin, or yielded to rows of columns or pillars—alternating frequently between groups of one and then the other. These formed colonnades with proportions never before seen in Mesoamerica, and gave the new Chichén Itzá a truly revolutionary look. The immense architectural complex known today as the Group of the Thousand Columns *(plates 328, 329)*, which was built in various stages, shows a surprising flexibility in the handling of spaces. Its great colonnades—bounded at times by the front of a building, or by thin walls—could form a spacious covered portico; provide a transitional element connecting two plazas; or even open over a wide *impluvium,* as in the case of the interior patio of what we call the Market, whose columns have a slimness unique in Mesoamerican architecture *(plates 326, 327)*.

At the opposite end from the Market, looking toward the central

332. *Chichén Itzá: Group of the Thousand Columns. Detail showing columns with bas-reliefs*

333. *Chichén Itzá: detail showing columns with bas-reliefs at the foot of the Temple of the Warriors* ▷

334. *Chichén Itzá: Temple of the Warriors. Detail of the entrance with serpent-shaped columns*

part of the esplanade, stands the Temple of the Warriors *(plates 328, 329),* whose general silhouette is reminiscent of Tula's Temple of Tlahuizcalpantecuhtli. This includes the pyramid-colonnade relationship, which reveals the same pillars that rise from the lower part of the stairway *(plates 276, 325).*

The sloping bodies of the base have *tableros* of a type more common to Teotihuacán buildings than to Toltec ones, but they are adorned with motifs from the Toltec repertory, such as eagles and jaguars devouring human hearts. Running along the foot of the base are typical attached benches, jutting out in some places like altars and enhanced by reliefs of plumed serpents and groups of richly dressed Toltec warriors. The theme of the Toltec warrior is repeated again and again *(plates 332, 333),* along with representations of the god Tlahuizcalpantecuhtli, on the four faces of the pillars that constitute the access portico to the temple. Many of the sculptures that in Tula were found mutilated or scattered can be seen here in their original context, including the typical dadoes or *alfardas* finials from the Mexican plateau —their heads of plumed serpents projecting forth menacingly *(plate 334)*—and a statue of a standard-bearer on the upper platform *(plate 335).*

In front of the entrance to the sanctuary *(plates 330, 331),* we find a *chac-mool* statue in its habitual reclining pose. The exterior walls of the facade display, over a Mexican *talud,* masks of Chac and fragments of beveled moldings springing from the Maya tradition. These last elements clearly illustrate the eclectic character of Maya-Toltec art, which in buildings such as the Caracol and the Castillo could achieve an intimate fusion—an authentic synthesis of two very divergent heritages—but which here, in the Temple of the Warriors, shows the elements of each of these traditions separately and in bold juxtaposition. Perhaps in this case it reflects a simple concession to local tradition, since all the other elements that comprise the interior of the sanctuary are also of Toltec origin—tall pillars covered in bas-relief, and the altar against the rear wall, adorned with plumed serpents and held aloft by small sculptures of atlantes.

Were it not for the technique and quality of their execution, many of Chichén Itzá's buildings would seem exclusively Toltec. Situated to the north of the Castillo, on the principal esplanade, are the Platform of the Jaguars and Eagles *(plates 336, 337)* and the Platform of Venus. With their large *tableros* of contrasting planes covered with bas-reliefs of Toltec themes, and with their four stairways flanked by *alfardas* in the form of plumed serpents, these two ceremonial platforms—which, according to the chronicler Fray Diego de Landa, were stages for theatrical representations "for the enjoyment of the

335. *Chichén Itzá : Temple of the Warriors*
336. *Chichén Itzá : Platform of the Jaguars and Eagles*

337. *Chichén Itzá : Platform of the Jaguars and Eagles. Detail of an alfarda in the form of a plumed serpent*
338. *Chichén Itzá : the ball court seen from the summit of the Castillo. In the foreground, right, the Platform of the Jaguars and Eagles (and behind it, the Tzompantli)*

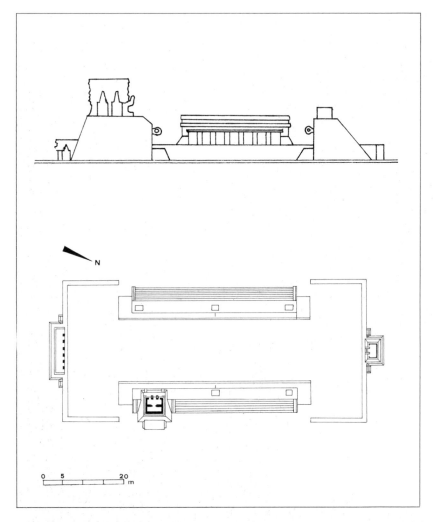

people"[12]—bear a noticeable similarity to the half-ruined altar occupying the center of the main plaza in distant Tula.

The same can be said of the immense *Tzompantli*—the altar of skulls—that rises near the Platform of the Jaguars and Eagles, displaying on its sides hallucinatory rows of human skulls strung on stakes. These images illustrate with dramatic impact the altar's macabre role in massive human sacrifice—an increasingly common practice in the last centuries before the Spanish Conquest.

Finally, there is the outsized ball court located near these structures, at one end of the principal esplanade *(plates 338–340)*; in many respects it is similar to Tula's larger court. Chichén Itzá's monumental ball court—its 550-foot (168-m.) length eclipsing that of the other 500 or more courts in Mesoamerica—astonishes us with its curious acoustical properties, and in other ways as well. Directly over one side of the court rises the Temple of the Jaguars, the fruit of a skillful sculptural integration in which Toltec elements predominate. Its heavy serpent-shaped columns *(plates 347, 348)* add a disquieting note to the universal architectural repertory of the independent support, and enable us to imagine how the columns of Tula's Temple of Tlahuizcalpantecuhtli probably looked before they lost the fanged head and the feathered rattlesnake tail that here protrude from the facade and rise above the lintel of the entrance.

From the elevated vertical walls that border the main section of the ball court *(plate 342)*, two rings jut out, decorated with the intertwined bodies of plumed serpents *(plate 343)*. The center and ends of the banquette running along the foot of these walls display finely carved bas-relief scenes depicting the sacrifice of a player by decapitation—the grand finale of one of these highly ritualistic encounters. We see both teams, their flashy outfits including protectors and other equipment. One of the players holds a knife in one hand and the head of his kneeling victim in the other, while six serpents and a plant with large stalks and graceful flowers spring symbolically from the victim's neck. Over a disc in the center of the scene we find the mask of the god of death, from whose jaws float the elegant scrolls that symbolize speech *(plate 341)*.

Thus, art in the new Chichén Itzá continued to flourish, its motifs reflecting the motley warrior apparatus and bloody ritual that the city's Toltec masters had grafted onto the old Maya foundations. The space of some two or three centuries witnessed the unbridled splendor of what Pollock describes as "a last flicker of life, tinged perhaps with the effects of cultural hybridization [and] . . . the finale of the great architectural tradition in the Maya area."[13]

341. *Chichén Itzá : ball court. Detail of a bas-relief carved on an interior banquette*

Mayapán

Exhausted by a series of wars that shook the peninsula, Chichén Itzá ceded its ruling position around the year 1200 to Mayapán, a city that would dominate the political panorama of the region for two centuries more, until the middle of the fifteenth century. Mayapán made a last attempt to revive some of the old Classic Maya traditions, erecting dated stelae and using quadrangular building layouts; but this city's ceremonial center never became, to any degree, but "a miniature copy of Chichén Itzá."[14] Indeed, we can detect in its artistic output a progressive deterioration that nothing could avert.

Even so, we find in the city of Mayapán factors that indicate an apparent evolution "toward a way of life in a progressively urban environment," a way of life in a sense much like our own.[15] We quote A. Ledyard Smith's description of a group of houses that must have belonged to a rich member of the local nobility: ". . . a main house for the master; various smaller ones for the family of some relative, and for the servants; a kitchen; a family chapel and a group of small altars for the favorite idols; . . . a house for the majordomo, or *caluac,* and another in which to store the provisions that the latter caused to be brought from regions under his master's dominion; cages to house birds and small animals; and, perhaps, an artificial garden—for as there was no earth in this area, only limestone, earth had to be brought in and retained by stone borders."[16]

Tulum and the Cities of the East Coast of the Yucatán

Among the last bulwarks of Maya culture on the Yucatán peninsula were the modest-sized cities—some partially or totally fortified—that, along with small watchtowers situated at strategic distances, dotted the east coast of the peninsula, and also islands such as Isla Mujeres and Cozumel (an important sanctuary existed during these last centuries on the latter island). Many cities of this region were probably founded in an earlier era, but their appearance today suggests the difficulties of Post-Classic times during which an unstable political balance called for defensive measures. Such is the case with Ichpaatún, and with Xelhá, located on a small peninsula whose narrow neck (410 feet, or 125 m.) was protected by a wall almost 10 feet (3 m.) high—described by Lothrop as having "a curious bastion that projected over the line of defense to protect the single portal."[17]

Of all the sites in this region, it is undoubtedly the walled city of Tulum that stands out *(plate 349)*—not only for its well-preserved fortifications, but also for its marked stylistic characteristics and because it is, as Hardoy says, "the one that most closely approximates in form and layout our own image of a city. [Here] . . . perhaps for

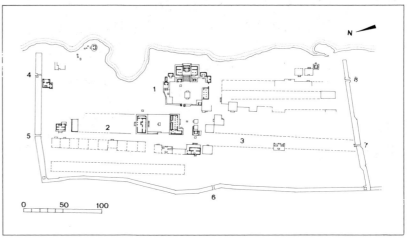

350. *Tulum: the Castillo (and the Temple of the Descending God seen from the north cliff)*
351. *Tulum: Castillo*
352. *Tulum: Temple of the Descending God* ▷

355. *Tulum: Temple 5*

356. *Tulum: Temple 35, probably dedicated to the god of water*

357. *Tulum: Temple 7 (Temple of the Descending God)*

the first time among Maya cities, we find clearly recognizable traces of two—and perhaps three—streets with urban characteristics, bordered by palaces, residences, and smaller buildings . . . reflecting a tendency to attempt alignment along a street that runs exactly the length of the city in a north-south direction."[18]

As in other shoreline cities, the serpent-shaped columns of Tulum's Castillo *(plates 350, 351)* and the colonnades that, along with slender walls, composed its buildings, all reveal the Maya-Toltec influence that Chichén Itzá had exerted on this region for several centuries. But despite this influence, and despite a certain poverty of construction, the architecture of the east coast shows a style of its own, recognizable mainly in the strong concave slope of the exterior walls. The building best illustrating this regional tendency is perhaps the small Temple of the Descending God *(plate 352)*, in which the curvature of the walls is accentuated by a marked leaning that finds its counterpart in the slightly trapezoidal doorway *(plates 355–357)*. Another variant can be seen in the upper part of the Temple of the Frescoes *(plates 353, 354)*, whose curved planes show a subtle break that further embellishes the structure. The frescoes, like other paintings of the east coast, are similar to the Maya codices, and at the same time reminiscent of Mixtec manuscripts.

Let us note, finally, as a distinctive feature of the local style, the great profiles carved on the corners of the lower portico *(plate 354)* and the frequent representations of the Descending God that usually appear in niches over the doorways.

Western and Northwestern Mexico

Western Mexico had a village culture from beginning to end, with no writing or numbering system that we know of, and with little monumental architecture of the type seen at Post-Classic Tzintzuntzan in Michoacán.

At this writing, the term "western Mexico" includes Michoacán, Guanajuato, the coastal states of Jalisco, Nayarit, Colima, Sinaloa, and Guerrero. A new classification will soon be necessary, for it is obvious that Guerrero with its Olmec cave paintings, abstract Mezcala stone carvings, unique clay figurines, and Maya-influenced centers such as Xochipala, is a culture different from the rest. For that matter Michoacán has traits that differ from those farther west, suggesting yet a third division.

Continuing village life accounts for the delightful clay figurines found especially in Colima. At first glance they represent only everyday activities—women combing their hair, mothers coddling babies, children playing with animals, fat cuddly dogs; but warriors and

359. *Tzintzuntzan: detail of a yácata*

360, 361. *Small terra-cotta models of houses from Nayarit, western Mexico. Mexico City, National Museum of Anthropology*

shamans are also portrayed. Shaft tombs typify architecture in Jalisco and Colima. El Ixtépete and Jalisco also reveal Teotihuacán influences.

Ixtlán del Río in Nayarit came into existence at a later period, as did the dramatic *yácata* complex in Michoacán. The Tarascans, great warriors and great artisans, were the builders of these *yácatas,* circular-combined-with-rectangular-form pyramids, such as are found at Tzintzuntzan, their capital. We call these people Tarascans because it is said that when the Spaniards came to Michoacán the lords there gave them their daughters in marriage and therefore called the Europeans *tarascue,* "sons-in-law." The Tarascans called themselves *Uasúsecha* ("Eagles") and today use the name *Purépecha,* "People of the Land."

Contemporaries of the Aztecs, the Tarascans—some chroniclers say—accompanied them on their pilgrimage from the Seven Caves in Aztlan, "since they were of the same band and all had come out of the seventh cave, all speaking the same language."[19] But when they reached Lake Pátzcuaro (in the present-day state of Michoacán), part of the group went in to bathe, leaving their clothes on the shore. The others stole the garments and fled. The bathers then learned to go about nude, for lack of clothing, and even changed their language so they would no longer be associated with the Aztecs.

This legend shows that Náhuat groups, related to the people of Jalisco, Nayarit, and Colima, settled here early in the Post-Classic period. Subsequent migrations brought different people who fused with the early settlers. Strong South American influence is evident in the Tarascan culture, visible in language similarities between Tarascan and some Peruvian tongues, and in pottery forms. Metal probably came to Mexico from the south also, being introduced into Oaxaca's Pacific coast and the western region, also via the Pacific, early in Post-Classic times. The Tarascans were great metallurgists and possessed other advanced Mesoamerican traits such as a calendar system, mathematics, and hieroglyphic writing. As warriors they were so outstanding that the Aztecs, who had conquered most of Mesoamerica, were not able to subdue them. These people worshiped the god of sun and fire, Curicáveri, above all other deities.

Northwestern Mexico might well be called an extension of the southwestern United States cultures if it were not for influences received here from the central highlands of Mexico. Cultural manifestations of this type date from the Late Pre-Classic and from the Post-Classic. These manifestations include temple bases and ball courts in Durango, a canal system of irrigation in Chihuahua, fortifications in Zacatecas and Durango, small ceremonial centers and polychrome pottery in Guanajuato, paint cloisonné decoration in Sinaloa, and ball courts and architectural remains in San Luis Potosí.[20] La Quemada in

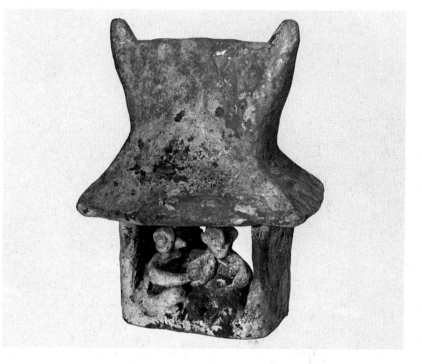

362. *Small terra-cotta model of a temple built on a platform, from western Mexico. Mexico City, National Museum of Anthropology*

Zacatecas and Casas Grandes in Chihuahua are the most important sites in the region.

In reviewing the relationship between the southwestern United States and northwestern Mexico, we must remember that millennia ago no maps existed and lines between cultural areas were not sharply drawn. Between 7000 and 5000 B.C. this area—which we will so designate—reflected the Desert pre-ceramic cultural tradition, and only after 5000 B.C. did the agricultural complex characteristic of Meso-america (bottle gourd, squash, corn, cotton, and beans) mark the rise of sedentary cultures to the south. It was not until the Late Pre-Classic (c. 100 B.C.) that the Southwest began to show influences from Mesoamerica, in the form of pottery making and the use of hybrid maize. Weaver believes that cultural traits may have passed along the Pacific coastal plain of Nayarit and Sinaloa to Sonora, or through the eastern slopes of the Sierra Madre occidental range, occupied by farming communities.[21] Around 900 A.D., at the time of the southwestern Anasazi expansion, the Aztatlán culture, reflecting Mixteca-Puebla traits, flourished in coastal Sinaloa.

Even in the sixteenth century northwestern Mexico and the southwestern United States formed an almost homogeneous region. The European conquistadors believed it to correspond to the Cíbola region, with its seven cities with silver palaces decorated in precious stones (the legend probably arose from Aztec descriptions of their own native land, with the Seven Caves—a veritable terrestrial paradise). Coronado, with a band of 300 Spaniards, 1,000 Indians, and 1,000 horses, launched an expedition to discover Cíbola, but found nothing except deserts, mountains, and groups of nomads.

POST-CLASSIC ARCHITECTURE IN WESTERN AND NORTHWESTERN MEXICO

Nayarit

In the rich output of ceramic products from Nayarit, we find miniature representations of buildings *(plates 360–362)* and happy group scenes that reflect a thousand facets of life as it was lived in the tropical villages of that region up to the end of the Classic period and the beginning of the Post-Classic era. As Von Winning recently demonstrated, there is a vast and varied documentation of the simple Nayarit architecture: houses, often of two floors and invariably built of perishable materials, their graceful roofs wearing a polychrome geometric decoration; and small temples, platforms, or altars.[22]

The masonry architecture of Ixtlán del Río may date from a later time. Among these buildings we find a large elevated platform on which two altars stand. It is round in shape, with sloping walls, and has a heavy parapet perforated with cruciform motifs *(plate 363)*.

Michoacán

It was in Michoacán, in the centuries just preceding the Spanish Conquest, that the powerful Tarascan kingdom emerged. Establishing itself in the lake region, its people became known for their elegant work in gold, silver, and copper, and for the delicacy of their ceramics. The Tarascans were creators of a vigorous hard-stone sculpture with abrupt angles, frequently inspired by such Toltec motifs as the *chac-mool*. Their great ceremonial complexes were dominated by *yácatas,* whose unmistakable regional style of stepped bases combined elongated rectangular masses with truncated-conical elements. Examples can be seen at Tzintzuntzan *(plates 358, 359)* and Ihuatzio, the last capitals of the Tarascan kingdom, built on the shores of Lake Pátzcuaro.

Northern Mexico

To the north we find regions of semidesert that generally remained outside the mainstream of Mesoamerican architectural developments. Lands inhabited by nomadic hunters whose incursions constituted a perpetual menace to agricultural communities, these regions had been touched by civilizing currents on more than one occasion, particularly in the north. It is also probable that the citizens of Teotihuacán, then the Toltecs, and finally the Aztecs, all maintained garrisons in strategic places in order to control the thrust of the nomadic hordes. Perhaps this was the case with La Quemada, a partially fortified city situated far north. Its existence may date from the time of Teotihuacán's splendor, but it tends to reflect a Toltec influence. Its pyramid, along with the great ball court, has a different shape from those we have seen in the south.

Not far from La Quemada lie the sites called Shroeder and Alta Vista de Chalchihuites. There are a multitude of other small sites, but only La Quemada and Chalchihuites have ball courts. To the north, Casas Grandes, in the state of Chihuahua, shows closer ties with the southwestern United States than with Mesoamerica, although since 1300 A.D. many Mesoamerican traits—I-shaped ball courts, platforms, truncated pyramids, motifs showing plumed serpents and human sacrifices—indicate a late expansion of this center.[23] Prior to this period, we see northern influences in the form of semisubterranean houses and ceremonial *kivas*.

NOTES / SYNOPTIC TABLES / SELECTED BIBLIOGRAPHY / INDEX
LIST OF PLATES / PHOTOGRAPHIC CREDITS

NOTES

Chapter One

[1]Fray Gerónimo de Mendieta, *Historia Eclesiástica Indiana*, edited by Salvador Chávez Hayhoe, Mexico, n.d., Vol. I, pp. 83–84.

[2]Paul Kirchhoff, "Mesoamérica. Sus límites geográficos, composición étnica y caracteres culturales," supplement of *Tlatoani*, 1960.

[3]E.R. Wolf, *Sons of the Shaking Earth*, Chicago, University of Chicago Press, 1959, pp. 15–16.

[4]Wigberto Jiménez Moreno, *Historia Antigua de México*, Mexico, Ediciones S.A.E. N.A.H., 1956, p. 13.

[5]E.R. Wolf, *op. cit.*, p. 37.

[6]Muriel Porter Weaver, *The Aztecs, Maya, and Their Predecessors*, New York-London, Seminar Press, 1972, p. 23.

[7]Michael D. Coe, *America's First Civilization: Discovering the Olmec*, New York, American Heritage Publishing Company and The Smithsonian Institution, 1968, p. 32.

[8]Fray Diego Durán, *Book of the Gods and Rites and the Ancient Calendar*, translated and edited by Fernando Horcasitas and Doris Heyden, preface by Miguel León-Portilla, Norman, University of Oklahoma Press, 1971, p. 317.

Chapter Two

[1]Muriel Porter Weaver, *The Aztecs, Maya, and Their Predecessors*, New York-London, Seminar Press, 1972, p. 35.

[2]Román Piña Chán, *A Guide to Mexican Archaeology*, Mexico, Ediciones Minutiae Mexicana, 1971, p. 42.

[3]Muriel Porter Weaver, *op. cit.*, pp. 64–65.

[4]Miguel Covarrubias, *Indian Art of Mexico and Central America*, New York, Knopf, 1957, p. 28.

[5]Ibid., p. 83.

[6]Michael D. Coe, *America's First Civilization: Discovering the Olmec*, New York, American Heritage Publishing Company and The Smithsonian Institution, 1968.

[7]Isabel Kelly, "Vasijas de Colima con boca de estribo," *Boletín del Instituto Nacional de Antropología e Historia*, No. 42, December 1970.

[8]Personal communication from Arturo Oliveros.

[9]Muriel Porter Weaver, *op. cit.*, p. 76.

[10]K.V. Flannery, A.V. Kirkby, M.J. Kirkby, A.W. Williams, "Farming Systems and Political Growth in Ancient Oaxaca, Mexico," *Science*, No. 158, 1967.

[11]Muriel Porter Weaver, *op. cit.*, p. 58.

[12]Román Piña Chán, *Una visión del México prehispánico*, Mexico, Universidad Nacional Autónoma de México, 1967, p. 131.

[13]Michael D. Coe, "La Victoria, an Early Site on the Pacific Coast of Guatemala," *Peabody Museum Archaeological and Ethnological Papers*, Harvard University, Cambridge, Mass., 1961. See also B.J. Meggers, C. Evans, E. Estrada, "Early Formative Period of Coastal Ecuador: The Valdivia and Machalilla Phases," *Smithsonian Contributions to Anthropology*, No. 1, Washington, D.C., 1965.

[14]Muriel Porter Weaver, *op. cit.*, p. 285.

[15]Ignacio Bernal, *The Olmec World*, Berkeley and Los Angeles, University of California Press, 1969, p. 112.

[16]See the chapter on the Maya for an explanation of the "Long Count."

[17]Michael D. Coe, *The Jaguar's Children: Pre-Classic Central Mexico*, New York, Museum of Primitive Art, 1965.

[18]Matthew Stirling, quoted in Peter T. Furst, "The Olmec Were-Jaguar Motif in the Light of Ethnographic Reality," *Dumbarton Oaks Conference on the Olmec, 1967*, Washington, D.C., 1968, p. 144.

[19]Michael D. Coe, *America's First Civilization: Discovering the Olmec*, New York, American Heritage Publishing Company and The Smithsonian Institution, 1968, p. 110.

[20]Not only do the relief carvings representing Aztec heads still exist in Mexico City's Chapultepec Park, but Fray Diego Durán, in his sixteenth-century chronicle, says that the Aztecs made stone statues of great men to perpetuate their memory. See D. Durán, *Historia de las Indias de Nueva España e Islas de la Tierra Firme*, edited by Angel M. Garibay, Mexico City, Porrúa, 1967, Vol. II, pp. 99, 122. See also Paul Gendrop, *El México Antiguo: Ancient Mexico*, Mexico, Trillas, 1972, p. 27.

[21]Michael D. Coe, *America's First Civilization: Discovering the Olmec*, pp. 111–13.

[22]Ibid., p. 188.

[23]Charles R. Wicke, *Olmec: An Early Art Style of Precolumbian Mexico*, Tucson, University of Arizona Press, 1971.

[24]Jorge Angulo, "Señalando el concepto olmeca como religión" in *Religión en Mesoamérica*, Round Table XII, Mexico, Sociedad Mexicana de Antropología, 1972.

[25]These subterranean rooms have a primitive vaulted roof. In another center in the Puebla Valley, Tlalancaleca, we find the beginnings of urban planning (with probable traces of roads) and early stepped bases in stone in which the stairways are already flanked with *alfardas*, or lateral protections. In this center, too, between 300 and 100 B.C., we find the first examples known in Mesoamerica of the *talud-tablero* combination, an architectural element that reached its apogee later in Teotihuacán.

[26]Doris Heyden, "What is the Meaning of the Mexican Pyramid?," paper presented at the XL International Congress of Americanists, Rome, September 1972.

[27]William Holland, *Medicina Maya en los Altos de Chiapas*, translated by Daniel Cazés, Mexico, Instituto Nacional Indigenista, 1963, pp. 68–110.

Chapter Three

[1]René Millon, "Teotihuacán: Completion of Map of Giant Ancient City in the Valley of Mexico," *Science*, December 4, 1970, Vol. 170, pp. 1077–82.

[2]William T. Sanders and Barbara J. Price, *Mesoamerica: The Evolution of a Civilization*, New York, Random House, 1968, p. 141.

[3]René Millon, *op. cit.*

[4]Ibid.

[5]Fray Bernardino de Sahagún, *Florentine Codex. General History of the Things of New Spain*, translated into English from the Náhuatl by Arthur J.O. Anderson and Charles E. Dibble, Santa Fe, New Mexico, The School of American Research and The University of Utah, 1950–69, Book 7, p. 4.

[6]René Millon, *op. cit.*

[7]Bernardino de Sahagún, *op. cit.*, Book 10, p. 192.

[8]René Millon, Bruce Drewitt, and James A. Bennyhoff, "The Pyramid of the Sun at

Teotihuacán: 1959 Investigations," *Transactions of the American Philosophical Society*, n.s., Vol. 55, Part 6, Philadelphia, 1965, p. 10.

[9]George Kubler, "The Iconography of the Art of Teotihuacán," *Studies in Pre-Columbian Art and Archaeology*, No. 4, Washington, D.C., Dumbarton Oaks, 1967, p. 10.

[10]Laurette Séjourné, "Pensamiento y Religión en el México Antiguo," *Breviarios*, No. 128, Mexico, Fondo de Cultura Económica, 1964, p. 158.

[11]This is a hypothetical picture of the old Classic society at a time in which few peripheral centers possessed their own temples or public buildings.

[12]René Millon, "Teotihuacán," *Scientific American*, June 1967, Vol. 216, No. 6, p. 43.

[13]René Millon, *Science*, December 4, 1970, Vol. 170, pp. 1077–82.

[14]Ibid.

[15]William T. Sanders, "Life in a Classic Village," *Teotihuacán*, Round Table XI, Mexico, Sociedad Mexicana de Antropología, 1966, pp. 123–32.

[16]William T. Sanders, *op. cit.*, p. 132.

[17]René Millon, *Scientific American*, June 1967, Vol. 216, No. 6, p. 46.

[18]Attempts at deciphering Teotihuacán's glyphs were made by A. Caso, C. Millon, E. Pasztory, G. Kubler, G.H. von Winning, E. Rattray, R. Chadwick, L. Séjourné, and D. Heyden.

[19]Muriel Porter Weaver, *The Aztecs, Maya, and Their Predecessors*, New York-London, Seminar Press, 1972, p. 139.

[20]Robert H. Cobean, Michael D. Coe, Edward A. Perry, Jr., Karl K. Turekian, Dinkar A. Kharkar, "Obsidian Trade at San Lorenzo Tenochtitlán, Mexico," *Science*, Vol. 174, No. 4010, November 12, 1971, p. 666.

[21]Ibid., p. 670.

[22]Jaime Litvak, "La problemática de la arqueología en el Estado de Morelos," paper presented at the conference of the Sociedad Mexicana de Antropología, Mexico, November 11, 1972.

[23]Román Piña Chán, *A Guide to Mexican Archaeology*, Mexico, Ediciones Minutiae Mexicana, 1971, p. 57.

[24]William T. Sanders, *The Cultural Ecology of the Teotihuacán Valley. A Preliminary Report of the Results of the Teotihuacán Valley Project*, Department of Sociology and Anthropology, The Pennsylvania State University, September 1965, p. 129.

[25]So called because the Aztecs who came along after Teotihuacán's decline believed that the altars they found were tombs.

[26]René Millon, "Extensión y población de la ciudad de Teotihuacán en sus diferentes períodos: un cálculo provisional," *Teotihuacán*, Round Table XI, Mexico, Sociedad Mexicana de Antropología, 1966, p. 5.

[27]The construction technique of the small pyramidal bases that run along the quadrangular platform of the Citadel consists of a fill of earth, covered with stone, upon which a covering of adobes was laid (personal communication from Evelyn Rattray).

[28]René Millon, *op. cit.*, pp. 75–76.

[29]Matthew Wallrath, "The Calle de los Muertos Complex: a Possible Macrocomplex of Structures near the Center of Teotihuacán," *Teotihuacán*, Round Table XI, Mexico, Sociedad Mexicana de Antropología, 1966, p. 115.

[30]Jorge Hardoy, *Ciudades Precolombinas*, Buenos Aires, Ediciones Infinito, 1964, p. 91.

[31]Otto Schöndube, "Teotihuacán, Ciudad de los Dioses," *Imagen de México*, No. 3, Mexico, 1971, p. 18.

[32]René Millon, *Science*, December 4, 1970, Vol. 170, pp. 1077–82.

[33]Jorge Hardoy, *op. cit.*, p. 89.

[34]Bruce Drewitt, "Planeación en la Antigua Ciudad de Teotihuacán," *Teotihuacán*, Round Table XI, Mexico, Sociedad Mexicana de Antropología, 1966, pp. 86–87.

[35]René Millon, *Scientific American*, June 1967, Vol. 216, No. 6, p. 41.

[36]Jorge R. Acosta, *El palacio de Quetzalpapálotl*, Mexico, Instituto Nacional de Antropología e Historia, 1964.

[37]Laurette Séjourné, *Un Palacio en la Ciudad de los Dioses*, Mexico, Fondo de Cultura Económica, 1959; *Arquitectura y Pintura en Teotihuacán*, Mexico, Siglo XXI Editores, 1966.

[38]Fray Juan de Torquemada, *Monarquía Indiana*, edited by Salvador Chávez Hayhoe, Mexico, 1943, Vol. I, p. 252.

[39]George Kubler, "La iconografía del arte de Teotihuacán," *Teotihuacán*, Round Table XI, Mexico, Sociedad Mexicana de Antropología, 1972, pp. 69–85.

Chapter Four

[1]Personal communication from Norberto González and Rodolfo Velázquez Cano.

[2]Florencia Müller, "El Origen de los barrios de Cholula," *Proyecto Puebla-Tlaxcala*, Mexico, Instituto Nacional de Antropología e Historia, 1972 (mimeographed copy).

[3]Ignacio Marquina, *Arquitectura Prehispánica*, Instituto Nacional de Antropología e Historia, 1951, p. 115.

[4]Fray Diego Durán, *Historia de las Indias de Nueva España e Islas de la Tierra Firme*, edited by Angel M. Garibay, Mexico, Porrúa, 1967, Vol. II, p. 243.

[5]Fray Diego Durán, *Book of the Gods and Rites and the Ancient Calendar*, translated and edited by Fernando Horcasitas and Doris Heyden, preface by Miguel León-Portilla, Norman, University of Oklahoma Press, 1971, pp. 91–92.

[6]Tatiana Proskouriakoff, *Varieties of Classic Central Veracruz Sculpture*, Carnegie Institution, Washington, D.C., 1954, pp. 63–100.

[7]Miguel Covarrubias, *Indian Art of Mexico and Central America*, New York, Knopf, 1957, p. 173.

[8]Michael D. Coe, "The Archaeological Sequence at San Lorenzo Tenochtitlan," *Contributions of the University of California, Archaeological Research Facility*, No. 8, 1970, pp. 27–29.

[9]Fray Diego Durán, *op. cit.*, 1971, p. 316.

[10]Ibid., pp. 312–19.

[11]Octavio Paz, "Risa y penitencia," *Magia de la Risa*, Veracruz University, 1962, p. 12.

[12]Jorge Hardoy, *Ciudades Precolombinas*, Buenos Aires, Ediciones Infinito, 1964, pp. 134–35.

[13]Octavio Paz, *op. cit.*, p. 12.

[14]Ignacio Bernal, "La presencia olmeca en Oaxaca," *Culturas de Oaxaca*, No. 1, Mexico, Museo Nacional de Antropología, 1967, p. 2.

[15]John Paddock, *Ancient Oaxaca*, Stanford, Stanford University Press, 1966, p. 99.

[16]Personal communication from John Paddock.

[17]René Millon and Robert E. Longacre, "Proto-Mixtecan and Proto-Amuzgo-Mixtecan Vocabularies: a preliminary cultural analysis," *Anthropological Linguistics*, Vol. II, Part 4, 1961, pp. 1–44.

[18]John Paddock, *op. cit.*, p. 120.

19John Paddock, information from *Ancient Oaxaca, op. cit.*; "A beginning in the Ñuiñe," *Bulletin of Oaxaca Studies*, Mitla, Frissell Museum of Zapotec Art, No. 6, April 30, 1970, pp. 2–21; and from "El Esplendor de los Mixtecos," *Culturas de Oaxaca*, No. 4, Mexico, Museo Nacional de Antropología, 1967.

20Jorge Hardoy, *op. cit.*, p. 138.

21Ibid.

22Raúl Flores Guerrero, *Arte Mexicano: Epoca Prehispánica*, Mexico, Hermes, 1962, p. 133.

23Paul Westheim, *Arte Antiguo de México*, Mexico, Fondo de Cultura Económica, 1950, p. 280.

24Raúl Flores Guerrero, *op. cit.*

25Ibid.

Chapter Five

1*Popol Vuh: The Sacred Book of the Ancient Quiché Maya*, English translation by Delia Goetz and Sylvanus G. Morley, from the Spanish translation by Adrián Recinos, Norman, University of Oklahoma Press, 1950.

2George W. Brainerd, *The Maya Civilization*, Los Angeles, Southwest Museum, 1954, p. 7.

3Miguel Covarrubias, *Indian Art of Mexico and Central America*, New York, Knopf, 1957, p. 204.

4Frederick A. Peterson, *Ancient Mexico*, London, Allen and Unwin, 1969, p. 193.

5Román Piña Chán, *Una visión del México Prehispánico*, Mexico, Universidad Nacional Autónoma de México, 1967, p. 168.

6Miguel Covarrubias, *op. cit.*, p. 208.

7Betty Bell, "An Appraisal of the Maya Civilization," *The Ancient Maya*, by Sylvanus G. Morley, Stanford, Stanford University Press, 1956, p. 427.

8Ibid., p. 437.

9On the occasion of the October 1971 symposium of the School of American Research of the National Science Foundation at Santa Fe, New Mexico, which dealt with new interpretations of the decline of Maya civilization in the eighth century. See Gordon R. Willey and Demitri B. Shimkin, "Why did the Pre-Columbian Maya Civilization Collapse?," *Science*, Vol. 173, No. 3997, August 13, 1971, pp. 656–58. The five hypotheses on this subject were set forth in this symposium.

10J. Eric S. Thompson, *Maya History and Religion*, Norman, University of Oklahoma Press, 1970, p. 43.

11Muriel Porter Weaver, *The Aztecs, Maya, and Their Predecessors*, New York-London, Seminar Press, 1972, p. 155.

12Jorge Hardoy, *Ciudades Precolombinas*, Buenos Aires, Ediciones Infinito, 1964, p. 252.

13W.A. Haviland, "Tikal, Guatemala, and Mesoamerican Urbanism," *World Archaeology*, Oxford, 1970, pp. 186–98; cited by Muriel Porter Weaver, *op. cit.*, p. 155.

14William R. Coe, "Tikal, Ten Years of Study of a Maya Ruin in the Lowlands of Guatemala," *Expedition*, Vol. 8, No. 1, 1965, p. 47.

15Paul Westheim, *Arte Antiguo de México*, Mexico, Fondo de Cultura Económica, 1950, p. 308.

16William R. Bullard, Jr., "Maya Settlement Patterns in Northeastern Petén, Guate-

mala," *American Antiquity*, Vol. XXV, No. 3, 1960, pp. 355–72.

17Jorge Hardoy, *op. cit.*, p. 294.

18Ibid., pp. 265–66.

19Nicholas M. Hellmuth, *Report on First Season Explorations and Excavations at Yaxhá, El Petén, Guatemala, 1970*, New Haven, 1971.

20Beatriz de la Fuente, *La escultura de Palenque*, Mexico, Universidad Nacional Autónoma de México, 1965, p. 179.

21Raúl Flores Guerrero, *Arte Mexicano: Epoca Prehispánica*, Mexico, Hermes, 1962, p. 216.

22Jack D. Eaton, *Chicanná, an Elite Center in the Río Bec Region*, New Orleans, Tulane University Press, 1971.

23H.E.D. Pollock, "Architecture of the Maya Lowlands," *Handbook of the Middle American Indians*, vol. 2, part I, Austin, University of Texas Press, 1965.

24David E. Potter, *Architectural Style at Becán during the Maya Late Classic Period*, New Orleans, Tulane University Press, 1972.

25Marta Foncerrada de Molina, *La escultura arquitectónica de Uxmal*, Mexico, Universidad Nacional Autónoma de México, 1965, p. 39.

26Another similar case, in the conception of the volumes if not in the decoration, is that of Culucbalom, in the Río Bec region.

27Marta Foncerrada de Molina, *op. cit.*

Chapter Six

1George Kubler, "The Iconography of the Art of Teotihuacán," *Studies in Pre-Columbian Art and Archaeology*, No. 4, Dumbarton Oaks, Trustees for Harvard University, 1967, pp. 12–13.

2Fray Diego Durán, *The Aztecs: The History of the Indies of New Spain*, translated and annotated by Doris Heyden and Fernando Horcasitas, New York, Orion Press, 1964, p. 11.

3David C. Grove, "The Olmec Paintings of Oxtotitlan Cave, Guerrero, Mexico," *Studies in Pre-Columbian Art and Archaeology*, Dumbarton Oaks, Trustees for Harvard University, 1970. See also Emily Edwards, *Painted Walls of Mexico: From Prehistoric Times until Today*, photographs by M. Alvarez Bravo, Austin, University of Texas Press, 1966, p. 43.

4Florencia Müller, "Chimalacatlan," *Acta Antropológica*, Vol. III, Part 1, Mexico, 1948.

5Personal communication from Don Juan Guadalupe Martínez.

6Jaime Litvak, "Xochicalco en la caída del Clásico," *Anales de Antropología*, Instituto de Investigaciones Históricas, Universidad Nacional Autónoma de México, Vol. VII, 1970, pp. 131–44.

7Román Piña Chán, *A Guide to Mexican Archaeology*, Mexico, Ediciones Minutiae Mexicana, 1971, p. 58.

8Jorge Hardoy, *Ciudades Precolombinas*, Buenos Aires, Ediciones Infinito, 1964, pp. 126–29.

9Ibid., p. 129.

10César A. Sáenz, "Exploraciones en Xochicalco," *Boletín del Instituto Nacional de Antropología e Historia*, 1966, No. 26, p. 27.

11Fray Bernardino de Sahagún, *Florentine Codex. General History of the Thin*

New Spain, translated into English from the Náhuatl by Arthur J.O. Anderson and Charles E. Dibble, New Mexico, The School of American Research and The University of Utah, 1950–69, Book I, p. 2.

[12]Paul Kirchhoff, "Quetzalcóatl, Huémac y el fin de Tula," *Cuadernos Americanos*, 1955, pp. 163–96.

[13]Muriel Porter Weaver, *The Aztecs, Maya, and Their Predecessors*, New York-London, Seminar Press, 1972, pp. 204–5.

[14]George Kubler, *The Art and Architecture of Ancient America*, Harmondsworth, Penguin Books, 1961, pp. 176–77.

[15]Richard A. Diehl, *Preliminary Report, University of Missouri Archaeological Project at Tula, Hidalgo, Mexico, 1970–71 Field Season*, December 1, 1971.

[16]Michael W. Spence and Jeffrey R. Parsons, "Prehispanic Obsidian Exploitation in Central Mexico: a Preliminary Synthesis," *Miscellaneous Studies in Mexican Prehistory*, Ann Arbor, University of Michigan, 1972, No. 45, pp. 1–33.

[17]Personal communication from Eduardo Matos.

[18]Wigberto Jiménez Moreno, "Síntesis de la historia pretolteca de Mesoamérica," *Esplendor del México Antiguo*, Mexico, Center for Anthropological Studies of Mexico, Vol. II, 1959, pp. 1019–95.

[19]Jaime Litvak, "Mesoamérica y la Economía Azteca," *Los Aztecas: Su Historia y Su Vida*, Mexico, Museo Nacional de Antropología, 1965, pp. 5–6.

[20]Jacques Soustelle, *The Daily Life of the Aztecs*, Harmondsworth, Penguin Books, 1964, p. 208.

[21]Fray Diego Durán, *Book of the Gods and Rites and the Ancient Calendar*, translated and edited by Fernando Horcasitas and Doris Heyden, preface by Miguel León-Portilla, Norman, University of Oklahoma Press, 1971, p. 432.

[22]Ibid., p. 78.

[23]Ibid.

[24]Ignacio Marquina, *Arquitectura Prehispánica*, Mexico, Instituto Nacional de Antropología e Historia, 1951, pp. 186–98.

[25]Edward E. Calnek, *The Internal Structure of Cities in America. Pre-columbian Cities: The Case of Tenochtitlán*, contribution to the XXXIX International Congress of Americanists at Lima, August 1970. Mimeographed copy. Department of Anthropology of the University of Rochester, New York.

[26]Ibid.

[27]Ibid., p. 8; cites René Millon, personal communication from the author.

[28]Bernal Díaz del Castillo, *Historia Verdadera de la Conquista de la Nueva España*, Mexico, Porrúa, 1967, pp. 147–48.

[9]Luis Nicolau D'Owler, "Cartas de Relación de Hernán Cortés al Emperador Carlos V: Segunda Relación, 30 de octubre de 1520," *Cronistas de las Culturas Precolombinas, Antología*, Mexico, Fondo de Cultura Económica, 1963, pp. 178–79.

Fray Juan de Torquemada, *Monarquía Indiana*, edited by Salvador Chávez Hayhoe, vols., Mexico, 1943, Vol. I, p. 451; Vol. II, pp. 142, 146.

Miguel Covarrubias, "Las raíces del arte de Tenochtitlán," *México en el Arte*, No. 8, 49.

Luis Nicolau D'Owler, *op. cit.*

Bernal Díaz del Castillo, *op. cit.*, pp. 160–61.

Luis Nicolau D'Owler, *op. cit.*

Fray Diego Durán, *Historia de las Indias de Nueva España e Islas de la Tierra Firme*, edited by Angel M. Garibay, Mexico, Porrúa, 1967, Vol. II, p. 48.

Miguel León-Portilla, *Los Antiguos Mexicanos a través de sus Crónicas y Cantares*, México, Fondo de Cultura Económica, 1961, pp. 76–77.

Chapter Seven

[1]Florencia Müller, "El Origen de los barrios de Cholula," *Proyecto Puebla-Tlaxcala*, Mexico, Instituto Nacional de Antropología e Historia, 1972. Mimeographed copy.

[2]Sergio López Alonso, Zaid Lagunas Rodríguez, and Carlos Serrano Sánchez, "Datos Preliminares sobre los Enterramientos Humanos Prehispánicos de Cholula, Puebla," *Proyecto Puebla-Tlaxcala*, Mexico, Instituto Nacional de Antropología e Historia, 1972, pp. 3–10.

[3]Bernal Díaz del Castillo, *The True History of the Conquest of Mexico*, translated by Maurice Keating, New York, McBride & Co., 1927, pp. 153–54.

[4]Fray Diego Durán, *Book of the Gods and Rites and the Ancient Calendar*, translated and edited by Fernando Horcasitas and Doris Heyden, preface by Miguel León-Portilla, Norman, University of Oklahoma Press, 1971, pp. 128–30.

[5]Bernal Díaz del Castillo, *op. cit.*, p. 132.

[6]Fray Diego Durán, *op. cit.*, p. 163.

[7]Ibid., p. 68.

[8]Alfonso Caso, *Los Señoríos de Yanhuitlán*, proceedings and records of the XXXV International Congress of Americanists, Vol. I, Mexico, 1964, p. 448.

[9]J. Eric S. Thompson, *Maya History and Religion*, Norman, University of Oklahoma Press, 1970.

[10]Román Piña Chán, *A Guide to Mexican Archaeology*, Mexico, Ediciones Minutiae Mexicana, 1971, p. 109.

[11]Román Piña Chán, *Historia, Arqueología y Arte Prehispánico*, Mexico, Fondo de Cultura Económica, 1972, pp. 75–83.

[12]Fray Diego de Landa, *Relación de las Cosas de Yucatán*, edited by Pedro Robredo, Mexico, 1938, p. 218.

[13]H.E.D. Pollock, "Architecture of the Maya Lowlands," *Handbook of Middle American Indians*, edited by Gordon R. Willey, Vol. 2, Part I, Austin, University of Texas Press, 1965, p. 395.

[14]Ibid.

[15]Jorge Hardoy, *Ciudades Precolombinas*, Buenos Aires, Ediciones Infinito, 1964, p. 281.

[16]A. Ledyard Smith, *Residential Structures, Mayapán, Yucatán, Mexico*, Washington, D.C., Carnegie Institution, 1962, pp. 166–319.

[17]S.K. Lothrop, *Tulum: an Archaeological Study of the East Coast of Yucatán*, Washington, D.C., Carnegie Institution, 1924.

[18]Jorge Hardoy, *op. cit.*, pp. 282, 284.

[19]Fray Diego Durán, *The Aztecs: The History of the Indies of New Spain*, translated and annotated by Doris Heyden and Fernando Horcasitas, New York, Orion Press, 1964, pp. 14–16.

[20]J.C. Kelley, "Settlement Patterns in North-Central Mexico," *Prehistoric Settlement Patterns in the New World*, edited by Gordon R. Willey, Viking Fund Publications in Anthropology, No. 23, 1956, pp. 128–39. See also Muriel Porter Weaver, *The Aztecs, Maya, and Their Predecessors*, New York-London, Seminar Press, 1972, pp. 218–19.

[21]Muriel Porter Weaver, *op. cit.*, pp. 277–78.

[22]Hasso von Winning, "Keramische Hausmodelle aus Nayarit, Mexiko," *Baessler-Archiv*, n.s., Vol. XIX, 1971.

[23]Muriel Porter Weaver, *op. cit.*, p. 280.

PERIODS		WESTERN MEXICO	CENTRAL PLATEAU OF MEXICO		OAXACA	GULF OF MEXICO
			VALLEY OF MEXICO AND NEIGHBORING REGIONS	PUEBLA AND MORELOS VALLEYS		OLMEC HEARTLAND
MIDDLE PRE-CLASSIC	B.C. 1200		Tlatilco		Olmec influences	SAN LORENZO earliest planned ceremonial centers
	1100					
	1000	Olmec influences in Guerrero	Olmec influences	Olmec influences	San José Mogote	LA VENTA intense cultural diffusion into other areas
	900				Guadalupe	
LATE PRE-CLASSIC	800				Montenegro	ritual ball game
	700	isolated Olmec influences in other regions			earliest use of columns	
	600		Cerro del Tepalcate		MONTE ALBÁN	TRES ZAPOTES
	500				Building of the *Danzantes*	CERRO DE LAS MESAS
	400	Mezcala	CUICUILCO		Dainzú	
	300		Tlapacoya		Mound J	
PROTO-CLASSIC	200		TEOTIHUACÁN	Totomihuacan TLALANCALECA stairways with *alfardas* and beginnings of the *talud-tablero*	glyphic inscriptions and development of funerary architecture	glyphic inscriptions
	100	underground tombs dug	Pyramids of the Sun and the Moon			
	0			Cholula		
	A.D. 100		development of the *talud-tablero*		first moldings on bases	CENTRAL VERACRUZ
	200	Chupícuaro	Temple of Quetzalcóatl			EL TAJÍN
EARLY CLASSIC	300	Colima	triple complexes	Teotihuacán influence	development of the "scapulary" *tablero*	
	400		urban development	Manzanilla		
MIDDLE CLASSIC	500	isolated Teotihuacán influences	period of greatest splendor		Teotihuacán and Maya influences	Teotihuacán (and Maya?) influences
	600		partial destruction (A.D. 650)	Xochicalco		*tableros* with niches or stepped frets
	700	Nayarit	gradual abandonment	Temple of the Plumed Serpents	Lambityeco	
LATE CLASSIC	800		temporary cultural decline in the Valley of Mexico	CHOLULA	definitive aspect of the Great Plaza	Pyramid of the Niches
	900	clay models of buildings		XOCHICALCO		Building of the Columns Las Higueras frescoes
EARLY POST-CLASSIC	1000	Ixtlán del Río	TULA colonnades, serpent-shaped columns, atlantes, combined *tableros*		Mixtec occupation; Tomb 7	Building 3
	1100	El Ixtépete				Building A
	1200					
LATE POST-CLASSIC	1300	Ihuatzio	TENAYUCA twin temple TENOCHTITLAN foundation of the Aztec capital (A.D.1325)	religious predominance by Cholula	Yagul MITLA	influences from the Mexican plateau Misantla
	1400		Aztec empire expands (A.D. 1428)			Teayo Cempoala
	1500	Tzintzuntzan			Aztec hegemony	Aztec hegemony

SOUTHERN AREA	CENTRAL AREA			NORTHERN AREA		
	USUMACINTA	EL PETÉN	MOTAGUA	RÍO BEC, CHENES	PUUC	OTHER REGIONS
Olmec influences	Olmec influences	Olmec influences	Olmec influences	Olmec influences	Olmec influences	Olmec influences
						Dzibilchaltún
IZAPA						
Chiapa de Corzo moldings on bases		UAXACTUN stucco masks "apron" moldings		Santa Rosa, Xtampak		
Kaminaljuyú		TIKAL masonry walls				Dzibilchaltún
			COPÁN			
		first vaults on tombs; development and diffusion of the corbel vault, roof-comb, and dated monuments				Acancéh
KAMINALJUYÚ strong Teotihuacán influences	PIEDRAS NEGRAS					
few corbel vaults	YAXCHILÁN	Temple 23	earliest corbel vaults in this area	Becán, Santa Rosa, Xtampak: earliest corbel vaults in this area	Oxkintok: earliest corbel vaults in this area	earliest corbel vaults in this area
	PALENQUE earliest vaulted chambers in this area	Temple 22	perfection of the calendar			DZIBILCHALTÚN Temple of the Seven Dolls
first Pipil migrations	Temples of the Sun, of the Cross, of the Foliated Cross, and of the Inscriptions	Teotihuacán influences	Teotihuacán influences	XPUHIL, RÍO BEC HORMIGUERO	EDZNÁ Teotihuacán influences	Teotihuacán influences Kohunlich COBÁ
		Temples I and II Temple IV Temple of the Inscriptions	Hieroglyphic Stairway	TABASQUEÑO	SAYIL	
	PIEDRAS NEGRAS Bonampak		Temples 11 and 22	BECÁN, CHICANNÁ	LABNÁ	
				DZIBILNOCAC	KABÁH	CHICHÉN ITZÁ
successive influences from the Mexican plateau	YAXCHILÁN Toniná		QUIRIGUÁ	HOCHOB	UXMAL	Tulum
	progressive abandonment of the ceremonial centers	progressive abandonment of the ceremonial centers	progressive abandonment of the ceremonial centers	progressive abandonment of the ceremonial centers		CHICHÉN ITZÁ Toltec occupation and Maya-Toltec art
Zaculeu		Topoxté			UXMAL	
Cahyup						MAYAPÁN
Chuitinamit						TULUM and other cities of the east coast
Mixco Viejo						
Iximché		Tayasal				

SELECTED BIBLIOGRAPHY

Abbreviations: E.N.A.H. = Escuela Nacional de Antropología e Historia; I.I.E. = Instituto de Investigaciones Estéticas; I.N.A.H. = Instituto Nacional de Antropología e Historia; M.A.R.I.T.U. = Middle American Research Institute, Tulane University; M.N.A. = Museo Nacional de Antropología; U.N.A.M. = Universidad Nacional Autónoma de México

ACOSTA, JORGE R., "Técnicas de la construcción," in *Esplendor del México Antiguo*, Vol. II, Mexico, 1959.

——, *El palacio de Quetzalpapálotl*, Mexico, I.N.A.H., 1964.

——, "Exploraciones arqueológicas en Cholula," *Artes de México*, No. 140, 1971.

——, and MOEDANO KOER, HUGO, "Los juegos de pelota," in *México Prehispánico*, Mexico, E. Hurtado, 1946.

ADAMS, R.E.W., "Suggested Classic Period Occupational Specialization in the Southern Maya Lowlands," *Monographs and Papers in Maya Archaeology*, Peabody Museum, Harvard University, Cambridge, Mass., 1970.

AMABILIS, MANUEL, *La arquitectura precolombina de México*, Mexico, Orión, 1952.

ANDREWS, E. WYLLYS, *Dzibilchaltún Program*, New Orleans, M.A.R.I.T.U., 1965.

——, "Archaeology and Prehistory in the Northern Maya Lowlands, an Introduction," in *Handbook of Middle American Indians*, Vol. II, Part 1, New Orleans, M.A.R.I.T.U., 1965.

——, *The Emergence of Civilization in the Maya Lowlands, Observations on the Emergence of Civilizations in Mesoamerica*, University of California Archaeological Facility, Publication No. 11, Berkeley, 1970.

ANGULO, JORGE, "Señalando el concepto olmeca como religión," in *Religión en Mesoamérica*, Round Table XII, Sociedad Mexicana de Antropología, Mexico, 1972.

BELL, BETTY, "An Appraisal of the Maya Civilization," in Sylvanus G. Morley, *The Ancient Maya*, Stanford University Press, 1956.

BERNAL, IGNACIO, "Evolución y alcance de las culturas mesoamericanas," in *Esplendor del México Antiguo*, Vol. I, Mexico, 1959.

——, *Ancient Mexico*, London, Thames and Hudson, 1968.

——, *The Olmec World*, Berkeley and Los Angeles, University of California Press, 1969.

——, "The Olmec region—Oaxaca," in *Observations on the Emergence of Civilizations in Mesoamerica*, Berkeley, 1970.

——, and GENDROP, PAUL, *L'arte precolombiana dell' America Centrale*, Florence, Sansoni, 1971.

BORHEGYI, STEPHAN F. DE, "Archaeological Synthesis of the Guatemala Highlands," in *Handbook of the Middle American Indians*, Vol. II, New Orleans, M.A.R.I.T.U., 1965.

BRAINERD, GEORGE W., *The Maya Civilization*, Southwest Museum, Los Angeles, 1954.

BULLARD, WILLIAM R., JR., "Maya Settlement Patterns in Northeastern Petén, Guatemala," *American Antiquity*, Vol. XXV, No. 3, 1960.

CALNEK, EDWARD E., *The Internal Structure of Cities in America. Pre-Columbian Cities: The Case of Tenochtitlan.* Contribution to the XXXIX International Congress of Americanists, Lima, 1970. Mimeographed copy, Department of Anthropology, University of Rochester, New York.

CARVER, NORMAN F., JR., *Silent Cities: Mexico and the Maya*, Tokyo, Shokokusha, 1966.

CASO, ALFONSO, *The Aztecs: People of the Sun*, Norman, University of Oklahoma Press, 1958.

——, "Los Señoríos de Yanhuitlán," in *XXXV Congreso Internacional de Americanistas, Actas y Memorias*, Vol. I, Mexico, 1964.

COBEAN, ROBERT H.; COE, MICHAEL D.; PERRY, EDWARD A., JR.; TUREKIAN, KARL K.; KHARKAR, DINKAR AÑ, "Obsidian Trade at San Lorenzo Tenochtitlán, Mexico," *Science*, Vol. 174, No. 4010, November 12, 1971.

COE, MICHAEL D., "La Victoria, an Early Site on the Pacific Coast of Guatemala," *Peabody Museum Archaeological and Ethnological Papers*, Harvard University, Cambridge, Mass., 1961.

——, *The Jaguar's Children: Pre-Classic Central Mexico*, New York, Museum of Primitive Art, 1965.

——, *Mexico*, Collection Ancient Peoples and Places, Vol. 29, New York, 1966.

——, *The Maya*, New York, Praeger, 1966.

——, *America's First Civilization: Discovering the Olmec*, New York, American Heritage Publishing Company and The Smithsonian Institution, 1968.

——, "The Archaeological Sequence at San Lorenzo Tenochtitlán," Contributions, No. 8, University of California Archaeological Research Facility, Berkeley, 1970.

COE, WILLIAM R., "Tikal, Ten Years of Study of a Maya Ruin in the Lowlands of Guatemala," *Expedition*, Vol. 8, No. 1, Philadelphia, The University Museum of Pennsylvania, 1965.

——, *Tikal: A Handbook of the Ancient Maya Ruins*, Philadelphia, The University Museum of Pennsylvania, 1967.

——, "Cultural Contact Between the Lowland Maya and Teotihuacán," in *Teotihuacán: Onceava Mesa Redonda*, Vol. II, Sociedad Mexicana de Antropología, Mexico, 1972.

CONTRERAS, EDUARDO, "La zona arqueológica de Manzanilla, Puebla," *Boletín del I.N.A.H.*, No. 21, 1965.

——, "Trabajos de exploración en la zona arqueológica de Ixtlán del Río, Nayarit," *Boletín del I.N.A.H.*, No. 25, 1966.

——, "Trabajos en la zona arqueológica de Ixtlán del Río, Nayarit, Temporada 1967," *Boletín del I.N.A.H.*, No. 29, 1967.

COVARRUBIAS, MIGUEL, "Las raíces del arte de Tenochtitlan," *México en el Arte*, No. 8, Mexico, 1949.

——, *Indian Art of Mexico and Central America*, New York, Knopf, 1957.

DÍAZ DEL CASTILLO, BERNAL, *The True History of the Conquest of Mexico*, translated by Maurice Keating, New York, McBride & Co., 1927.

DIEHL, RICHARD A., *Preliminary Report, University of Missouri Archaeological Project at Tula, Hidalgo, Mexico, 1970-71 Field Season*, December 1, 1971.

DOCKSTADER, FREDERICK J., *Indian Art of Central America*, London, Cary, Adams, and Mackay, 1964.

D'OWLER, LUIS NICOLAU, "Cartas de Relación de Hernán Cortés al Emperador Carlos V: Segunda Relación, 30 de octubre de 1520," in *Cronistas de las Culturas Precolombinas, Antología*, Mexico, Fondo de Cultura Económica, 1963.

DREWITT, BRUCE, "Planeación en la Antigua Ciudad de Teotihuacán," in *Teotihuacán: Onceava Mesa Redonda*, Sociedad Mexicana de Antropología, Mexico, 1966.

DURÁN, FRAY DIEGO, *The Aztecs: The History of the Indies of New Spain*, translated and annotated by Doris Heyden and Fernando Horcasitas, New York, Orion Press, 1964.

——, *Historia de las India de Nueva España e Isla de la Tierra Firme*, edited by Angel M. Garibay, 2 vols., Mexico, Porrúa, 1967.

——, *Book of the Gods and Rites and the Ancient Calendar*, translated and edited by Fernando Horcasitas and Doris Heyden, preface by Miguel León-Portilla, Norman, University of Oklahoma Press, 1971.

DÜRER, ALBRECHT, *Tagebuch der Reise in die Niederlande Anno 1520, in seine Briefen und Tagebüchern*, Frankfurt 1925.

DU SOLIER, WILFRIDO, *Estudio arquitectónico de los edificios Huaxtecos, Anales del I.N.A.H.*, Vol. I, 1954.

EATON, JACK D., *Chicanná, an Elite Center in the Río Bec Region*, Tulane University Press, New Orleans, 1971.

EDWARDS, EMILY, *Painted Walls of Mexico: From Prehistoric Times until Today*, photographs by M. Alvarez Bravo, Austin, University of Texas Press, 1966.

FERDON, EDWIN N., *A Trial Survey of Mexican-Southwestern Architectural Parallels*, New Mexico School of American Research, Santa Fe, 1955.

FERNÁNDEZ, JUSTINO, "El Arte," in *Esplendor del México Antiguo*, Vol. I, Mexico, 1959.

FLORES GUERRERO, RAÚL, *Historia General del Arte Mexicano: Epoca Prehispánica*, Mexico, Hermes, 1962.

FORD, JAMES A., *A Comparison of Formative Cultures in the Americas*, The Smithsonian Institution, Washington D.C., 1969.

FUENTE, BEATRIZ DE LA, *La escultura de Palenque*, Mexico, U.N.A.M., 1965.

FURST, PETER T., "The Olmec Were-Jaguar Motif in the Light of Ethnographic Reality," in *Dumbarton Oaks Conference on the Olmec, 1967*, Dumbarton Oaks Research Library and Collection, Trustees for Harvard University, Washington, D.C., 1968.

GARCÍA COOK, ANGEL, "Algunos descubrimientos en Tlalancaleca, Estado de Puebla," *Comunicaciones*, No. 9, Fundación Alemana para la Investigación Científica, Puebla, 1973.

GARIBAY, ANGEL MARÍA, *La literatura de los Aztecas*, edited by Joaquín Mortiz, Mexico, 1964.

——, *Historia de la Literatura Náhuatl*, 2 vols., Mexico Porrúa, 1953-54.

GARZA TARAZONA DE GONZÁLEZ, SILVIA, *Análisis de la Arquitectura Representada en los Códices Mixtecos*, graduate thesis, Mexico, E.N.A.H., 1970.

GENDROP, PAUL, "Esthétique de l'art précolombien au Mexique," *Boletín del A.F.M.I.T.*, Vol. XII, No. 1, 1966.

———, "Arquitectura Prehispánica, la Estética," *Cam-Sam*, Vol. I, No. 1, Colegio de Arquitectos Mexicanos, 1968.

———, "Tikal, Copán y Palenque, el triángulo maya clásico," *Sandorama*, No. 2, Mexico, 1968.

———, "Labná," *Sandorama*, No. 5, 1969.

———, *Arte Prehispánico en Mesoamérica*, Mexico, Trillas, 1970.

———, "Murales Prehispánicos," *Artes de México*, No. 144, 1971.

———, "La crestería en la arquitectura maya," *Revista de la Universidad de México*, Vol. XXVII, No. 4, 1972.

———, "Arte precolombino de México," in *Historia del Arte*, Nos. 121–123, Barcelona, Salvat, 1973.

———, *A Guide to Architecture in Ancient Mexico*, Mexico, Ediciones Minutiae Mexicana, 1974.

GONZÁLEZ, NORBERTO, *Reporte de la excavación 1972 en Manzanilla este*, Universidad de las Américas, Cholula, Puebla, 1973 (in course of publication).

GRAHAM, IAN, *Archaeological Explorations in El Petén, Guatemala*, Publication 33, New Orleans, M.A.R.I.T.U., 1967.

GRAHAM, JOHN A., *Ancient Mesoamerica*, Palo Alto, Peak Publications, 1966.

———; GREENE ROBERTSON, MERLE; and RANDS, ROBERT L., *Maya Sculpture of the Southern Lowlands, Highlands, and Pacific Piedmont*, Berkeley, Lederer, Street & Zens, 1972.

GUILLEMIN, JORGE F., *Iximché, capital del antiguo reino Cakchiquel*, Instituto de Antropología e Historia de Guatemala, 1968.

HARDOY, JORGE, *Ciudades Precolombinas*, Buenos Aires, Ediciones Infinito, 1964.

———, *Planning and Cities: Urban Planning in Pre-Columbian America*, New York, Braziller, 1968.

———, *Pre-Columbian Cities*, New York, Walker & Co., 1973.

HARTUNG, HORST, "Notes on the Oaxaca Tablero," *Bulletin of Oaxaca Studies*, No. 27, 1970.

———, *Die Zeremonialzentren der Maya*, Graz, Akademische Druck-U. Verlagsanstalt, 1972.

HAVILAND, W.A., "Tikal, Guatemala, and Mesoamerican Urbanism," *World Archaeology*, 1970.

HEIZER, ROBERT; DRUCKER, PHILIP; and GRAHAM, JOHN A., "Investigaciones de 1967 y 1968 en La Venta," *Boletín del I.N.A.H.*, No. 33, 1968.

HELFRITZ, HANS, *Mexican Cities of the Gods*, New York, Praeger, 1970.

HELLMUTH, NICHOLAS, *Possible Streets at a Maya Site in Guatemala*, New Haven, 1971.

———, *Preliminary Report on Second Season Excavations at Yaxhá, Guatemala*, New Haven, 1971.

———, *Report on First Season Explorations and Excavations at Yaxhá, El Petén, Guatemala, 1970*, New Haven, 1971.

HEYDEN, DORIS, "Teotihuacán," in *Guía General al Museo Nacional de Antropología*, Mexico, I.N.A.H., 1967.

———, "Una deidad del agua de las obras del Metro," *Boletín del I.N.A.H.*, No. 40, 1970.

———, "Un adoratorio a Omácatl," *Boletín del I.N.A.H.*, No. 42, 1972.

———, "What is the Meaning of the Mexica Pyramid?," paper presented at the XL International Congress of Americanists, Rome, 1972.

———, "A Chicomoztoc in Teotihuacán?," paper presented at the XXXVIII Annual Reunion of the Society for American Archaeology, San Francisco, 1973.

———, "El Preclásico Superior y el Protoclásico," in *Antropología e Historia de México*, Mexico, I.N.A.H. (in course of publication).

———, *Algunos grupos étnicos mesoamericanos y la arquitectura de sus templos: Teotihuacán, sus templos y deidades*, Round Table XIII, Sociedad Mexicana de Antropología, Mexico, Xalapa, 1973 (in preparation).

———, and BERNAL, IGNACIO, "Art: Pre-Columbian," in *Handbook of Latin American Studies*, Nos. 23–26, 28, The Hispanic Foundation, The Library of Congress, Washington, D.C., and Gainesville, Florida Press, 1961-66.

HOLLAND, WILLIAM, *Medicina Maya en los Altos de Chiapas*, translated by Daniel Cazés, Instituto Nacional Indigenista, Mexico, 1963.

JIMÉNEZ MORENO, WIGBERTO, *Historia Antigua de México*, Mexico, Ediciones S.A.E.N.A.H., 1956.

———, "Síntesis de la historia pretolteca de Mesoamérica," in *Esplendor del México Antiguo*, Vol. II, Mexico, 1959.

———, "Mesoamerica Before the Toltecs," in *Ancient Oaxaca*, Stanford University Press, 1966.

KELLEY, J.C., "Settlement Patterns in North-Central Mexico," in *Prehistoric Settlement Patterns in the New World*, edited by G.R. Willey, Viking Fund Publications in Anthropology, No. 23, 1956.

KELLY, ISABEL, "Vasijas de Colima con boca de estribo," *Boletín del I.N.A.H.*, No. 42, 1970.

KIRCHHOFF, PAUL, "Quetzalcóatl, Huémac y el fin de Tula," *Cuadernos Americanos*, 1955.

———, *Mesoamérica. Sus límites geográficos, composición étnica y caracteres culturales*, supplement of *Tlatoani*, Mexico, 1960.

KRICKEBERG, WALTER, *Las Antiguas Culturas Mexicanas*, Mexico, Fondo de Cultura Económica, 1961.

KUBLER, GEORGE, "La función intelectual," in *Esplendor del México Antiguo*, Vol. I, Mexico, 1959.

———, *The Art and Architecture of Ancient America*, Harmondsworth, Penguin Books, 1961.

———, "The Iconography of the Art of Teotihuacán," *Studies in Pre-Columbian Art and Archaeology*, No. 4, Dumbarton Oaks Research Library and Collection, Trustees for Harvard University, Washington, D.C., 1967.

LANDA, FRAY DIEGO DE, *Relación de las Cosas de Yucatán*, edited by Pedro Robredo, Mexico, 1938.

LEHMANN, HENRI, *Les civilisations précolombiennes*, Paris, P.U.F., 1958.

———, *Mixco Viejo, Guía de las ruinas de la plaza fuerte Pocomam*, Guatemala, 1968.

LEONARD, CARMEN COOK DE, "La escultura," in *Esplendor del México Antiguo*, Vol. II, Mexico, 1959.

LEÓN-PORTILLA, MIGUEL, "La fílosofia," in *Esplendor del México Antiguo*, Vol. I, Mexico, 1959.

———, *Los Antiguos Mexicanos a través de sus Crónicas y Cantares*, Mexico, Fondo de Cultura Económica, 1961.

———, *El reverso de la Conquista*, Mexico, Joaquín Mortiz, 1964.

LITVAK, JAIME, "Mesoamérica y la Economía Azteca," in *Los Aztecas: Su Historia y Su Vida*, Mexico, M.N.A., I.N.A.H., 1965.

———, "Una maqueta de piedra hallada en Xochicalco, Morelos," *Boletín del I.N.A.H.*, No. 22, 1965.

———, "Xochicalco en la caída del Clásico," *Anales de Antropología*, Vol. VII, Instituto de Investigaciones Históricas, Mexico, U.N.A.M., 1970.

———, "La problemática de la arqueología en el estado de Morelos," paper presented at the conference of the Sociedad Mexicana de Antropología, Mexico, November 11, 1972.

LIZARDI RAMOS, CÉSAR, "El calendario maya-mexicano," in *Esplendor del México Antiguo*, Vol. I, Mexico, 1959.

LÓPEZ ALONSO, SERGIO; LAGUNAS RODRÍGUEZ, ZAID; and SERRANO SÁNCHEZ, CARLOS, "Datos Preliminares sobre los Enterramientos Humanos Prehispánicos de Cholula, Puebla," in *Proyecto Puebla-Tlaxcala*, Mexico, I.N.A.H., 1972.

LOTHROP, S.K., *Tulum: an Archaeological Study of the East Coast of Yucatán*, Carnegie Institution, Washington, D.C., 1924.

———; FOSHAG, W.F.; and MAHLER, JOY, *Pre-Columbian Art: The Robert Woods Bliss Collection*, London, Phaidon Press, 1957.

LOWE, GARETH W., and MASON, J. ALDEN, "Archaeological Survey of the Chiapas Coast, Highlands, and Upper Grijalva Basin," in *Handbook of Middle American Indians*, Vol. II, Part 1, Austin, University of Texas Press, 1965.

MALER, TEOBERTO, *Recently Discovered Ruins in Yucatan*, Peabody Museum, Harvard University, Cambridge, Mass., n.d.

———, "Researches in the Central Portion of the Usumasintla Valley," *Memoirs of the Peabody Museum*, Vol. II, Nos. 1 and 2, Harvard University, Cambridge, Mass., 1901 and 1903.

MARGAIN, CARLOS R., "Sobre sistemas y materiales de construcción en Teotihuacán," in *Teotihuacán: Onceava Mesa Redonda,* Vol. I, Mexico, Sociedad Mexicana de Antropología, 1966.

MARISCAL, FEDERICO, *Estudio arquitectónico de las ruinas Mayas de Yucatán y Campeche,* Mexico, Secretaria de Educación Pública, 1928.

MARQUINA, IGNACIO, *Estudio Arquitectónico comparativo de los Monumentos arqueológicos de México,* Mexico, 1928.

———, *Arquitectura Prehispánica,* Mexico, I.N.A.H., 1951 (enlarged edition, 1964).

———, *El Templo Mayor de México,* Mexico, I.N.A.H., 1960.

———, "Influencia de Teotihuacán en Cholula," in *Teotihuacán: Onceava Mesa Redonda,* Vol. II, Sociedad Mexicana de Antropología, Mexico, 1972.

MATOS, EDUARDO, "Exploraciones en Totomihuacan, Puebla," *Boletín del I.N.A.H.,* No. 19, Mexico, 1965.

MAUDSLAY, A.P., "Biologia Centrali Americana," in *Archaeology,* Vol. IV, London, 1902.

MEDELLÍN ZENIL, ALFONSO, *Exploraciones en Las Higueras, Veracruz,* Instituto de Antropología de la Universidad Veracruzana, Xalapa, 1971.

MEGGERS, B.J.; EVANS, C.; and ESTRADA, E., "Early Formative Period of Coastal Ecuador: The Valdivia and Machalilla Phases," *Smithsonian Contributions to Anthropology,* No. 1, Washington, D.C., 1965.

MENDIETA, FRAY GERÓNIMO DE, *Historia Eclesiástica Indiana,* edited by Salvador Chávez Hayhoe, Vol. I, Mexico, n.d.

MILES, S.W., "Sculpture of the Guatemala-Chiapas Highlands and Pacific Slopes and Associate Hieroglyphs," in *Handbook of Middle American Indians,* Vol. II, Part 1, Austin, University of Texas Press, 1965.

MILLON, RENÉ, "La agricultura como inicio de la civilización," in *Esplendor del México Antiguo,* Vol. II, Mexico, 1959.

———, "Cronología y periodificación: datos estratigráficos sobre períodos cerámicos y sus relaciones con la pintura mural; El problema de integración en la sociedad teotihuacána; Extensión y población de la ciudad de Teotihuacán en sus diferentes períodos: un cálculo provisional," in *Teotihuacán: Onceava Mesa Redonda,* Vol. I, Sociedad Mexicana de Antropología, Mexico, 1966.

———, "Teotihuacán," *Scientific American,* Vol. 216, No. 6, June 1967.

———, "Teotihuacán: Completion of Map of Giant Ancient City in the Valley of Mexico," *Science,* Vol. 170, December 4, 1970.

———; DREWITT, BRUCE; and BENNYHOFF, JAMES A., "The Pyramid of the Sun at Teotihuacán: 1959 Investigations," *Transactions of the American Philosophical Society,* n.s., Vol. 55, Part 6, 1965.

MOLINA, MARTA FONCERRADA DE, *La escultura arquitectónica de Uxmal,* Mexico, I.I.E., U.N.A.M., 1965.

MORLEY, SYLVANUS G., *The Ancient Maya,* Stanford, 1956.

MÜLLER, FLORENCIA, "Chimalacatlán," *Acta Antropológica,* Vol. III, Part 1, Mexico, 1948.

———, *Atlas Arqueológico de la República Mexicana: Campeche,* Mexico, I.N.A.H., 1960.

———, "El Origen de los barrios de Cholula," in *Proyecto Puebla-Tlaxcala,* Mexico, I.N.A.H., 1972, mimeographed copy.

NATIONAL GEOGRAPHIC SOCIETY, *Archaeological Map of Middle America, Land of the Feathered Serpent,* Washington, D.C., 1968.

NICHOLSON, H.B., "Religion in Pre-Hispanic Central Mexico," in *Handbook of Middle American Indians,* Vol. 10, Austin, University of Texas Press, 1971.

NICHOLSON, IRENE, *Mexican and Central American Mythology,* London, Hamlyn, 1967.

NORIEGA, RAÚL, "Sabiduría, Matemática, Astronomía y Cronología," in *Esplendor del México Antiguo,* Vol. I, Mexico, 1959.

OUTWATER, OGDEN, JR., "Técnicas de la cantería," in *Esplendor del México Antiguo,* Mexico, 1959.

PADDOCK, JOHN, "Mixtec Ethnohistory and Monte Albán V," in *Ancient Oaxaca,* Stanford University Press, 1966.

———, "El Esplendor de los Mixtecos," *Culturas de Oaxaca,* No. 4, Mexico, M.N.A., I.N.A.H., 1967.

———, "A Beginning in the Ñuiñe," *Bulletin of Oaxaca Studies,* No. 6, 1970.

———, "Distribución de rasgos teotihuacanos en Mesoamérica; El ocaso del clásico," in *Teotihuacán: Onceava Mesa Redonda,* Vol. II, Sociedad Mexicana de Antropología, Mexico, 1972.

PAZ, OCTAVIO, and MEDELLÍN ZENIL, ALFONSO, *Magía de la Risa,* Xalapa, Universidad Veracruzana, 1962.

PETERSON, FREDERICK A., *Ancient Mexico,* London, Allen & Unwin, 1969.

PIÑA CHÁN, ROMÁN, *Mesoamérica,* Mexico, I.N.A.H., 1960.

———, *Una visión del México prehispánico,* Instituto de Investigaciones Históricas, Mexico, U.N.A.M., 1967.

———, *A Guide to Mexican Archaeology,* Mexico, Ediciones Minutiae Mexicana, 1971.

———, *Historia, Arqueología y Arte Prehispánico,* Mexico, Fondo de Cultura Económica, 1972.

———, and NAVARRETE, CARLOS, "Archaeological Research in the Lower Grijalva River Region, Tabasco and Chiapas," *Papers of the New World Archaeological Foundation,* No. 22, Provo, Brigham Young University, 1967.

POLLOCK, H.E.D., "Architecture of the Maya Lowlands," in *Handbook of Middle American Indians,* Vol. 2, Part 1, Austin, University of Texas Press, 1965.

———, "Architectural Notes on Some Chenes Ruins," *Monographs and Papers in Maya Archaeology,* Peabody Museum, Harvard University, Cambridge, Mass., 1970.

POPENOE HATCH, MARION, *An Hypothesis on Olmec Astronomy, with Special Reference to the La Venta Site,* Contributions, No. 13, University of California Archaeological Facility, Publ. No. 11, Berkeley, 1970.

Popol Vuh: The Sacred Book of the Ancient Quiché Maya, English translation by Delia Goetz and Sylvanus G. Morley, from the Spanish translation by Adrián Recinos, Norman, University of Oklahoma Press, 1950.

POTTER, DAVID E., *Architectural Style at Becán during the Maya Late Classic Period,* Tulane University Press, New Orleans, 1972.

Prehistoric Settlement Patterns in the New World, edited by Gordon R. Willey, New York, Johnson Reprint Corp., 1967.

PROSKOURIAKOFF, TATIANA, *An Album of Maya Architecture,* Carnegie Institution, Washington, D.C., 1946.

———, *A Study of Classic Maya Sculpture,* Carnegie Institution, Washington, D.C., 1950.

———, *Varieties of Classic Central Veracruz Sculpture,* Carnegie Institution, Washington, D.C., 1954.

———, "Sculpture and Major Arts of the Maya Lowlands," in *Handbook of Middle American Indians,* Vol. II, Part 1, Austin, University of Texas Press, 1965.

———, "Early Architecture and Sculpture in Mesoamerica," in *Observations on the Emergence of Civilizations in Mesoamerica,* Berkeley, 1970.

RIVET, PAUL, *Maya Cities: Ancient Cities and Temples,* New York, Putnam, 1962.

ROBERTSON, DONALD, *Pre-Columbian Architecture,* New York, Braziller, 1963.

ROBINA, RICARDO DE, *Estudio preliminar de las ruinas de Hochob,* Mexico, Atenea, 1956.

———, "La arquitectura," in *Esplendor del México Antiguo,* Vol. II, Mexico, 1959.

RUIZ, SONIA LOMBARDO DE, *El Espacio en la arquitectura prehispánica en México,* Universidad Ibero-Americana, Mexico, 1965.

RUPPERT, KARL, and DENISON, J.H., JR., *Archaeological Reconnaissance in Campeche, Quintana Roo, and Petén,* Carnegie Institution, Washington, D.C., 1943.

RUZ LHUILLIER, ALBERTO, "Estudio de la cripta del templo de las Inscripciones en Palenque," *Tlatoani,* Vol. I, Nos. 5–6, 1952.

———, *La civilización de los antiguos mayas,* Mexico, I.N.A.H., 1963.

———, "Tombs and Funerary Practices of the Maya Lowlands," in *Handbook of Middle American Indians,* Vol. II, Part 1, Austin, University of Texas Press, 1965.

SÁENZ, CÉSAR A., "Nuevos descubrimientos en Xochicalco, Morelos," *Boletín del I.N.A.H.,* No. 11, 1963.

———, "Exploraciones en Xochicalco," *Boletín del I.N.A.H.,* No. 20, 1965; No. 26, 1966.

———, "Exploraciones y restauraciones en Yucatán," *Boletín del I.N.A.H.,* No. 31, 1968.

SAHAGÚN, FRAY BERNARDINO DE, *Historia General de las Cosas de la Nueva España,* notes by E. Seler, introduction by W. Jiménez Moreno, 5 vols., Mexico, Robredo, 1938.

———, *Florentine Codex. General History of the Things*

of New Spain, translated into English from the Náhuatl by Arthur J.O. Anderson and Charles E. Dibble, 12 vols., The School of American Research and The University of Utah, Santa Fe, New Mexico, 1950–69.

SALAZAR, PONCIANO, "Maqueta prehispánica teotihuacana," Boletín del I.N.A.H., No. 23, 1966.

SANDERS, WILLIAM T., The Cultural Ecology of the Teotihuacán Valley. A Preliminary Report of the Results of the Teotihuacán Valley Project, Department of Sociology and Anthropology, The Pennsylvania State University, September 1965.

———, "Life in a Classic Village," in Teotihuacán: Onceava Mesa Redonda, Vol. 1, Sociedad Mexicana de Antropología, Mexico, 1966.

———, and PRICE, BARBARA J., Mesoamerica: The Evolution of a Civilization, New York, Random House, 1968.

SCHÖNDUBE, OTTO, "Teotihuacán, Ciudad de los Dioses," Imagen de México, No. 3, Mexico, 1971.

SEGOVIA, VICTOR, "Kohunlich," Boletín del I.N.A.H., No. 37, Mexico, 1969.

SÉJOURNÉ, LAURETTE, "Pensamiento y Religión en el México Antiguo," Breviarios, No. 128, Mexico, Fondo de Cultura Económica, 1964.

———, Arquitectura y Pintura en Teotihuacán, Mexico, Siglo XXI Editores, 1966.

SHARP, ROSEMARY, "Early Architectural Grecas in the Valley of Oaxaca," Bulletin of Oaxaca Studies, No. 32, 1970.

SHOOK, EDWIN M., "Archaeological Survey of the Pacific Coast of Guatemala," in Handbook of Middle American Indians, Vol. II, Part 1, Austin, University of Texas Press, 1965.

———, and PROSKOURIAKOFF, TATIANA, "Settlement Patterns in Mesoamerica, and the Sequence in the Guatemalan Highlands," in Prehistoric Settlement Patterns in the New World, New York, Johnson Reprint Corp., 1967.

SMITH, A. LEDYARD, Residential Structures, Mayapán, Yucatán, Mexico, Carnegie Institution, Washington, D.C., 1962.

———, "Architecture of the Guatemalan Highlands," in Handbook of Middle American Indians, Vol. II, Part 1, Austin, University of Texas Press, 1965.

SODI, M. DEMETRIO, La Literatura de los Mayas, Mexico, Joaquín Mortiz, 1964.

SOUSTELLE, JACQUES, La pensée cosmologique des anciens Mexicains, Paris, Hermann, 1940.

———, L'art du Mexique ancien, Paris, Arthaud, 1959.

———, The Daily Life of the Aztecs, Harmondsworth, Penguin Books, 1964.

———, "Les quatre soleils," Collection Terre Humaine, Paris, Plon, 1967.

SPENCE, MICHAEL W., and PARSONS, JEFFREY R., "Prehispanic Obsidian Exploitation in Central Mexico: a Preliminary Synthesis," in Miscellaneous Studies in Mexican Prehistory, Anthropological Papers of the Museum of Anthropology, University of Michigan, No. 45, Ann Arbor, 1972.

SPINDEN, HERBERT J., "A Study of Maya Art: Its Subject Matter and Historical Development," Memoirs of the Peabody Museum, Vol. VI, Harvard University, Cambridge, Mass., 1913.

SPRANZ, BODO, "Descubrimientos en Totimehuacán, Puebla," Boletín del I.N.A.H., No. 28, 1967.

STEIMBOMER KENDALL, DOROTHY, Maya Town Planning: a Visual Survey, University of the Americas, Cholula, 1972.

STEPHENS, JOHN LLOYD, Incidents of Travel in Central America, Chiapas and Yucatan, New York, Dover, 1963.

STIERLIN, HENRI, Maya: Architecture Universelle, Fribourg, Office du Livre, 1964.

———, Mexique ancien: Architecture Universelle, Fribourg, Office du Livre, 1967.

STIRLING, MATTHEW, "Early History of the Olmec Problem," in Dumbarton Oaks Conference on the Olmec, 1967, Dumbarton Oaks Research Library and Collection, Trustees for Harvard University, Washington, D.C., 1968.

STRESSER-PEAN, GUY, Les indiens Huaxtèques, Mexico, 1963.

THOMPSON, J. ERIC S., Maya Archaeologist, Norman, University of Oklahoma Press, 1963.

———, "Archaeological Synthesis of the Southern Maya Lowlands," in Handbook of Middle American Indians, Vol. II, Part 1, Austin, University of Texas Press, 1965.

———, Maya Hieroglyphic Writing, Norman, University of Oklahoma Press, 1966.

———, The Rise and Fall of Maya Civilization, 2nd ed., Norman, University of Oklahoma Press, 1966.

———, Maya History and Religion, Norman, University of Oklahoma Press, 1970.

TOBRINER, STEPHEN, "The Fertile Mountain: an Investigation of Cerro Gordo's Importance to the Town and Iconography of Teotihuacán," in Teotihuacán: Onceava Mesa Redonda, Vol. II, Sociedad Mexicana de Antropología, Mexico, 1972

TORQUEMADA, FRAY JUAN DE, Monarquía Indiana, edited by Salvador Chávez Hayhoe, 2 vols., Mexico, 1943.

TOSCANO, SALVADOR, Arte Precolombino de México y de la América Central, Mexico, I.I.E., U.N.A.M., 1952.

TOTTEN, GEORGE D., Maya Architecture, Washington, D.C., 1926.

VILLAGRA CALETI, AGUSTÍN, "La pintura mural," in Esplendor del México Antiguo, Vol. II, Mexico, 1959.

WALLRATH, MATTHEW, "The Calle de los Muertos Complex: a Possible Macrocomplex of Structures near the Center of Teotihuacán," in Teotihuacán: Onceava Mesa Redonda, Vol. I, Sociedad Mexicana de Antropología, Mexico, 1966.

WAUCHOPE, ROBERT, Modern Maya Houses: a Study of Their Architectural Significance, Carnegie Institution, Washington, D.C., 1938.

———, Lost Tribes and Sunken Continents, The University of Chicago Press, 1963.

WEAVER, MURIEL PORTER, The Aztecs, Maya, and Their Predecessors, New York and London, Seminar Press, 1972.

WEBSTER, DAVID L., The Fortifications of Becán, Campeche, Mexico, Department of Anthropology, Tulane University, New Orleans, 1971.

WESTHEIM, PAUL, Arte Antiguo de México, Mexico, Fondo de Cultura Económica, 1950.

———, Ideas fundamentales del arte prehispánico en México, Mexico, Fondo de Cultura Económica, 1957.

WICKE, CHARLES R., "Tomb 30 at Yagul and the Zaachila Tombs," in Ancient Oaxaca, Stanford University Press, 1966.

———, Olmec: An Early Art Style of Precolumbian Mexico, Tucson, University of Arizona Press, 1971.

WILLEY, GORDON R., and BULLARD, WILLIAM R., JR., "Prehistoric Settlement Patterns in the Maya Lowlands," in Handbook of Middle American Indians, Vol. II, Part 1, Austin, University of Texas Press, 1965.

———, and SHIMKIN, DEMITRI B., "Why did the Pre-Columbian Maya Civilization Collapse?," Science, Vol. 173, No. 3997, 1971.

WINNING, HASSO VON, Pre-Columbian Arts of Mexico and Central America, New York, Abrams, 1968.

———, "Keramische Hausmodelle aus Nayarit, Mexiko," Baessler-Archiv, n.s., Vol. XIX, 1971.

WOLF, E.R., Sons of the Shaking Earth, University of Chicago Press, 1959.

The authors gratefully acknowledge the cooperation of the Instituto de Investigaciones Arquitectónicas, Escuela Nacional de Arquitectura of the Universidad Nacional Autónoma de México.

INDEX

LIST OF PLATES

PHOTOGRAPHIC CREDITS

NOTE: *The numbers listed refer to the plates.*

Acosta, Jorge R., Mexico City: 24.

Allen, John, Chattanooga, Tenn.: 53, 55, 57.

Artes de México, Mexico City: 141.

Bonnavent, Jacques, Mexico City: 247, 348.

British Museum, London: 140, 169, 191.

Courtesy of the Carnegie Institution, Washington, D.C.: 199.

Compañia Mexicana Aerofoto, Mexico City: 18, 19, 25, 37, 38, 80, 82.

Cordry, Donald: 78, 282, 315, 344, 345, 346.

Dumbarton Oaks, Washington, D.C.: 179, 180.

Fuente, Beatriz de la, Mexico City: 152.

Gendrop, Paul, Mexico: 4, 17, 21, 26, 27, 31, 32, 34, 36, 48, 63, 65, 69, 71, 72, 73, 77, 92, 96, 147, 153, 154, 158, 159, 165, 177, 178, 190, 209, 210, 214, 218, 223, 227, 235, 236, 237, 240, 242, 243, 260, 263, 266, 267, 268, 269, 273, 276, 277, 284, 285, 291, 310, 327, 329, 336, 338, 352, 354, 359, 363.

Heyden, Doris, Mexico: 8, 9, 10, 13, 23, 33, 41, 42, 54, 66, 67, 79, 85, 105, 107, 109, 116, 119, 120, 121, 143, 148, 150, 151, 155, 156, 160, 161, 162, 163, 168, 172, 173, 174, 175, 176, 181, 182, 183, 184, 185, 187, 188, 189, 192, 193, 194, 195, 206, 220, 225, 231, 232, 238, 239, 246, 251, 252, 254, 255, 258, 271, 272, 276, 279, 281, 303, 304, 305, 306, 318, 319, 320, 330, 331, 332, 333, 334, 335, 340, 341, 342, 343, 350, 351, 355, 356, 357.

Instituto Nacional de Antropología e Historia, Mexico City: 6, 7, 11, 12, 15, 22, 40, 49, 50, 51, 60, 70, 83, 84, 86, 93, 94, 95, 98, 142, 149, 164, 166, 198, 213, 215, 216, 234, 244, 249, 257, 264, 265, 278, 280, 283, 286, 287, 288, 289, 290, 292, 293, 294, 295, 311, 312, 321, 347, 360, 361, 362.

Maler, Instituto Nacional de Antropología e Historia, Mexico City: 115, 135, 138, 139, 202, 203, 204, 212, 253.

Medina de los Reyes, José, Museo Nacional de Antropología de México, Mexico City: 296, 297, 298, 299, 300, 301.

Muñoz, Alfonso, Mexico City: 64, 217, 230, 233, 250, 313, 353.

Museo Etnografico, Basel: 111.

National Geographic Society, Washington, D.C.: 196, 201.

Nissley, Carmen, San Diego, Cal: 274, 275.

Nonis, Louis, Mexico City: 219.

Peabody Museum, Harvard University, Cambridge, Mass.: 129

Piña Chán, Román, Mexico City: 14, 170, 197, 207, 208, 358.

Potter, David E., Boulder, Colo.: 200.

Sáenz, César A., Mexico City: 245.

Stierlin, Henri, Geneva: 221, 222, 224, 226, 241, 337.

University Museum, Philadelphia: 103, 104, 108, 110, 113, 118, 130, 131, 132, 133.